Julio de Santa Ana / Towards a Church of the Poor

Julio de Santa Ana, editor

Towards a Church of the Poor

The Work of an Ecumenical Group on the Church and the Poor

ORBIS BOOKS

Maryknoll, New York 10545

The Catholic Foreign Mission Society of America (Maryknoll) recruits and trains people for overseas missionary service. Through Orbis Books Maryknoll aims to foster the international dialogue that is essential to mission. The books published, however, reflect the opinions of their authors and are not meant to represent the official position of the society.

Acknowledgments

— To Mr Daniel Caselli for the illustrations.
— To Mr J. Victor Koilpillai for his assistance in giving this book its final form.
— To Miss Erna Haller and Mrs Carol Lunt for their untiring attention to production details of this book throughout its progress.

Library of Congress Cataloging in Publication Data
Main entry under title:

Towards a church of the poor.

Reprint of the ed. published by the World Council of Churches, Geneva.
Sponsored by the Commission on the Churches' Participation in Development of the World Council of Churches.
Includes bibliographical references.
1. Church and the Poor. I. Santa Ana, Julio de.
II. World Council of Churches. Commission on the Churches' Participation in Development.
BV639.P6T68 1981   261.8'3456   80-25667
ISBN 0-88344-502-6 (pbk.)

U.S. edition 1981 by Orbis Books, Maryknoll, NY 10545

Typeset in Switzerland; printed and bound in the United States of America

"For this reason the human righteousness required by God and established in obedience — the righteousness which according to Amos 5 : 24 should pour down as a mighty stream — has necessarily the character of a vindication of right in favour of the threatened innocent, the oppressed poor, widows, orphans and aliens. For this reason, in the relations and events in the life of His people, God always takes His stand unconditionally and passionately on this side and on this side alone: against the lofty and on behalf of the lowly; against those who already enjoy right and privilege and on behalf of those who are denied and deprived of it. What does all this mean? It is not really to be explained by talking *in abstracto* of the political tendency and especially the forensic character of the Old Testament and the biblical message generally. It does in fact have this character and we cannot hear it and believe it without feeling a sense of responsibility in the direction indicated."

KARL BARTH, *Church Dogmatics*, II/1, p. 386. Edinburgh: T. & T. Clark, 1957.

Contents

Preface

That it is the poor sections of society which provide the dynamic for the process of national development was clear from the beginning of the World Council of Churches' experiment in the Commission on the Churches' Participation in Development (CCPD). Hence the emphasis in CCPD programmes on the importance of popular participation in development, the need for appropriate technology to express this, and the priority given to structural changes to counteract conditions of domination and dependence. All these are factors making possible a process of economic growth which is organically related to the struggle for social justice and the quest for self-reliance.

This approach, with its special emphasis on the poor and its demonstrable biblical and evangelical roots, was ratified by the Fifth Assembly of the World Council of Churches in Nairobi, 1975. It was noted there that human development is the fruit of the oppressed people's own efforts for liberation and justice. In the hearing on "Justice and Development", therefore, the members of the Assembly proposed as a priority task for CCPD that it should aid the poor and the oppressed in their struggles, and at the same time help the churches to manifest their solidarity with the poor and to second their efforts for a more just and participatory society.

When the CCPD Core Group met in Bossey in May 1976, it had to define this vision, with its clear option in favour of the popular sectors, with more precise reference to the CCPD programmes of participation in development. It was clear that at that time few examples existed of Church participation in development in keeping with this option. But from that time onwards, the churches in various parts of the world, in "developing" countries as well as in the "developed" ones, increasingly began to reflect this line of action in solidarity with the poor and the oppressed. CCPD considered it essential, however, to start an action-reflection process on the basis of the actual practical experience of Christian communities. This would enable the member churches of the WCC to conduct a significant discussion of this option, with a view to giving current experiments greater depth and initiating such experiments where it was judged to be necessary. This naturally gave an enhanced importance to the current programmes of CCPD's partner groups in India, Cameroon and Indonesia, as well as to the new experiments being conducted with the support of the CCPD in certain Latin American churches in the field of ecumenical leadership training programmes for participation in human development in the countries of this region.

At the level of theological reflection, a study on "The Church and the Poor" was initiated. The first results of this were published in *Good News to the Poor*,[1] in which problems of relations with the poor were examined for the early centuries of Church history and in the late medieval period. This initial stage of the study served to underline the importance of the messianic idea of God's justice in which the poor and the oppressed occupy a privileged place and are often themselves the instruments of this justice. This messianic idea is not only a fundamental dimension of the biblical message but it has also been the source of decisive choices by many churches in the course of Christian history.

A second stage followed in which a study was made of relations between the poor and the Church in the crucial period of western colonial expansion and the industrial revolution. A group of specialists contributed the chapters of the book *Separation Without Hope?*,[2] showing that although the poor maintained a foothold in the life of the churches, they tended to be relegated to the least important and most oppressed positions. During this period the churches failed more than ever before to be the champions of the poor. This explains in part the growing indifference of the lowest sections of society to the proclamation of the Christian Gospel in the course of the last century. Finding that their struggles for justice were not supported by the churches nor their cultural expressions approached with understanding by them, they more and more kept their distance from the churches just as the churches themselves remained aloof from these sections of society.

In our time, thank God, there are clear signs that this separation is not going to endure for ever. Both through the World Council of Churches as well as through regional and national ecumenical bodies, the ecumenical movement has demonstrated its practical solidarity *with* the poor, *with* people deprived of their human rights, *with* people who suffer from economic injustice and racist oppression. In face of the challenge presented to them by the poor, the churches are showing a new sensitivity, and this in turn is inspiring a new style of theological, missionary, ecclesiological and developmental reflection, one which takes as its starting point the distinctive perspective of the underprivileged and involves the abandonment of a mode of thought which was developed, and to some extent is still developed, on the basis of positions close to the centres of secular power.

As a third stage in this effort to fulfil the CCPD mandate from the Nairobi Assembly with an action-reflection process, a meeting was held at the Ecumenical Centre of Ayia Napa in Cyprus in September 1978. The main purpose of this meeting was to reflect on the main tendencies apparent today in relations between the poor and the churches, and to make proposals to the churches designed to reinforce their programmes in the direction indicated by the Nairobi Assembly, and strengthen their efforts to play their part in the development of the peoples to whom they belong and whom they are seeking to serve. Various partner groups of the CCPD and the churches were invited to send representatives to this meeting (see the list of participants at the end of this volume). Although small, the group was fully representative of the contemporary ecumenical movement both from a confessional and from a cultural point of view.

Ten papers were produced in preparation for the meeting (each in English, French and Spanish). These provided evidence of the way in which different churches and Christian groups are carrying out their tasks in favour of the poor and expressing their solidarity with them in different parts of the world. The ten papers were circulated among a large circle of friends and institutions related to the CCPD, besides being sent to those invited to the Ayia Napa meeting. They were all invited to send their comments to CCPD. This was most important and helpful since, on the basis of these contributions as well as the preparatory reports presented by each participant in the conference on experiences of solidarity as a member of some Christian community, it was possible to prepare an annotated agenda for discussion at the Cyprus meeting.

The meeting itself lasted two weeks and was in three parts. In the first, taking up the whole of the first week, we concentrated on discussion of the annotated agenda. At the end of the discussion of each proposed chapter of this book, a summary was made recording the consensus reached by the group. At the beginning of the second week, an editorial plan for 19 chapters was drawn up on the basis of the consensus achieved, and these chapters assigned to different members of the conference. Each was responsible for writing part of the manuscript. About 200 pages in length, it was discussed during the third part of the Cyprus meeting and suggestions duly noted down for improving the draft, filling gaps and making corrections.

The author of this preface was entrusted with the work of editing the manuscript a second time. This was a matter of providing the bibliographical references and a full set of footnotes to the main theses of the manuscript. This second edition was sent to all the participants in the Cyprus conference and to over a hundred other persons, with a request for their comments. Many people helped us at this stage with valuable suggestions which have been taken into consideration in the third and final revision. In addition, discussion sessions were arranged with staff members of the WCC sub-units, and we record here our appreciation of their contributions and comments.

At the end of February 1979 a group of six people nominated by the Cyprus conference met in Geneva to put the finishing touches to this third and final version of a manuscript representing the collective work of CCPD and representatives of related partner groups and churches. A week was spent in studying all the comments received and the text of this book was revised in the light of the consensus reached. Besides, a paper was prepared summarizing the more than three years of action-reflection process; this has been submitted to CCPD for consideration with a view to discussion by the WCC Central Committee in the summer of 1980.

In presenting this final version to the churches and their members for their reflection, it seems important to stress that this book is the fruit of a collective effort. Our constant point of reference throughout this work has been the poor and the oppressed. Our principal concern has been to keep faith with them but also with the churches to whom we now submit this book. It is our hope that it will provide food for thought which will enable them to work more effectively for the development of a more just and participatory society. It is our prayer that the movement of spiritual renewal in many Christian communities which are responding creatively to the challenge of the poor may spread throughout the whole people of God, and that the work accomplished by CCPD and so many friends may contribute in some measure to this end.

No claim to exhaustive analysis is made for this volume, nor was that ever its aim. The footnotes provide references to material that is more complete on the topics introduced in the various chapters of this book. Nor is this study an adequate guide to the peculiarities of regional phenomena: the distinguishing marks of the African situation as opposed to

Asia, the specific problems in the developed world as against Latin America, or the differences within any of these geographical areas are not explored at length.

This study rather challenges the churches to become involved with the poor in a struggle that has world dimensions. The proposals to the churches constitute, therefore, an integral part of the text. This document is an invitation to the churches to share more profoundly in action/reflection along with the poor, to experience within the dynamics of history the full significance of what it means to be a church of the poor. As a world phenomenon, poverty thus may be confronted by a world Church, in response to its Lord who made his own the cause of the poor.

I wish to conclude with a final word of acknowledgment and appreciation to C. I. Itty, the director of CCPD. If solidarity with the poor and the oppressed is now being expressed in a variety of ways in many churches and in the World Council of Churches in particular, we owe a tremendous debt of gratitude to the director for his deep sensitivity to the importance of this issue, and for having urged his immediate collaborators to explore its implications for the churches. Without his vision it is doubtful whether the programme could have advanced to the position reflected in the pages of this book.

JULIO DE SANTA ANA

NOTES

[1] Julio de Santa Ana. Geneva: WCC, 1977.
[2] Ed. Julio de Santa Ana. Geneva: WCC, 1978.

Introduction

During the last two decades the world community has been deeply concerned about the plight of the poor. The United Nations and its agencies have been at work to increase the economic performance of the poor countries. Most governments of poor countries have adopted policies and carried out measures to accelerate their growth rate, which some of them hoped would filter down to the poor and benefit them. Several voluntary agencies and most of the Christian churches have substantially expanded their efforts in the fields of service and development aimed at the poorest of the poor. Now, as the second development decade is drawing to a close, many concerned people, voluntary agencies, governments and intergovernmental bodies are assessing their achievements and mapping out their plans for the future. Therefore, it is right and proper that the churches too engage in such a review of the past and discern their future role in this field.

The poor of our time

What is the state of the poor in today's world compared to two decades ago? Have the efforts made by governments, intergovernmental bodies, voluntary agencies and churches during the last few years brought about much change in the overall situation of the poor in the world?

There is overwhelming evidence to conclude that the plight of the poor has deteriorated, their suffering become more acute than ever before and their number increased considerably during the last two decades. Today's poor suffer not only from worsening poverty. They are also subjected to increasing deprivation, exploitation and marginalization. The poor of our time are also the oppressed in our societies.

Almost all countries of the world have their own poor and oppressed. In the rich countries of North America and Europe those who suffer from material poverty are a small minority, but those who are discriminated against and marginalized are a much larger one. However, the bulk of the world's poor and oppressed live in the countries of the Third World. It is in their lives that the acuteness of poverty and oppression is most blatantly manifest. And they form the large majority of the third world population, almost half of the human family.

The poor majority in third world societies are often those who live in a primitive, underdeveloped state. Their poverty is attributed to the slow pace of the development process which has not yet reached them. In fact, the opposite is the case. The large majority of the poor people in the Third World are those who have been drawn into the development process or what is commonly called "modernization" and been impoverished by it. They are people who have been deprived of much of what they have — material things, their skills and know-how, their culture and dignity. The economic system that prevails in most third world countries creates poverty and locks the poor in a state of deteriorating poverty. The introduction of modern technology and new modes of production has made traditional skills and methods of production obsolete and redundant. The political structure and processes that operate in third world societies create marginalization. The impact of the dominant western culture and values has challenged the indigenous culture and values. The poor of today are those who have lost or are fast losing much of what they have, their pride, their identity and their dignity.

This process did not start two decades ago. Its origin goes back to the initial period of colonization of the Third World. What the "modernization" process has done to the poor majority of third world societies becomes vivid when one compares the state of the people before the colonial period with the present situation.

During the pre-colonial period, most societies in the Third World were characterized by self-subsisting, self-perpetrating local units — villages or tribal groupings. Often the means of production, mainly land, were socially owned. Production was geared to the basic needs of the people and was adequate, except in times of national calamity. What was produced was fairly distributed among the members of the village, caste or tribe. Often the local economy produced a net surplus which was appropriated by persons and groups who were entitled to it on the basis of social sanctions. As they used the surplus mainly for non-productive assets and services, the system was basically non-accumulative. Certain societies had a degree of inequality, mainly social although also economic. However, the economic inequality resting on ownership of property and appropriation of surplus was not increased by the production process.

Into such a situation the colonial enterprises introduced many seeds of change. The demand for goods for the metropolitan countries required not only additional production of traditional goods but also production of new goods not needed by the society. Conversely, certain new products and supplies from the metropolitan countries introduced new wants, replacing traditional needs. Thus, the traditional need-based economy began to get disturbed. The creation of a new labour market not only diverted the labour force from traditional economies but also gradually increased unemployment. Imported technology replaced traditional technology and skills. Most serious of all, as a result of the introduction of a new drive for accumulation and the law of the market, some of those who had command over non-human resources began to increase them by the surplus potential of the system, thus starting a process of accumulation. The propensity of the system, aided by the law of the market, began to pull not only new wealth produced but also the resources of the masses increasingly into the hands of those who controlled the new production process, the capital, technology, market distribution and political power. Most of it went to foreign enterprises and the rest to the newly-emerged indigenous entrepreneurs. Consequently, a new class of the rich emerged, as did a new class of the poor, deprived of land, property and traditional skills. This process, which began and progressed during the colonial period, accelerated during the last two decades and continues unabated, receiving added support from the prevailing international economic order.

The most blatant feature of the economic structure in most countries of the Third World is the highly skewed distribution of non-human resources or means of production. Take the case of India. In 1964 "the top 1% of households in the country owned 16%, the top 5% owned 40% and the top 10% owned 56% of land holdings, while the lower 50% owned only 4% of the land and the bottom 20% did not have any land at all. . . . As for ownership of industrial capital, it has been estimated that the top one-tenth of 1% of households when ranked by dividend income own more than half of the personal wealth in the form of shares."[1]

Most of the poor countries have not made any serious attempt to change this system. Growth-oriented development efforts helped to increase the national wealth, but the distribution of it followed existing lines. The result was to increase the wealth of the well-to-do and impoverish the poor. Both happened by the same process. A study undertaken in India compared the situation of the poor in 1960 and 1968 and concluded as follows: "The gains of development have remained largely confined to the upper middle class and the richer sections constituting the top 40% of the population. . . . The per capita consumption of the lower middle and the weaker sections constituting the bottom 40% of the urban population declined by as much as 15 and 20%. In the rural areas . . . the consumption of the poorest 5% actually declined by 1%."[2] Another study in the Philippines showed that, despite a growth in the country's per capita income, those of skilled and unskilled labour in 1978 were only 76 and 63% respectively of what they were in 1972.[3] Similar conclusions are reported from many other countries in the Third World. Thus a growth-oriented development process betrayed the aspirations of the poor.

Even governments and voluntary agencies attempting to serve the poor ended up serving the rich. The propensity of the social system was such that even the good efforts intended for the poor turned against them.

What is present in today's world is not a static state of poverty but a growing deterioration of the misery of the poor. What is alarming is that this happens partly as a result of the greedy efforts of the rich to acquire more. The process of accumulation of surplus, augmentation of wealth and the law of the market prevailing in many countries create and sustain wealth for the wealthy and poverty for the poor. It is the economic system and the values behind it that are at the root of present-day poverty.

The suffering of the poor is not limited to material needs. Their life is also characterized by dependency and oppression. They have very little opportunity for their own decision-making to shape their lives. What and when they eat, where and when they work, what wages they should receive and what price they should pay, where and how they should live, how many children they should have and how to bring them up, what they say and how they should say it, even when they should laugh and when they should cry and how — all these and many other aspects of life are determined or conditioned by the economic system, political power and religious sanctions controlled by the rich, the powerful and the influential. The poor live a life dominated by other human beings in their own society and even abroad. The other side of the picture is a collusion among those who have economic wealth, political power, social influence and even religious authority. This collusion among the dominating groups of different kinds makes the lives of the poor one of oppression and perpetual dependency.

Another aspect of the same vicious circle is the growing marginalization of the poor in the economic, political, social and even religious life of their societies. They do not count in the affairs of life. They have no voice in decision-making processes. They are considered ignorant and worthless. They are treated as expendable ones, the outcasts.

It is the experience of oppression, dependency and marginalization that makes the life of the poor more unbearable. But these experiences are not confined to those who are materially poor. Vast sections of the population of all societies in our world also suffer from similar experiences, though many of them do not face material scarcity to meet their basic needs. Racial and cultural minorities, migrant workers, dissident youth, the unemployed, women and many other groupings in our societies suffer from discrimination and marginalization. As part of the oppressed, they have a certain solidarity with the poor. In that sense the poor are more than the poor. The poor and the oppressed form one rank. That is the reason why the two terms, poor and oppressed, are mentioned together in most instances in this volume. The increasing power of governments, the modern organization of nation states, increasing militarism, the development of monopolies, urbanization, and so on, all add to the increasing oppression and even repression in our societies.

The struggle of the poor

What is the way out and how and by whom can this situation be changed? Much of the international thinking and many of the efforts in recent years have been geared to persuading the rich and the powerful to alleviate the sufferings of the poor and to undertake some reforms in the existing socio-economic structures. So far this path has led to an impasse, as the deteriorating situation of the poor testifies. The so-called development process has ended up in a deadlock. Why?

As pointed out earlier, the root cause of the present plight of the poor is systemic. A few adjustments and cosmetic changes in the system are not enough. What is needed is a total transformation of society, including drastic changes in the political, economic and social structures on national and international levels. This would mean a radical redistribution of resources and power. It is a vain attempt to ask the wealthy and the powerful of the existing societies to dispose of much of their resources and abdicate their positions of power. There are very few instances in history when the powerful have abrogated their power willingly and changed the system that protected their interests. Of course, what they could do and what they have done is to make some efforts to ease their conscience or pacify the poor and thereby prevent radical changes. At the same time, either deliberately or unwittingly, they have strengthened the existing structures and entrenched them against any eventual onslaught.

Most governments in the countries of the Third World have behaved the same way. They represent mainly the power interests in their own

countries and abroad. In a few countries, where those in charge of governments are concerned about the plight of their poor, the political will has
been lacking to take the necessary measures, due to pressure and threats
from those holding the reins of economic power and interests.

It must be admitted that there are governments, intergovernmental
bodies and voluntary agencies, including churches, with the support of
well-meaning people from the ranks of the rich and powerful, who have
genuinely tried to do their best for the poor and the oppressed. But often
they tend to look on the poor as objects of their charity and good efforts,
the passive recipients of their goodwill. Their efforts have mainly been *for*
the poor and seldom *with* the poor and have proved inadequate as they
fail to involve the poor as agents of change. More importantly, such
efforts do not take seriously the fact that what the poor are demanding is
that they be treated as subjects of their own history. What they are fighting
for is precisely recognition of themselves as people having the potential to
change their own situation and society as a whole. A people who are
fighting against marginalization in society do not want to be marginalized
in the efforts made for their own wellbeing.

Besides, groups and agencies from outside the ranks of the poor and
the oppressed are likely to see the situation and the problems from a
wrong perspective. For example, many from outside see the issue mainly
as poverty or scarcity of goods and services. From this perspective or
objectification and isolation of the issue, they design programmes to
increase the supply of goods and services. But that does not answer the
basic demands and aspirations of the people which are essentially their
liberation from oppression and dependency. For them poverty is only one
aspect of their plight. Similarly there are agencies which look at the issue
as one of human rights. Again, one aspect of the situation is isolated and
worked on without the total situation being looked at with the priority
needs of the people in their historical contexts.

Many consider the poor as the problem, and the rich and the powerful
as agents of the solution. The truth is the opposite. The present situation is
created and sustained by the rich and the powerful. Therefore, they and
the system they uphold are the problem. The situation of injustice, exploitation and oppression is of their making. As they are part of the problem,
they should not be expected to offer solutions. The poor who are victims
of the present situation will be the ones to find the way out.

But is this not a dream? If one takes history seriously it can be concluded that this is a practical possibility — perhaps the only possibility. It
is well known that most instances of social transformation that have taken

place in history happened through organized efforts of the victims of the *status quo*. Therefore, there is no reason to doubt that the future will follow the tested paths of history.

But do not the poor of today find themselves so helpless and powerless that they do not have the courage and strength to initiate and sustain such a hard and long struggle against the entrenched forces of present-day society? It is true that large sections of the poor are in such a resigned state. In fact they have been brainwashed into feeling and believing themselves to be helpless and impotent. They are also told to think that existing power structures are invincible and that any effort to challenge them would be crushed.

But change is in the air; the poor are awakening. The poor societies are in ferment. Many among them are becoming aware of their potential and the strength of organized mass struggle. They are realizing that there is no power (other than God) which is greater than people's power. They are affirming the historical subjectivity of the people in social transformation.

What is the evidence of this new awakening among the poor? It is evident in most countries, be it in the villages of Asia, the slums of Africa, among indigenous people in Latin America, minorities in North America or migrant workers in Europe. It is evident when the squatters in a slum in Manila resist eviction, when a village community in India organizes itself to resist exploitation by moneylenders, when the people of Soweto protest against racial discrimination, when the Indians in Brazil resist encroachment on their land by transnational corporations, when the aboriginals of Australia refuse mining in their territory. It is also evident when communities at local levels organize themselves into cooperatives to improve their living conditions, increase their productivity and enhance their purchasing and bargaining power. It is evident too when people innovate and master technology that is appropriate to their situation and refuse to be mystified by foreign technology and dependent on outside experts. It is seen when trade unions demand greater participation in the affairs of their industries, when peasants demand land for the tillers, when women demand equal wages for equal work and when groups work for human rights. It also finds expression in political movements for structural changes towards a just, participatory society. It is manifested in the renaissance of popular religion, culture and language. These and many other expressions of the newly-awakened poor testify to the growth of people's movements and organizations of the poor.

Obviously the immediate goals they pursue and the strategies they adopt differ according to the contexts and strength of their organization. But most of these movements have much in common. They are anxious to resist further violation of their rights, responsibilities and resources. They are eager to win more space for their organized efforts and to expand their power base. They are keen to achieve certain immediate goals in order to prove their potential and sustain the hope of their people. They are committed to lessen and, if possible, eliminate poverty, oppression and injustice and bring about a just, participatory society.

The churches and the poor

Throughout history, churches have had a deep concern for the poor and the oppressed. They cannot do otherwise and maintain their faith in Jesus Christ who came "to preach good news to the poor and set at liberty the oppressed". In recent years, the churches within the fellowship of the World Council of Churches have been seized with a new sense of urgency to do what they can to alleviate the sufferings of the poor and the oppressed. Many churches have expanded their programmes in the field of development and expended more resources. Many have come out championing the cause of racial justice and fundamental human rights. There is no doubt that these efforts had some effect in a number of local situations and in raising the public conscience on a global level. However, as mentioned earlier, the plight of the poor is deteriorating; forces of oppression and injustice are becoming stronger and more entrenched. Some Christians are inclined to give up their efforts out of despair and frustration. Some are feeling tired and weary of repeated calls to help the poor. Some have lost the sense of urgency they seemed to feel a decade ago. Many are confused as to what to do and how to go about manifesting their concern for the poor.

But this is not the whole picture. More and more Christians, especially in the countries of the Third World, are deepening their commitment to the struggle of the poor and the oppressed. Some of their experiences and insights have provided the inspiration and data for this volume. A few of these insights are mentioned here, not as a summary of what follows, but as an appetizer for further reading.

Their commitment is based on their faith in Christ, their biblical under-standing of the poor and the oppressed and their acute sense of the plight of the poor and their perception of history. They believe that the God of the Old Testament is the God of the poor and the oppressed, one who heard the cry of the enslaved people of Israel, who liberated them from

Egypt, who sustained them in exodus and in exile and who continued to act in history to establish justice and righteousness. He is the one who gave laws of justice, raised kings to administer justice and prophets to condemn injustice. The God of the New Testament is the same God, who sent his son Jesus Christ to be born in a manger, to live the life of a carpenter, to preach good news to the poor, care for the sick and the needy and comfort them in sorrow. He is the one who allowed himself to be victimized by the religious and political powers, be crucified like a criminal and die in agony. Yet this man who was poor, who owned nothing, who was void of all worldly desires and ambitions, was glorified by God who raised him from death. Through his resurrection his offer of his Kingdom to the poor and the oppressed was vindicated. And He continues to be present as the living Spirit in and among all those who are hungry, sick and enslaved. And He will come again to gather his people to his kingdom and judge the nations according to their treatment of the least of his brethren. It is this faith in Christ, who is on the side of the poor and the oppressed, that is at the heart of their commitment.

They are also acutely aware of the deep sufferings of the millions who are poor and oppressed. They hear their cry for liberation; they hear the call of God, "Let my people go". Their cry and his call become one spur for the same commitment. They recognize that their commitment to the cause of the poor and the oppressed is a commitment to the liberation of all people. Those who oppress, exploit and enrich themselves at the expense of the poor are also God's people. But it is as the poor and the oppressed are liberated that the rich and the oppressors will also find their liberation.

Their commitment to the struggle of the poor and the oppressed is also supported by scientific analysis and interpretation of historical realities and the process of social transformation.

They manifest their commitment by participating in the organized struggle of the poor and the oppressed. Those of them who do not belong to the poor and the oppressed make it a point not to take up leadership positions. They see their role as helpers in the struggle and communicators to the outside society. Some of them who are intellectuals assist the organization with their insights into history, in the formulation of strategies and the training of cadres. Depending on their role in society, they perform a certain function of advocacy for the cause of the poor and the oppressed. Through their membership in the churches, they try to enlist the support of Christians both in the country and abroad for the struggle. They strive to manifest their solidarity with the poor and the oppressed through their political options, choice of work, pattern of consumption, use of resources and style of life.

Their participation in the struggle of the poor and the oppressed does not mean commitment to any absolutist ideology or closed theories of history. Their commitment is primarily to the people and their struggle. But their participation requires a process of action and reflection. It is through action towards the transformation of society that knowledge is tested and gained. It is through reflection that action is reviewed and formulated. Thus they maintain an openness to new insights without weakening their commitment to the revolutionary struggle.

As Christians they pay attention to the questions and challenges that the poor and the oppressed pose to the churches. They in turn reflect on the life of the churches from the perspective of the poor and communicate these to the churches to which they belong. They are concerned about the alliances that the churches have with the rich and the powerful in society. They question the captivity of theology by the ideologies of dominating classes. They find the churches reflecting social differentiations similar to those in society. They find the structures of the churches heavy and non-participatory. They feel that the churches alienate the poor and marginalize the oppressed in very much the way the social institutions do. They find the churches behaving like the rich and acting as a power. They are concerned that the poor do not feel wanted or at home in many of the churches.

Their commitment to the struggle of the poor and the oppressed implies not merely providing support but also making a unique contribution as Christians. It also implies a certain degree of critical participation, especially when the direction of the struggle involves compromising Christian convictions. By being involved with the struggle and by being in solidarity with the poor and the oppressed, they earn the right and opportunity to make their Christian witness to those poor and oppressed who do not share the Christian faith. Besides, the struggle itself requires constant vigilance to keep it on course. The Christian faith that considers love and *koinonia* as the ultimate goals of human relationships can make a contribution to the struggle which might otherwise be content with the establishment of just societal structures. Similarly, the Christian view of the sinfulness of human beings and the ambiguity of all powers can be a constant reminder of the relative character of all human achievements and structures. Above all the necessity to view all powers and historical processes as subject to the guidance of the Lord of history and for all human beings to relate to God in Christ for the experience of true humanity are aspects of the Christian faith of which those in the struggle need to be made aware.

The most exciting and rewarding experience of those Christians who have joined the struggle of the poor and the oppressed is that within that context they found new ecclesial communities. Sometimes, these communities evolved as they themselves got together in his name to share their experiences and to seek together the resources of faith to sustain them. Sometimes they emerged as the poor and the oppressed within a neighbourhood began to form their own fellowships for prayer or Bible study or intercession. Whatever the factors at the beginning, most of these communities have much in common. Their membership is largely drawn from the poor and the oppressed. Their gatherings try to relate Christian faith to their daily life and struggle for justice. They consider common Bible study as a great source of inspiration. They evolve new songs, new liturgies and new ways of celebration which correspond to their language, milieu and aspirations. Their gatherings and community life are based on full participation of all members in which each and every one has a contribution to make.

Such new ecclesial communities have emerged in large numbers in several countries of the world. They point to a new action of the Holy Spirit in our time to renew his Church and to transform it into a home for the poor and the oppressed, "the weary and the heavy laden". They point in the direction of a "Church of the Poor".

NOTES

[1] The Report of the Mahalanobis Committee on the Distribution of Income and Levels of Living (1964), quoted in C. T. Kurien, *Poverty, Planning and Social Transformation*. Madras: Indian Council of Social Science Research, 1978.

[2] *The Study of Poverty in India* by V. M. Dandekar and N. Rath, 1971, quoted in *Poverty, Planning and Social Transformation, op. cit.*

[3] A memorandum circulated to UNCTAD V delegates by four Philippine church groups: the National Council of Churches, Association of Major Religious Superiors of Men and Women, National Secretariat for Social Action and the Justice and Peace Commission of the Catholic Bishops' Conference, quoted in *Ecumenical Press Service*, No. 12, 10 May 1979.

1.
The Churches and the Plight of the Poor

I · Two Voices but a Single Cry

"In a wilderness of idolatrous destruction the great voice of God still cries out for life."

The scandal of poverty in a world of abundance is crying out. Development decade after development decade passes by, but the poor are still dying. They die from starvation, from deprivation, from oppression. But it is their life and labour which create the wealth of the few.

In a world of scarcity in which everyone is in want, poverty would be a common challenge to everybody. But in a world of abundance in which many people are poor in order that a few others may stay rich, poverty — or better, wealth — is an infamy. Where the rich refuse to give up their privileges and share their plenty, their situation asks for reproach.

But the cry of this scandal does not seem to be heard. The people who have the power to change do not use their authority for justice, and in many cases use it to reinforce injustice. Even God seems to pay no heed to the prayer of the poor, as Job in his despair utters bitterly (Job 24 : 12).

Poverty is not an accident. It is a fundamental, incisive phenomenon in our society which destroys humanity, that is, God's creation. This phenomenon can only be attacked at its roots. The root of all evil things is, according to Paul in I Timothy 6 : 10, the love of money. Jesus calls it Mammon, an idol.[1] It promises wealth, but creates poverty; it suggests humanity, and its effect is separation; it speaks of liberty, but enslaves people. It is multinational, pervasive, and demands allegiance of the hearts of humankind. And Jesus simply says: "Mammon and God cannot be served together."[2]

The task of changing these patterns seems to be too heavy and the willingness to do so too weak. But certainly, the Lord Yahweh has heard the appeal of the poor for rescue from their slavery. What is more, the voices of the poor and the voice of God have become one great cry, questioning the rich: "Why are you so rich? Where are you?"[3]

Far ahead of his Church, which He created as his *avant-garde*,[4] the Son of God goes on his way towards the renewal of our earth. And over his shoulder He looks back and calls to his Church: "Why are you standing still? Follow me on my pilgrimage; only in obedience will you know me. For obedience is the only knowledge of God."[5]

On this pilgrimage a new and far-reaching step has to be taken. With all their ambiguities, sectors of the churches have always helped the poor in one way or another. They even learned to be with them. But nowadays the situation of the poor forces us to rediscover the old reality of the Church as originally a Church of the poor themselves.[6]

It is the aim of this book to demonstrate the necessity of this endeavour. To be a church *for* the poor is not enough. To be a church *with* the poor, however necessary this may be, is not sufficient. The situation of the poor in our world helps us to rediscover the origin of the Church in New Testament times as a church *of* the poor and asks us to become again such a Church of the poor themselves — to be a Church living on the grace of Jesus Christ who for our sake "became poor, so that through his poverty you might become rich" (II Cor. 8 : 9).

Signs of hope

In many parts of the world several groups and movements have heard the cry of the poor. Many of them operate outside the churches. However, a growing number of them can nowadays also be found within the Church. They have become sensitive to the situation of the poor today and to their demands and hopes. It is as if a wind were blowing at the same time in many places, clarifying the situation and helping the churches to realize that they cannot remain passive once they see the implications of the situation of the underprivileged in our time.

Some parishes, church groups and communities, realizing the present conditions of the poor, know that they must decide consciously to identify themselves with the poor and to live in solidarity with those who suffer from the mechanisms which create and freeze the situation of poverty. They are aware that, to those who believe in Jesus Christ as the incarnation of a loving God whose purpose is justice and equality (II Cor. 8 : 14), the present patterns of poverty are a scandal. Among Christians and, still more important, among churches, this indefensible situation is stimulating a movement (still unorganized, often somewhat spontaneous, but growing in both developed and developing countries) which decides clearly in favour of the poor. Scandalous though the condition of the poor may be, it is seen as one in which people are more open to God's grace than are those who are rich. This confirms biblical views of the poor. Not that poverty is idealized.[7] The very fact that these people align themselves with the poor in their struggles and strive to eradicate poverty by attacking its root causes shows how realistic they are in their decision. This realism makes them aware, however, that the poor with their hopes and expectations are much more open to God than are the rich.

Another aspect of the life of the churches in our time is the increasing involvement of certain sectors in the struggle for freedom and against injustice. There is a growing realization in these quarters that the prevailing condition of the poor cannot be solved by charity alone. The charitable approach may still be needed to deal with certain more urgent cases but the very character of structural poverty demands that its root causes be tackled by appropriate methods at the structural level. In other words, the factors which generate deprivation of life and prevent the satisfaction of basic human needs, which result in human inequality and dependence, must be tackled at the level of their causes rather than at the level of their effects.

As a result of this growing involvement of church groups in the struggle for justice, Christian communities are more visibly committed to the movement to defend people's rights than they were a decade ago. For those who share this commitment, the rights of the poor are as "the rights of God". There are sectors of the Christian churches which have decided to become "representatives of the poor". The poor have always been present in the churches, though in the last centuries they seem not to have been very much involved in the life of the Christian communities.[8] But the presence of the poor at Christian celebrations and services is one thing; for the churches to become churches of the poor is quite another thing. To make the Church "the voice of the voiceless", is what Dom Helder Camara, the Roman Catholic Archbishop of Olinda and Recife in Brazil, for example, has been trying to do for the past fifteen years.[9] This explains the growing number of Christian communities which in recent years have come to share the struggles of the poor and the oppressed for justice and liberation.

What does this mean for the life of the Universal Church? Basically, these choices, these commitments, these experiences are to be understood as "signs of hope". In what follows we present briefly some of the signs being manifested in various parts of the world. We call them signs, not examples. They are not blueprints that can be initiated easily, but signals of a new commitment and a new self-understanding of the Church.

STORIES OF THE CHURCH OF THE POOR

St Mark's Cathedral, Bangalore, India

Built in the early nineteenth century, the cathedral long retained the marks of its origin. But in recent times, the Indian clergy have tried to break through these limitations. In a city where 40% of the population live below the poverty line, it is nevertheless difficult for most of the congregation to come into direct contact with the poor. But as they became aware of the plight of the needy and sensitized to their living conditions, people began to respond to the challenge of the poor. Contact with the poor has led to an understanding of mission as commitment to liberation. Solidarity with the poor came to mean meeting Jesus in service. The pilgrimage has already begun . . . Various forms of communication are used to make people aware of the sufferings and struggles of the poor. Young people have taken the initiative in relating worship to two specific issues: the poor and the unemployed poor. An employment service was established and this became a meeting point for the congregation and the desperately poor; new possibilities of service and solidarity were consequently opened up and the congregation enabled to move forward. Prophetic tasks were envisaged and work in the slums led to direct engagement in the struggle for justice and in the organization of the poor. The movement is slow and often frustrating but the effort to become and be the Church for the poor continues . . .[10]

The Aymara Church in Bolivia

On the south eastern shores of the Titicaca Lake there are many villages inhabited by Aymara communities. They are people whose ancestors ruled the Kollasuyo Empire, many years before the Spanish *conquistadores* came to dominate the High Andes in the sixteenth century. When the western invaders arrived, an age of pain, suffering and oppression began for the Aymaras as well as for other indigenous peoples: slavery, forced labour, separation of families and communities, were some of the hardships they had to live with. The Aymaras resisted as much as they could, but they were unable to overcome the power of the *conquistadores*, the colonizers and those who came into power after political independence. Their situation did not change basically with that political change. The churches, in the best cases, had a paternalistic attitude towards them. They saw the Church as an institution of *gringos*, of white people. For the Aymaras the Christians did not bring "good news" but rather very bad news.

At the end of the nineteenth century the Methodist Church began its work of evangelization and service among the Aymara communities of the Bolivian coast of the Titicaca Lake. The missionaries and Bolivian pastors (most of them whites) tried to help the Aymaras, but paternalism continued to characterize their action. However, in increasing numbers, the Aymara people began to be more and more involved in church life. They became the majority of the Methodist community in Bolivia.

Awareness of the oppression practised on them for centuries moved the Aymaras of the Methodist Church to give constructive expression to it. Development activities were planned and carried out by the Aymaras themselves; health care programmes were implemented with their participation at decision-making levels and — what is indeed most important — an Aymara bishop was nominated to lead the church. Working together with a "Council of Amantas" ("wise people"), the Methodist Church in Bolivia is becoming an institution of the indigenous peoples in that country. Prestige projects are no longer considered most important. Now priority is given to training Aymara leadership, to work with peasants and with indigenous movements. The effort towards a church of the Indians is an expression of the search for a church of the poor. The message of the liberating gospel of Jesus Christ has gained a deeper meaning for these peoples; it is no longer a manifestation of paternalism from the Church, but rather a proclamation which helps them to understand better how to reaffirm their deep convictions and values. The Gospel is no longer a thing of *gringos*, but something which the Aymaras feel is addressed directly to themselves.

Nobody who visits them can be surprised if they spend a whole night praying in their chapels, if they organize cooperatives for economic production, if they begin to reinterpret Aymara history (which they were supposed to forget, according to the wishes of the white dominators) in the light of the Gospel, if they fight for their rights, if they join forces with the mining workers in social struggles for a better life. There is a new life springing up among the Aymaras of Bolivia. Their church is not only a poor church, it is above all a church of the poor in which the liberating Spirit of God is at work.

In the southern mountains of Appalachia, USA

The people of the southern mountains of Appalachia are among the poorest in the USA. They work hard in the coal mining industry where organized labour meets with many difficulties in securing its objectives, and where disease, accident and the changing market make opportunities for work uncertain. In this part of the country, evangelical Christianity is increasingly becoming pentecostal in character. There are many services which the churches are able to provide. They seem to be mostly of a very down-to-earth kind, like "washing feet". Yet they are greatly needed. People discover that the Church is with them. They feel at home in the church. Something of the promise of ministering as disciples of Christ is discovered as the community of faith is built up, when prayer meetings take place in the homes of poor people. The poor begin to feel that Jesus is liberating them from their various forms of bondage. They receive strength to persevere in their continuing struggle. In this context, the Church keeps hope alive.[11] It is the church of the poor, not of the powerful. The choice it has made finds expression in the kind of worship that is then celebrated. It is an expression of human liberation in popular liturgical forms.[12]

Churches' participation in Indonesian development

Two-thirds of the world's absolute poor live in four countries in Asia, and Indonesia is one of them. The plight of the poor has challenged the Church in Indonesia into positive response and action. Emphasizing the need to motivate the people who are too poor and powerless to speak up for themselves, the Development Centre of the Council of Churches in Indonesia (DGI) through its village motivators programme seeks to bring a new awareness among the poor of their condition, and helps them to struggle for a better life through their own efforts by means of community building development programmes, giving them a sense of dignity, a sense of achievement and a sense of hope.

The motivators, who work in teams of three in remote villages of Indonesia, primarily aim to be with the people — sharing their everyday life and winning their confidence. Their presence helps the villagers to reflect and analyse their situations, ask questions not asked before, and thus begins a common search for a constructive programme of development by the people themselves. These motivators often deal with tribal people whose culture is distinctly different from their own. They search hard for a way that would preserve their culture while helping them to meet the challenge of modernization. The motivators are trained in imparting skills, in simple technology and in agricultural development with which they give practical guidance to rural people to develop themselves.

The motivators are drawn from the churches in Indonesia which responded to the challenge to be with the poor and serve them. In a very practical way, the Church goes out among the poor, to be with them in their plight and serve them in their struggle for a better life. In some respects, these young motivators have characteristics of a religious order, since they make a covenant to remain poor in the villages to which they are sent. They are formed into a community of committed young Indonesians reaching out to fulfil an ideal that the Christian Church is holding up to them.

In the south of the USA

In the United States the Presbyterian Church in the US, a relatively small regional denomination "born in schism" at the time of the Civil War, is struggling to face in mission the challenges of today's world. In a mission consultation in 1978 the denomination's delegates heard the voices from the Third World (one-third of those present were from outside the US) and interpreted them as the voice of Jesus Christ calling them to greater faithfulness in facing today's challenges. The report pointed to capitalism as an economic system that was sinful and labelled complicity with it a sin. It called upon the church and its members to change their life-styles, identify and change the harmful system and its effects upon human beings, and to focus mission efforts towards international economic justice in work abroad and at home. The report puts on the agenda for the church's study and action the whole question of justice for the poor, and challenges this church of the relatively well-to-do to face that question. Resistance and evasion are already evident, but the voice of the poor, when heard clearly, can pose the challenge even to a middle-class church.[13]

The Church of Nampula, Mozambique

From 8 to 13 September 1977, the Church of Mozambique organized in Beira a national pastoral assembly. This gathering was the result of intense preparatory work which lasted for two years. Its aim was to analyse the situation of the Church in the new context of Mozambican society. The assembly was attended by bishops, priests, religious and lay people. Each diocese sent its delegates and presented a report on the results of collective work at the diocesan level. Each district had sent detailed reports which had then been discussed and compiled during a diocesan assembly. The extracts which follow were published in *Libertar*, a newsletter of Christian grassroots communities in Portugal, in its January 1978 issue.[14]

The communities

1. When we talk of communities in our diocese, we mean those groups of people who meet regularly and share their life, who celebrate the Word of God and, whenever possible, the eucharist, and who also have community leaders. The number of persons forming such groups varies greatly; the average is between twenty and forty.

2. Using these criteria, we have in our diocese some 524 communities. Their geographical distribution is very irregular.

3. For a deeper knowledge of the practice in the life of these communities, some points have to be taken into account:

    There is the experience of *radical change* brought about by the event of independence lived as a liberation which must be total and reach all the levels at which people have suffered oppression. With regard to the Church, this liberation was concretized in the following ways:
    a) separation of religion and state and the withdrawal of privileges formerly granted to the Catholic Church;
    b) nationalization of education and health systems, thus accelerating the end of "missions";
    c) open criticism of the Church as an ally of colonialism.

    This process has been somehow painful and required great abnegation and the discovery of what is essential in the life of the Church and in evangelization.
    The above-mentioned developments had some repercussions within the Church. Many missionaries left Mozambique; many Christians abandoned all practice of religion; the teachers ceased to be community leaders; community leaders were absorbed as political cadres.

4. Within this process of change, a *new consciousness* is emerging among Christians. Passivity and fear, clericalism and sacramentalism, the lack of instruction or conviction, the lack of the sense of responsibility and the fear of exercising ministries are considered serious deficiencies which must be overcome.

5. In order to overcome these deficiencies, it seems urgently necessary, *relying on our own resources*, to find new ways for:
    — a deeper approach to the Word of God (we ask the bishops to provide us Bibles in Portuguese printed in Mozambique);
    — the celebration of the sacraments, particularly the reconciliation and the eucharist.
6. It seems to us that this will bring to full maturity some fruits which have already started appearing in the communities, which are:
    — the progressive transition from being-Christian-by-force to being-Christian-by-conviction;
    — the transition from a childish faith to the faith of adult people.

In South Korea

It is one of the most moving experiences of the recent history of Asian Christianity to be witnessing the birth of new messianic communities. Compared with other communities in Asia, the significance of the Korean communities lies in their being within a country-wide, historically contradictory context of struggle. This struggle is a political struggle between the masses of the poor and a few rich people, between the oppressed and the oppressors. In the midst of this struggle, unique in its intellectual and physical intensity, the new messianic communities have emerged.

The nucleus for all other new congregations was the "Thursday Prayer Meeting", beginning in April 1974. The actual reason was the wave of detentions of Christians which began that year. Ham, the "Korean Gandhi" who had suffered in South Korean as well as in North Korean prisons, discovered the prayer meeting as a tool of resistance. In the midst of detentions and trials, he called for "prayer meetings", on the eve of the weekly trial sessions, that is, Thursday evening.

The first time only the families of the detained attended, about 50 people, but later hundreds came. In the beginning there were only Christians; later Taoists and Buddhists joined. "We are praying for all accused and detained." In 1975 eight men were sentenced to death and executed. They were accused of belonging to a forbidden party. "Although their fathers and sons were executed although they were innocent, and the parents and wives, children, brothers and sisters were crying during the prayers, our service was a celebration of life and hope. We are linked to each other in mutual confidence and love."

All those who are excluded from public life, relatives and friends of detained and those suffering in prison, join in the service and prayer every Thursday. During the meetings names as well as painful situations are mentioned, by a wife, a son. Those who pray are themselves being pursued and spied upon. They are dismissed professors and students, slum-dwellers and peasants, pastors and social workers: human beings without property, people who have their life only in their new community.

At the end of 1975, a few slum-dweller families who used to join the prayer meetings lost their huts because of the government programme to "make our town more beautiful". The families resisted and built tents in order to defend their rights. One small tent was used for prayers. This was the beginning of another new community: Sarang-Dang Room of Love. Once the whole community was detained. Later six women and ten men were sentenced to prison and also their prayer leader. Sarang-Dang is a living community in the wilderness, however, with hope as a new community of those who are no longer lonely.

There are other newly emerging communities with a similar history and similar stories, like "Galiläa", "Yumin", "Peace market", "House of dawn". Others are the non-localized communities gathering around "The spirit of March 1: Samil Chul" or the women of the "Group of 18", all wives of those sentenced in connection with the famous "Myong Dong Trials", solidarity groups for the "Dong A. Iebo" journalists, and others.

The new communities are living in the confidence that God is present and active in the struggle. At the new year service of 1978 with the released "1 March Declaration" victims, they told the community: "We are with the poor. We are therefore ready to be put into prison at any time. To be imprisoned is even a new manifestation of our community." [15]

The church of the poor in an affluent society

In the Netherlands, an affluent society, a bitter problem has nevertheless existed for many years. Thousands of people are waiting for housing. There are many reasons for this shortage, one of the major and most smarting being the destination of whole blocks of houses to commercial non-dwelling purposes. Houses intended to be lived in are forced to be left empty. The inhabitants are urged to leave and make way for business offices, shops or for speculation in landed property, especially in the urban centres where land now has more value than the buildings. But some people have not accepted this rule. Younger people especially, who have been waiting for years to find a home, broke into the empty residences. They restored them, fixed them up and refurnished them, but without the consent of the owners. They broke the law which protects private properties better than people in need of housing. Police forces try to expel these squatters.

In the old city of Amsterdam the biggest squatter residence is the Leeuwenburg building. It consists of 15 houses with some big industrial premises. The building is more than two hundred years old but is still in good condition. It had been used for wholesale trading in metallics. In 1969 the metallics trade came to an end, as investors bought everything in order to demolish the premises and build a hotel. In 1972 the inhabitants were expelled and the interiors of the mansions were pulled down to make them unfit for habitation. The people of the area protested, reminding the municipality of its promises to establish new houses in that neighbourhood. The local council of churches joined in this protest but nothing happened. The building remained empty.

The next year squatters, with the help of people in the area and of church people, broke into the houses and restored them at their own expense, working together in a completely self-reliant way. Now about a hundred people are living there in 60 apartments. In the meantime the entire property was again resold. The profit was about one million guilders. The new inhabitants are again threatened with expulsion. Together with the group of the Amsterdam Council of Churches they have decided to stay where they are and to resist the police.

In 1978 a study group of the Council of Churches in the Netherlands made a report on this and other stories, called *Squatters in the Netherlands*, in which they pleaded against a new law on squatting which the Dutch government was preparing. This law protects the owners and makes way for new speculation. After long discussions the Dutch Council of Churches has accepted the report and has objected to the government on the anti-squatter law. For the first time private property, being inviolable, is attacked by the churches and humanity is considered to be more important than the laws of the market. The squatters themselves have so far not received any security.

Biblical data for a church of the poor

These stories of churches again becoming churches of the poor have an interesting resemblance to the stories of the churches we read of in the New Testament. The traditions of both Old and New Testaments show us a profound and radical counter-movement against a development which separates humankind into oppressors and oppressed, into rich and poor, into wealthy and needy people.[16] The Bible attacks those who are in power and accuses them of not using their power in favour of the powerless, but on the contrary of adding power to the oppressors.[17] When the new Church arises, it shows a radical style of living together in which poverty is eradicated (Acts 2 : 42-47; 4 : 32-35). Paul demonstrates in his letters a Church based on God's election of the poor. "God has chosen things low and contemptible, mere nothings, to overthrow the existing order" (I Cor. 1 : 28 NEB).[18] So does the Letter of James. The Bible generates a counter-force against the prevailing power structures of this world.[19] It does so in a manifold way. Through the prophets and the legislation of the Torah it tries to establish rules for the practice of justice by which God's land and its wealth are honestly shared, and people who are threatened with poverty can find their way back into society.

In describing Israel and the Church as the people of God concrete solidarity is evoked and practised in a new brotherhood. This justice and solidarity are fundamentally based on a profound spirituality. It is the spirit of God and of Jesus Christ who gave himself away and who taught people not to rely on family, land or houses (Matt. 19 : 29) but on the love of God (Matt. 6 : 25-34, Luke 12 : 22-32). This spirituality creates the room in which the humble and the needy find their freedom. At the same time it makes it possible for the rich to participate.[20] In the Bible the rich are never locked up in their wealth. They are called to free themselves from being the slaves of their property, and are asked to make it available for the sake of justice and, if necessary, to get rid of it. In a process of conscientization and conversion the rich are invited to join the struggle of the poor. They are called to share this new community, but only on the condition of God's election of the poor, who are the bearers of the Gospel, not because as such they are nearer to God, but because God is nearer to them. The good message becomes clear in them; they are the basis of God's recreation.[21]

The poor outside the Church

In the first place, to become again a church of the poor means to become humble again. To speak of the Church as the party of the people is surely a plain fallacy, not only because of the ambiguities of the Church, but because of the fact that in most countries the Church is only a small minority.[22] Liberation is not only a church affair. Neither is the option to become a church of the poor primarily to do with the elaboration of a new fashion in theology. That would be using the poor again for our own purposes. A "theology of the underdog" can and does only arise from careful listening to their voices,[23] which together with God's word are becoming a single cry.

Nor should we want to "baptize" the poor too early. Becoming a church of the poor is not a means of repairing lost positions, nor a new method of church growth. It is a challenge to become faithful to the witness of Jesus Christ; it is an act of conversion.[24]

The captivity of our churches should be broken. Our closed churches should be opened to be creative institutions in a movement of liberation, in all the deep senses of that biblical word, including material liberation.

Within this process of the people, the Church, according to the calling of the Lord, should be the main agent.[25] It cannot be the Church without the poor, Christ being present in them. A church without the poor is a place He has obviously left.[26] Therefore the Church should be open to the claims of the poor. It should bear their burden and ask the deprived outside the Church in what ways the Church can support their cause.

As a sign of witness to Jesus Christ, the Church must remain attentive to the poor who appeal to it. In trying to respond to the needs of the poor, the Church must use all the possibilities at its disposal to solve their problems. Participation in social action on their behalf implies a response to socio-economic suffering. Basically, structural poverty can only be tackled from a political perspective, and the struggle against it asks for political involvement.[27]

Direct encounter with the poor, not as objects of charity, but as subjects of change, will renew the structures of our churches. It will act like a mirror in which the Church sees itself. Its credibility, even the credibility of the Gospel, will be tested. It will change its theological, missiological and ecclesiological concepts and will lead towards a new understanding of the Lord of the Bible.[28] The priorities of the agenda of the churches will be changed as can be seen in several parts of the world where the Church has become faithful to the witness of Jesus Christ in becoming the church of the poor.[29]

The poor within the Church

As a part of the society, the Church is not free from the antagonisms of this world. The contradictions in relations between rich churches in the developed countries and poor churches in the developing countries create severe problems. But also within a local community of the Church anywhere there are enormous gaps sometimes between the income, properties and wealth of the members, who of course call themselves brothers and sisters in Christ.[30] Often the poor are domesticated. They do not participate in decision-making. They are accepted on the conditions of the stronger groups. Within the Church a mentality of growth, prestige and personal profit exists which affects fellowship and separates people. The Law of the Market has its grip on the church community as much as on the larger society.[31]

The need to transform the institutional ecclesiastical bodies into real communities in Christ is urgent, though this cannot be dissociated from the transformation of society. On the margins of the official churches new communities arise in which new values are being tested. The Church itself should accept this challenge. Being a model of the new Kingdom of God it should be a healing community in social and economic matters also. Solidarity is a basic option of the people of God. It was the identity and raison d'être of Israel. In losing this solidarity Israel was destroyed and taken into captivity.[32] "The aim is equality", II Corinthians 8 : 14 tells us. The first church in Jerusalem practised this equality as a sign of its freedom and resurrection.[33]

Within this new community the vicious circle of greed can be broken. Private property is not an order of creation. New experiments in sharing earnings could be arranged in which institutions and organizations could be a step ahead of the surrounding society.[34] This should not be a new law but a sign of freedom and an example of the new order Jesus Christ has created.

The poor within ourselves

The human being has become a product of political trading for particular interests. Mass communication systems, commercials, the laws of the market, are creating unnecessary needs and unwanted desires. A permanent and vague feeling of guilt is evoked to make people want to consume, distracting them from the realities of life.

Most educational systems are based on progress and success, thus oppressing the less successful parts of ourselves.[35] The Church sometimes tends to strengthen these feelings of guilt by reducing the liberation of God to a morality in which the abundance of God himself is forgotten and the fullness of life is replaced by a masochistic weariness. Our failures, the things of which we are afraid, and our handicaps, are pushed down. We do not dare to encounter the poor in ourselves or the poor outside ourselves. We are afraid of them and do not want to be reminded that we might belong to that world from which we want to escape. We are forced to climb the ladder of success. Our attachment to power and property is so overwhelmingly strong because our faith in God and in ourselves is so weak. That is to say, we marginalize and oppress the poor within our own beings, as the poor are marginalized and oppressed on social, economic and political levels of society. It is part of the same process.

However, God is our liberator. Instead of vague feelings of guilt He confronts the rich with the reality of their sin, enabling them to break with it and find redemption. He comforts the poor. In blessing them He assures them that they are already precious children of God, enabling them to become self-confident and self-reliant. Jesus calls himself gentle and humble-hearted, the key words of the poor (Matt. 11 : 29). His vicarious poverty — being the Lord's Servant, who made himself nothing, assuming the nature of a slave (Phil. 2 : 7) — does not idealize poverty or make it sacrosanct but opens a new way in which people can liberate themselves from self-destruction and despair. He turns the ladder round.

This new spirituality links the poor within ourselves with the poor outside ourselves, and in this way the separation of dominant and dominated can be changed. The poor in spirit (Matt. 5 : 3) and the materially poor (Luke 6 : 20) basically belong to each other. The oppression of the materially poor is the oppression of the poor in ourselves. The Church in its pastoral care, its worship and evangelization, should create a place of freedom in which the salvation of Christ the Liberator is lived *(koinonia)*, served *(diakonia)*, and communicated (evangelization).

NOTES

[1] Cf. Matt. 6 : 24; Luke 16 : 13. Cf. JACQUES ELLUL: *L'Argent.* Neuchâtel and Paris: Delachaux et Niestlé, 1960.

[2] THOMAS CULLINAN, OSB, states very well in *The Roots of Social Injustice*: "If we idolize wealth, then we create poverty; if we idolize success, then we create the inadequate; if we idolize power, we create powerlessness. And these processes are inevitable." London: Catholic Housing Aid Society, 1973, p. 4.

[3] Even among the rich there are voices raising questions of this kind. This is what JOHAN GALTUNG points out when he says that "there is the idea of *a limit to inequality*. When some countries or some people, and particularly, when some people in some countries, have much more of these goods than others, they possess a resource that can be converted into power. For instance, if the elite in a country has access to better health services than others (or easier access to the same health

services, which amounts to the same), this may increase their life expectancy. Lower morbidity may make them more efficient and lower mortality makes them last longer; to last longer, in turn, means more time to accumulate experience that can be converted into power over others. Thus, the argument has been and will continue to be, that there is a limit to how much inequality the world as a whole and the individual country can stand without becoming a caricature of what a society with a minimum of built-in social justice should be like." In MARC NERFIN (ed.): *Another Development: Approaches and Strategies*, p. 107. Cf. the chapter by PAUL SINGER and BOLIVAR LAMOUNIER: "Brazil: Growth through Inequality." Uppsala: Dag Hammarskjöld Foundation, 1977. This leads people concerned with justice in rich countries to ask for a "new life style". Cf. CCPD Dossiers Nos. 10 and 11: *In Search of the New*, I-II. Geneva: CCPD/WCC, 1976-77.

4 Cf. James 1 : 18: "Of his (the Father's) own will He brought us forth by the word of truth that we should be a kind of first fruits of his creatures."

5 Cf. JOSÉ MÍGUEZ BONINO: *Christians and Marxists: the Mutual Challenge for Revolution*, p. 40: "Obedience is not a *consequence* of our knowledge of God, just as it is not a pre-condition for it: obedience is included in our knowledge of God. Or, to put it more bluntly: obedience *is* our knowledge of God. There is not a separate *noetic* moment in our relationship to God. There is an imperfect faith, but there cannot be, in the nature of the case, a believing disobedience — unless it is the 'dead faith' of which James speaks and which profits 'nothing'. This is what is meant by emphasizing the intrinsic demand for Christian truth to become historical, to be 'truth in the facts'. We do not know God in the abstract and then deduce from his essence some consequences. We know God in the synthetic act of responding to his demands." London: Hodder & Stoughton, 1976.

6 Acts 2 : 42-47; 4 : 32-37. Also JULIO DE SANTA ANA: *Good News to the Poor*, Ch. 4. Geneva: WCC, 1977.

7 Cf. HUGO ECHAGARAY: *Derechos del pobre, derechos de Dios*, in *Páginas*, Vol. III, special issue, 11-12, pp. 12-17, Lima: CEP, 1977, and in CEI, Biblia Hoje, August 1978.

8 Cf. JULIO DE SANTA ANA (ed.): *Separation Without Hope?* Geneva: WCC, 1978.

9 Cf. DOM HELDER CAMARA: *Les Conversions d'un Evêque*. Paris: Ed. du Seuil, 1977.

10 Cf. ALEX DEVASUNDARAM: "The Experience of St Mark's Cathedral, Bangalore." CCPD Dossier No. 12: *Good News to the Poor*. Geneva: CCPD/WCC, 1978.

11 Cf. the pastoral letter by the Catholic bishops of Appalachia, *Powerlessness in Appalachia*, pp. 12-13:

"Action on behalf of justice
and participation in the transformation
of the world
fully appear to us
as a *constitutive dimension*
of the preaching of the Gospel,
or, in other words,
of the church mission
for the redemption of the human race

and its liberation from every oppressive
situation.

Thus,
there must be no doubt,
that we, who must speak the message
of him who summoned Moses
and who opened his mouth
in Jesus of Nazareth,

and who keeps the Spirit alive
on behalf of justice
for so many centuries
can only become advocates of the poor.

This is not to be simplistic,
to see all in black and white,
to be ignorant of economics
and the contribution of other human
sciences,

but in a profound sense
the choices are simple
and stark:
— death or life;
— injustice or justice;
— idolatry or the Living God.
We must choose life.
We must choose justice.
We must choose the Living God.

Prestonburg, Kentucky: Catholic Committee of Appalachia, 1978.

[12] Cf. the preparatory paper for the CCPD workshop on "The Church and the Poor", Ayia Napa, Cyprus, September 1978, by JAMES SOMERVILLE: *My Involvement in the Struggle.*

[13] Cf. the report of the 1978 consultation of the Presbyterian Church in the United States, *One Mission under God,* ed. Office of the Stated Clerk, Atlanta, Georgia, 1978. Cf. also *Presbyterian Survey: a Third World Look at the Mission Consultation,* September 1978, pp. 41-42.

[14] From *Idoc International: New Series,* Bulletin 2-3. Rome: IDOC, February/ March 1978, p. 15.

[15] This is a summary of a chapter of WOLFGANG SCHMIDT's book *Der lange Marsch zurück,* to be published in 1980 by Christian-Kaiser-Verlag, Munich.

[16] Cf. JULIO DE SANTA ANA: *Good News to the Poor.* And COEN BOERMA: *Rich Man, Poor Man and the Bible.* London: SCM Press, 1979.

[17] Cf. Psalm 72 : 1-4; 12-14; several places in Isaiah, Jeremiah, Micah, Amos.

[18] Cf. *To Break the Chains of Oppression.* Geneva: CCPD/WCC, 1975, pp. 36-44, esp. p. 40. Cf. also Raul Vidales: "People's Church and Christian Ministry". *International Review of Mission,* Vol. LXVI, No. 261 on "Ministry with the Poor", January 1977, p. 39: "For our part, we are convinced that this is the inescapable historical 'moment' (Matt. 16 : 1-4ff; Luke 19 : 41-44) in which we Christians have to make a clear and effective choice: to live the Gospel of Jesus Christ, as a struggle for the liberation of all the poor, as a concrete expression of our faith, and as a permanent commitment to the message. The price of this choice has always been, and still is, the accusation inferred in the expression 'rendering a service to God' (John 16 : 2: 'Whoever kills you will think he is offering service to God')."

[19] Cf. the report of Section VI of the WCC Fifth Assembly, Nairobi, 1975, on "Human Development: Ambiguities of Power, Technology, and Quality of Life", in DAVID M. PATON, (ed.): *Breaking Barriers: Nairobi 1975,* p. 130. Grand Rapids, Mich.: Wm. B. Eerdmans, & London: SPCK, 1976.

[20] See JULIO DE SANTA ANA: *Good News to the Poor.* Ch. 3, pp. 33ff.

[21] Cf. WILLIAM R. COATS: *God in Public: Political Theology beyond Niebuhr,* p. 133: "... in the New Testament the poor are related, not to the world and the systems of man, but to the Kingdom of God. Only from this perspective can the cruelty and the blindness of man be exposed and judged. The poor possess the secret of the Kingdom, for they are the judgment of the present age ... the poor exist as a sign of promise. In the New Testament God acts precisely through those who have nothing to expect from the world, and for whom the structure and life of the world

have become enemies. God acts through the outcast, the despised, through those without possibilities, without any future, through those who, in possessing nothing on earth, bear the promise of a new age in which all people can possess everything equally." Grand Rapids, Mich.: Wm. B. Eerdmans, 1974.

[22] This is valid not only in countries of Asia, Africa, the Middle East and the Pacific, where Christians are a minority in society. It can also be applied to Europe, North and South America and the Caribbean, where religious practices demonstrate that those participating more or less regularly in church services are a small sector of society, and generally not very close to organized people's movements.

[23] Cf. GUSTAVO GUTIÉRREZ: *Teología desde el Reverso de la Historia*, p. 31. Speaking of theological thinking in Latin America he says: ". . . The popular movement (despite the oppression to which it is subjected) continues to assert itself at the grassroots. The political awareness of the dispossessed masses is becoming deeper and more mature, gaining in independent organization and learning new ways of work. The achievements and failures are instructive experiencies. The blood of those — whether they figure in newspaper headlines or not — who rose against age-old injustice gives even more titles to ownership of land that is more and more in the hands of others but at the same time increasingly laid claim to by those that the Bible calls the poor 'people of the land'. The popular movement experiences setbacks and uncertainties, typical of every historical process, but also knows firmness, hope, political realism and a capacity for resistance which the defenders of the established order find hard to understand and which even baffles the revolutionary elites who have undertaken — with serious setbacks — certain actions in recent years in Latin America. This is the context in which the theology of liberation originated and is growing to maturity. It could not come into existence before a certain development of the popular movement and before its historical praxis of liberation matured. These struggles are the scene of a new way of being man and woman in Latin America, and consequently a new way of living faith and encounter with the Father and the brethren. This spiritual experience (in Paul's sense of 'living according to the Spirit') in the very midst of social conflict and in solidarity with those absent from history, is at the source of this theological endeavour." Lima: CEP, 1977.

[24] Cf. JOSÉ MÍGUEZ BONINO: *Revolutionary Theology Comes of Age*, p. 159: "A Christian committed to liberation becomes therefore involved in the struggle for the reformation of the Church, or to put it more drastically, for the reconstitution of a Christianity in which all forms of organization and expression will be humanized and liberating." London: SPCK, 1975.

[25] Cf. JÜRGEN MOLTMANN: *The Church in the Power of the Spirit*, pp. 225-226: "The messianic community belongs to the Messiah and the messianic word; and this community, with the powers that it has, already realizes the possibilities of the messianic era, which brings the gospel of the Kingdom to the poor, which proclaims the lifting up of the downtrodden to the lowly, and begins the glorification of the coming God through actions of hope in the fellowship of the poor, the sad and those condemned to silence, so that it may lay hold on all men." London: SCM Press, 1977.

[26] BENOIT DUMAS: *Los dos rostros alienados de la Iglesia una*, p. 20: ". . . the Church is not entirely within the Church — as long as the poor who await their liberation do not know the name of Jesus Christ and do not recognize him in his visible Body

committed together with them; as long as those who hope in Christ and know his name do not know to meet him, to name him, and to wait for him in the liberation of the poor." Buenos Aires: Latinoamerica Libros, 1971. Cf. Matt. 25 : 31-46.

[27] Cf. Ch. XIII of this book.

[28] Cf. the article by JORGE PANTELIS: "Implications of the Theologies of Liberation for the Theological Training of the Pastoral Ministry in Latin America". *International Review of Mission*, Vol. LXVI, No. 261, January 1977, pp. 14-21.

[29] Cf. Ch. XI of this book.

[30] Cf. Ch. V of this book.

[31] DAVID E. JENKINS: *The Contradiction of Christianity*, p. 49. London: SCM Press, 1976.

[32] Ezek. 22 : 29-30. See also Ch. X of this book.

[33] In the New Testament the demand for solidarity is given to the Church through the image that it is the body of Christ: Cf. I Cor. 12; Rom. 12 : 3-13. On the practice of solidarity in the Early Church, cf. JULIO DE SANTA ANA: *Good News to the Poor*, Ch. 4, and COEN BOERMA, *op. cit.*

[34] Some experiments of this kind have been indicated by IAN M. FRASER: *The Fire Runs*, pp. 3-41. London: SCM Press, 1975. Also by the same author: "Room to Answer Back: Salvation and the Struggles of the Poor." *Study Encounter*, Vol. IX, No. 1, 1973, pp. 1-15.

[35] Cf. PAULO FREIRE: *Pedagogy of the Oppressed.* New York: Herder & Herder, 1970.

II · The Plight of the Poor

"We eat only once a day, a ball of millet with a few chillies," says the prematurely aging man squatting on the wet pavement in the city, where he has come to live from the village, looking in hope for a better life. "After going round me and my nine children, precious little is left for my wife," he adds, looking at his emaciated wife, struggling to suckle a baby on her lap, a wrinkled, malnourished little human body. The children are either naked or near naked and sprawl on newspaper for beds. On this sparse diet they — the whole family, including children — work from morning till late in the night. At the street corner waits the burly money-lender, who gave them loans at exorbitant interest when the father was sick, when his daughter had to be married off and when he had to make some repairs to this ramshackle tin and cardboard structure he calls his home. The money-lender takes away the major portion of the family's income merely for interest and that means their taking another loan from him. All their lives they toil, without hope.

Emerging from his one-room tenement in the slum where his large family lives, another man recalls with nostalgia the time when they had small enterprises within the community, all of them eking out a living but masters of their own destiny — until the big corporation came. "The big company swallowed us," he says. "Today we work and work and have no recompense. We know our labour is going to make someone somewhere rich, while we perish in this slush and mud all our lives. Is there any hope for us?"

"Why do you people defecate all around here? Don't you know it's bad for your health?" "Mister, you'd do the same if you had one lavatory a furlong away for 500 people!"

In a family planning session in a village a woman talks: "You ask me to limit my family. But I need children, more children, see? They are the ones who help me with the family income. If I want three children to remain alive, I have to produce at least ten." She is right. She lost many children and she speaks from experience. Her children start working at the age of 5. Some roll incense sticks (bidis) or local leaf cigarettes, some are in road gangs pouring hot tar on crushed stones all through the hot day. For these children, there is no such thing as childhood. Everyday life is a continuous anguish for this family, not knowing where they are to live, when they will eat next ... "I do not bathe for months," brags the man who gets his pittance as a labourer. "I work the whole day in the hot sun and I need water to wash myself. In this slum we had water before but now it belongs to the landlord who has taken over the place. Who can afford a bath if you have to pay for every pot of water?"

A woman, after a lifetime of labour in the tea gardens, dies, and is buried in the tea gardens in a cask made out of tea chests. Over her grave will grow bushes of tea, whose leaves will refresh many ... In life and in death, people like her could never hope for an identity that befits a human being.

These are people. And like them there are millions and millions in our midst, making up the gruesome spectacle of mass poverty today.

A World Bank report of 1978 states: "The past quarter century has been a period of unprecedented change and progress in the developing world. And yet despite this impressive record, some 800 million individuals continue to be trapped in what I have termed absolute poverty: a condition of life so characterized by malnutrition, illiteracy, disease, squalid surroundings, high infant mortality and low life expectancy as to be beneath any reasonable definition of human decency." [1]

As never before in human history, humankind today confronts the stark reality of abject poverty amidst plenty, with one quarter of the world's population living in unprecedented affluence, while the rest is condemned to poverty, an impressive number of them living in absolute poverty. [2] The painful awareness that their number increases day by day, their situation worsening to a dangerous level where survival itself comes under constant threat, calls for urgent attention by all concerned. [3] On the other hand, the affluence and standard of living of the rich minority have been increasing steadily, widening the gap between the rich and the poor. [4] Ironically, in spite of a tremendous advance in science and applied technology, giving humankind the wherewithal to master nature and provide for its members, in spite of planned efforts for development on a global level, the number of the poor has been increasing, while the escalating demands of an affluent minority on natural resources pose a threat to the environment as well as to future generations of humankind. [5] The world, fast becoming a global village with unprecedented increase in wealth, projects the age-old problem of the poor and the rich on a global scale, focusing attention on the process of impoverishment, in relation to affluent nations and their hold on the poor countries of the world.

Disembodied figures in the form of statistical data do not often bring to the imagination the human dimension of the suffering in which millions — in Asia, Africa, the Middle East and Latin America — live on "the very margin of existence — with inadequate food, shelter, education and health care".[6] There the masses are deprived increasingly of the material wherewithal to meet the elementary needs of human existence. For instance four large countries in Asia — Bangladesh, India, Indonesia and Pakistan — contain about two-thirds of the world's absolute poor. In human terms, this means families have to go without food for days or subsist on one meal a day. They live in inhuman dwelling conditions, on the pavements or in one-room shacks, constantly contending with sickness produced by malnutrition and an insanitary environment. They have no access to education or health services. Everyday life becomes a critical struggle for basic survival needs such as food, defecation, drinking water and shelter.[7]

In India, the percentage of those who live under the poverty level has risen to 62% out of a population of over 600 million people;[8] 25 million are reported to go blind each year due to malnutrition and lack of vitamin A. In spite of great efforts to increase educational facilities, 73% of the population are illiterate. There are places where there is one doctor for 20,000 people. Over 40% of the population of about 7 million in Bombay live in the open, on pavements or in one-room slum tenements. But the irony becomes more poignant, for India produces a variety of goods, ranging from radios, television, aircraft, to nuclear energy — the country has even launched a satellite. Only the privileged minority is able to benefit from these advances. Conditions are similar in other poor countries. In Africa and Latin America, the number of those who live below poverty level is constantly increasing. Nearly 70% of Liberia's 1.6 million people are poor, surviving on an income of $70 a year. Eighty per cent of the population are illiterate. Forty per cent of Latin America is below the poverty line. All development efforts in these countries benefit only the small percentage at the top, never reaching the majority for whom they are intended. In these countries the social structures are organized in such a way that the labour and resources of the country are used to benefit a small elite who, by virtue of holding undue economic power in their hands, make the political, social, religious and cultural institutions in the system work for their own benefit.[9] However the poor toil, their labour goes to enrich the few at the top, while the majority is deprived of even the material means of life.[10] The poor, for this reason, are bypassed by economic growth in many countries; they have only weak links with the organized market economy; they own fewer productive assets; they are less educated and in poor health. Poverty, then, seems to be the consequence of a process within the operation of a system in which a few economically powerful people wield political power to control institutions for their own private profit. What is true of individual nations holds good on a global scale in a common system of exploitation. The resources and economic growth of the world seem to be exploited by a global system in which a few economically powerful sectors of society manipulate the system for profit, bringing about, in the process, impoverishment for millions of people living in poor nations. It was love of economic gain and profit that drove powerful nations armed with weapons and technology to subdue other nations and people rich in resources and culture, resulting in a political process of colonialism and imperialism. That period is over, yet the same process is in operation today; that is, the lust for economic gain finds expression through political power which oppresses weak nations and lets loose oppressive regimes in individual nations to preserve and perpetuate the system that works for the exclusive benefit of the few.[11]

The same economic pursuit of gain in modern times was structured into emerging capitalism on a worldwide scale, in the form of neo-colonialism, and operates now through powerful transnational corporations. Belting the earth, these corporations wield enormous power; they grow by exploiting the resources of the world, in collusion with the national elites in every country, using cheap labour, with consideration neither for the impoverishment of the natural environment, nor for the equitable distribution of profits with the exploited countries.[12] The unprecedented increase in their economic wealth is seen from the 1973 UN report. It states that 650 corporations of this kind made sales in 1971 equivalent to one-third of the world's product.[13]

Every effort is made by the national elite and international oppressive forces to keep the system working for their benefit, thus maintaining the poor where they are. The rise and fall of oppressive, dictatorial and authoritarian regimes in countries in Asia, Latin America and Africa tended to institutionalize human rights violations as a necessary measure to maintain prevailing patterns of domination at home and abroad.[14]

Armaments produced by the rich nations are traded to the poor countries through the political influence the former wield through economic power. This encouraged the poor countries to fight among themselves, spending huge amounts on destructive violence. It is a scandal of our times that the poor nations are forced to spend a large part of their meagre income on arms purchase, while the majority of their peoples go without basic needs.[15]

Working within the exploitative social structure, the dominant few employ institutional elements — political, economic, social, cultural and religious — to devise a framework perpetually to contain the poor. Religion legitimizes the dominance of the few and safeguards the working of the system. The churches have sanctified/legitimized the domination of the elites in an effort to maintain their own position. They have sided with the oppressor. Their message has helped the poor accept their condition as God-given, and hope for a better life is projected on the world to come.[16]

Educational systems, entrusted with the task of socializing people, perpetuate values that keep the system going. They teach conformity to the *status quo*. Only those at the top have full access to the educational process, thereby perpetuating their domination. The majority of the poor find that the educational system only helps them join the ranks of the unemployed.[17]

Family structures prepare family members to take over the process of domination. Family empires in many countries have become inherited fiefs with a few individuals controlling their destiny and exercising enormous power and wealth. The economically rich control political power in every country.[18] Political institutions respond to the dominant few, ensuring the working of the social structure in their favour. Parties are brought to power or toppled, depending on their stand concerning the national and international domination by the few. Political institutions legitimize and put into operation the elite's economic aspirations. The process of impoverishment continues for the masses; the rich reap the reward.

Forms of social structures having a socio-cultural-religious sanction contribute to the perpetuation of poverty. Status fixed at birth, by religion, the colour of one's skin, or sex becomes the basis on which people are exploited. Twenty-six million untouchables in the caste system of India suffer this impoverishment in material terms and in their collective self-image as people. In spite of legislation, the majority of them continue to live a dehumanized existence. They perform menial tasks according to status fixed at birth (although this is changing rapidly); they continue to be oppressed by the higher castes.[19]

Economic domination expressed in social structures has resulted in the perpetuation of poverty on the basis of race.[20] Many Indians and blacks of America, Aborigines of Australia, Maoris of New Zealand know that "inferior", "discrimination", "unequal", "segregation", "deprivation", "dehumanization" are not mere words in a dictionary, but describe a way of life all too real for them. "Separate but equal" educational systems, separate public facilities, separate houses of worship, these and other arrangements legitimized racial discrimination. Not only physical impoverishment like poor housing, unemployment, poor health care, high infant mortality rate, but the most debilitating of all, poverty of mind and spirit, is the condition in which they live. The structures are built so that an opportunity to live a decent life in equality is denied on the basis of race.

Racism is seen in every part of the world, and in some countries it is more obvious in that it is legally enforced. Racism is also a factor in numerous violations of human rights and fundamental freedoms in many countries. It is a matter of shame for the Christian churches around the world which are all too often infested by racism. In worship, in relations, in sharing of resources and in programme priorities racism is a factor affecting attitudes and relationships directly or indirectly.

Oppressive racism in our time is mostly built into the institutional structures which reinforce and perpetuate themselves, generally to the great advantage of the few and the disadvantage of the many. Trade patterns and preferences are deliberately created which perpetuate discrimination on racial lines.

Arms and sophisticated weapons from strong military powers and other industrialized countries assist racist regimes. Irrespective of their social systems, powerful countries often support racial repression under the pretext of legally justified defence of their own national self-interest. Special attention is called to the fact that across the globe racist structures uphold and reinforce each other internationally: transnational corporations with their self-preserving policies, weapons or mercenaries supplied internationally to local elites, worldwide communication networks manipulated to reinforce racist attitudes and actions.

The scourge of racism is today kept alive through its institutional seepage, its revitalization by strong political and economic power and a widespread fear in the affluent world of loss of privilege.

Spiritual poverty

Mother Teresa, once speaking to a group in Great Britain, observed: "There is a poverty here greater than material poverty. This poverty of the spirit is more killing than the poverty of material things." In developed societies, material advancement has overtaken human values; there is a systematic impoverishment to which Mother Teresa was referring. Where societies function on values which support an extreme kind of selfish individualism — of anything for money, of cut-throat dog-eat-dog competition, of human work measured in terms of money — a new kind of poverty arises, a poverty of the spirit, a sense of purposelessness, of emptiness and of wanton destruction. Suicide and crime rates go up, and human warmth and concern become tragically scarce amidst material plenty. Mental illnesses and irrational behaviour fill hospitals. Year after year, young men and women from developed countries stage an exodus to exotic lands in search of spiritual meaning and purpose to their lives.

Poverty is consolidated in the class nature which our social structures take, to ensure the syphoning process of wealth created by the poor and the working masses to the privileged few at the top.[21] Cheap labour in plantations, mines, factories and manufactures are contained in that position by the social structure through restrictions and legislation. Political repression prevents the efforts by the poor to claim their just dues, and the obstacles placed against upward social mobility perpetuates them in their poverty and deprivation.[22]

Sexism is another form in which the values of the dominant find expression. In an exclusively male-dominated society, women are accorded an inferior status, and prevented from developing their potential or freeing themselves from poverty. In many poor countries, but also in some rich nations, tradition has condemned women to the status of a chattel or possession of man, expected to slave and serve him, bear his children and work to subsidize the family income. Obstacles are carefully woven into the social structure to frustrate women's legitimate aspirations to rise to positions of power, to participate in decision-making, or to have a voice in the administration of things affecting their life and destiny.[23]

Economic domination has resulted in cultural deterioration and alienation in the poor countries. Much that was unique to their societies, to their way of life and world view, was destroyed. It was replaced by cultural elements of the dominant nation or succession of dominant nations, thus placing poor countries in a subordinate and subservient position. Valuable elements in popular religion and culture were lost, leading to a serious problem of identity. The dominant nations have endeavoured to remake the poor in their own image, and have instilled in them the spurious superiority of their own culture for the poor to aspire to.[24] Coupled with economic affluence, this cultural value had great attraction for the young and educated in subject societies, resulting in the impoverishment of their own culture and hope for reconstruction. They migrated increasingly causing the "brain drain". Doctors, scientists and artists, who would have been of great help to their poor countries, take their skills, acquired at the cost of their own poor people, and migrate to affluent countries to serve there at lower wages than their counterparts.

As a concomitant to this spiritual poverty, there is yet another kind of poverty which is the product of the values present in the systems that function in developed societies. Nuclear families built on selfish acquisitive tendencies have no time for the care of the old and the infirm. In spite of the provisions for institutional care, many of the aged are left to lead rather lonely and blighted lives. The poverty of their existence at the evening of their lives amidst a life of plenty causes grave concern about the quality of human life.

Mass media, developed to sophisticated perfection, facilitate cultural invasion with a view to exploiting commercially whatever little the poor countries have.[25] It was said in India that Coca-Cola was available in the remotest village where even drinking water facilities had not been installed. Fashions and fads spread through high pressure advertisement have created unnecessary consumer wants, obscuring the priority of nation-building in poor countries, and helping the market potential of transnational corporations to suck their lifeblood.

The poor are thus trapped in a worldwide system of oppression operating at all levels, wielding enormous police and military power sanctioned by political influence, thwarting attempts to organize and struggle against injustice and for the eradication of poverty. The system, using freely the mass media and social institutions, frustrates the feeble attempts of the poor to free themselves. With a value system built in as bait, the system assimilates attempts to oppose its working, divides the poor to fight among themselves, and renders their efforts futile and hopeless.

The plight of the poor today is the consequence of a continuing process of exploitation and oppression. It is a structure operating in an interconnected way at the local, national and international levels, through mechanisms of domination based on economic considerations and enforced through political power.

Any attempt to tackle the problem of poverty must take seriously this structural reality. Attempts to change its operation without taking into account its built-in mechanisms of domination will only help increase its power and would only be self-defeating.

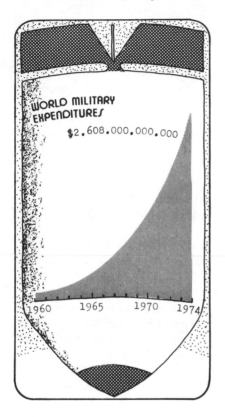

WORLD MILITARY EXPENDITURES
$2.608.000.000.000

1960   1965   1970   1974

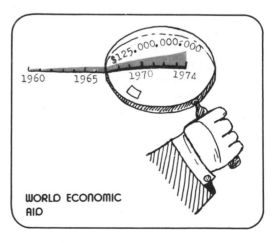

$125.000.000.000

1960   1965   1970   1974

WORLD ECONOMIC AID

NOTES

1 *World Development Report*, p. 11. Washington, DC: World Bank, August 1978.

2 *Ibid.*, pp. 33-34: "Given the obstacles they face, elimination of absolute poverty in the Low Income countries by the end of this century seems impossible. A more realistic target would be to reduce the proportion of their populations living in poverty to about 15 to 20% by the year 2000, which would still have nearly 400 million in absolute poverty. To realize even this gain will require massive efforts to raise the productivity and incomes of the poor ... While poverty could be reduced to low levels in the Middle Income countries by the end of this century, it will continue to plague the Low Income countries." Cf. also C. T. KURIEN: *Poverty and Development*, p. 14. Madras: Christian Literature Society, 1974. Another perspective, convergent with that of the World Bank, can be found in the book by CHARLES ELLIOTT, assisted by FRANÇOISE DE MORSIER: *Patterns of Poverty in the Third World*. New York, Washington, London: Praeger Publishers, 1975.

3 Cf. WCC Central Committee statement, *Threats to Survival*, Berlin, 1974. *Study Encounter*, Vol. X, No. 4, 1974. Also RUDOLF H. STRAHM: *Pays industrialisés — pays sous-développés*, p. 17: "One-third of the world population, living in the industrialized countries, controls seven-eighths of world income, while two-thirds of the world population in the underdeveloped countries of Asia, Latin America and Africa, has to be satisfied with one-eighth of world income (1968 figures). These ratios of course give no indication of the distribution of income inside each country." Neuchâtel, Switzerland: Ed. Baconnière, 1974.

4 Cf. *Anticipation*, No. 19: "Science and Technology for Human Development: the Ambiguous Future and the Christian Hope." Report of the 1974 Conference of Church and Society, Bucharest, Romania. Cf. also RICHARD D. N. DICKINSON: *To Set at Liberty the Oppressed*, pp. 10-12. Geneva: WCC, 1975.

5 World Bank: *op. cit.*, p. 1.

6 The situation is worse for women than for men. Cf. LISA LEGHORN and MARY ROODKOWSKY: *Who Really Starves? Women in World Hunger*, p. 21. New York: Friendship Press, 1977.

7 On the inadequacies of policies attacking poverty in India, cf. C. T. KURIEN, *op. cit.*, pp. 91-102.

8 *To Break the Chains of Oppression*, pp. 26-35. Geneva: CCPD/WCC, 1975.

9 CHARLES ELLIOTT: *Do the Poor Subsidize the Rich?*, p. 10: "Through indirect taxation the poor make some contribution to the finance of social consumption. Through falling real informal earnings (probably) and declining rural terms of trade (perhaps), resources are moved from the poor to the not-so-poor. We do not know with any precision how substantial these transfers are: nor do we know the extent of the poor's subsidization of the services enjoyed by the not-so-poor. But it is becoming increasingly clear that the poor are not only not benefiting from the expenditures which are supposed to be highly redistributive, e.g. health and education, but that they are also likely to be contributing towards the cost of services from which they are excluded." *Study Encounter*, Vol. IX, No. 4, 1973. Geneva: WCC, 1973.

10 *To Break the Chains of Oppression, op. cit.*, pp. 13-14: "Of course, the benefits of the system (and it would be more appropriate to call them privileges for some and

exploitation for the others) are far greater for those who own and manage the systems of production. In some cases they are individuals, in other cases companies, and sometimes countries. Although their own natural resources are meagre, their former colonial enterprises enabled them to accumulate such great wealth, knowledge and power that today they are much better off than those who, despite their potential wealth, vast territories and human resources, were dominated at one point or another."

[11] F. Fröbel, J. Heinricks, O. Krege and O. Sunkel: *The Internationalization of Capital and Labor*, pp. 14-55. This is a publication of the research group "Development and Underdevelopment" at the Max Planck Institut zur Erforschung der Lebensbedingungen der wissenschaftlich-technischen Welt, Sternberg, Federal Republic of Germany, 1973.

[12] United Nations: *Multinational Corporations in World Development.* It is also stated on p. 13, that "the enormous size and steadily growing importance of multinational corporations are clearly revealed when viewed in the context of world economic activities. Although the usual comparison of gross annual sales of multinational corporations with gross national *product* of countries exaggerates the relative importance of the activities of multinational corporations, the general conclusion that many multinational corporations are bigger than a large number of entire national economies remains valid. Thus, the value added by each of the top ten multinationals in 1971 was in excess of $3 billion or greater than the gross national product of over 80 countries. The value added of all multinational corporations, estimated roughly at $500 billion in 1971, was about one-fifth of world gross national product, not including the centrally planned economies." New York: UN, 1973.

[13] As stated at the Fifth Assembly of the WCC in the report of Section V on "Structures of Injustice and Struggles for Liberation": "The basic causes for these violations are to be found in the unjust social order, the abuse of power, the lack of economic development, and in unequal development. This leads to violations of unjust laws and rebellion by the dispossessed, to which political and military forces of 'law and order' respond with cruel repression." David M. Paton (ed.): *Breaking Barriers, Nairobi 1975*, p. 106. Grand Rapids, Mich.: Wm. B. Eerdmans, and London: SPCK, 1976.

[14] Cf. Ruth Leger Livard: *World Military and Social Expenditures 1976.* Leesburg, Virginia: WMSE Publications, 1976. Also the reports of the WCC consultations on *Militarism* (1977) and *Disarmament* (1976). Geneva: CCIA/WCC, 1978.

[15] Report of Section V of the WCC Fifth Assembly. David Paton (ed.), *op. cit.*, p. 106: "In some cases, the churches themselves have actively supported the oppressors or even become involved in the oppression itself, out of misguided conviction and/or attempts to safeguard their own privileges."

[16] Charles Elliott and Françoise de Morsier, *op. cit.*, pp. 228-262.

[17] Cf. comments by Samuel L. Parmar, entitled "Jesus in the Development Debate", in Richard N. Dickinson, *op. cit.*, p. 182.

[18] Max Weber: *Wirtschaft und Gesellschaft, Grundriss der verstehenden Soziologie.* Tübingen: Verlag J. C. B. Mohr, 1922.

[19] Heruàn Santa Cruz (special rapporteur): *Racial Discrimination*, p. 57. New York: UN, 1971.

[20] CHARLES ELLIOTT and FRANÇOISE DE MORSIER, *op. cit*, pp. 5-14.

[21] The Church and Society Conference on "Science and Technology for Human Development: the Ambiguous Future and the Christian Hope", Bucharest, 1974, stated: "Economic, technological and social dependence also implies political and military dependence. Those countries of Latin America which in the last decade were ready for social change were prevented from action by the intervention of military power. Coups d'état have in several cases been aided by, and have consolidated political dependence on, sources of foreign military assistance. The military group has proved most effective in making the kind of adjustment required by foreign investors in Latin America. If the dissatisfaction of the people were to find expression in social unrest foreign investment would not be forthcoming. Therefore there has been the increase of authoritarian regimes in the last ten years with consequent injustice. Unemployment is increasing in both rural and urban areas; distribution of GNP is favourable to privileged groups. ... Those who commit themselves in the struggle for change generally suffer persecution, prison, torture, exile, and often death. Violations of human rights occur at all levels." Cf. *Anticipation*, No. 19, p. 27. Geneva: WCC, November 1974.

[22] Cf. LISA LEGHORN and MARY ROODKOWSKY, *op. cit.* Also *Sexism in the 1970s: Discrimination Against Women*, report of a WCC consultation, West Berlin, 1974, pp. 45-55 and 113-115. Geneva: WCC, 1975.

[23] Cf. ANDREW GUNDER FRANK: *Capitalisme et sous-développement en Amérique Latine*, pp. 120-139. Paris: Maspero, 1968.

[24] TISSA BALASURIYA: *The Development of the Poor Through the Civilizing of the Rich*, p. 13. Colombo: Centre for Society and Religion, 1973.

[25] Cf. CEES HAMELINK: *The Corporate Village*, p. 134. Rome: IDOC, 1977.

III · Accumulation of Wealth — Growth of Poverty

(Mechanisms of Injustice)

In the previous chapter we were presented with the grim picture of the plight of the poor in our world today. Poverty appears to the poor as deprivation of life, as non-satisfaction of even basic human needs. Somehow their right to better life, to work, to be cared for, to be educated, to decent housing, to participate in making decisions affecting their destiny, all are denied to them. It is therefore necessary to look into this problem of increasing world poverty more closely to understand the root causes of this phenomenon of growth of poverty despite increasing wealth.

The poor have always been with us. They are found in all periods of history. Poverty is basically a systemic problem. In spite of development efforts over the centuries, poverty is on the increase and it behoves us to investigate the process or the mechanism which makes this happen.

Secondly, poverty is generated by the appropriation of the fruits of the labour of the poor by the few with capital, and our concern is about the people who labour and yet get poorer and poorer. This would mean that we examine also the system by which the labour of many is exploited so that a few might become richer.

At the end of the Second Development Decade, it must be confessed that very little has been achieved in the struggle against poverty: "In the past few years there have been many conscious efforts to give human development a conceptual clarity that it lacked, but the relation between the concept and reality seems to become more diffused and more evasive. The uncertainties and ambiguities resulting from this situation are made more pronounced because of the few certainties that cannot be evaded: that after two decades of efforts to remove poverty and reduce inequality there are today more people in the grips of dire poverty and the gap between the rich and the poor has widened; that in a world with tremendous technological possibilities, there is the persisting threat of famine...." [1]

If we really want to eradicate poverty, it must be attacked at its roots. We need to know the factors that cause it to exist, and that cause it to have a structural dimension in our world. The structural character of poverty is related to the functioning of prevailing mechanisms in the application of power in our societies,[2] which produce domination and/or oppression. We are called to make clear what kind of domination and oppression is meant.

The present situation of the poor in the world is related to the process of the modern world since the eighteenth century.[3] In this evolution, particular structures have been imposed by dominant powers on whole societies. Within this socio-economic structure there developed a new relationship between people, and also between humanity and nature, aimed at the appropriation of economic surplus and accumulation of wealth for those who handle and control the mechanism of power, to the detriment of the powerless. This is what has been called "capitalism".[4]

This structure arose in the name of freedom; however, the freedom referred to was not human freedom, but the freedom of trade and commerce. This is a form of freedom which today, perhaps more than ever before, continues to determine the ideology of domination. Freedom of prices, freedom of the dollar, freedom of commerce, freedom of enterprise: free prices, free dollars, free trade, free enterprise. Human liberty has come to be seen in terms of this freedom of the market.[5]

The more this free market progressed, the more market laws came to be spoken of as the laws of liberty. The reign of liberty became the reign of the free market and the laws of the free market became like divine laws. With the development of the free market, the concept of a natural law of private property, considered as divine law given by the Creator himself, made its first appearance in the history of Christianity.[6]

A metaphysics of market laws developed: virtues of the market and sins against the market, corrections of behaviour by reference to the laws of the market and economic miracles as rewards given by nature itself. The laws of the market, and with them commercial relationships, became the very root of a bourgeois Christianity imposed progressively as the right approach to a life of faith.[7] Then the love of God and respect for the laws of the free market came to be identified — stock exchanges were built in the form of churches, banks like Greek temples — love of money was concretely expressed in the love of Mammon, who dictated the laws of the free market and engraved them in nature itself. Human behaviour was the quest for maximum profit. The resulting structures covered all of humanity and very soon the entire world. Submission to market structures was preached in the name of the basic Christian value of humility.[8] However, while the free market included the whole world, it did not affect everyone equally. When everyone is subjected to these structures, some are winners and some are losers: equality has been lost.[9] Nevertheless, even those who came out winners were subject to this structure. When they were entrepreneurs, they thought of themselves as the humble servants of free enterprise. They fostered and defended this structure, although others suffered from the consequences in the oppression at the origin of the structural conditioning of poverty. Oppression became anonymous and impersonal: no personal relationships of oppression developed between oppressors and oppressed.[10] The free market structure therefore appeared to be the rule of a natural law which dictated its own precepts. Some were justified, others not. Reality itself was seen as the true judge: world history as the final judgment. Thomas Hobbes was one of the first to understand the emergence of this new structure of domination. He called it Leviathan — the Beast.[11]

The law of the market was promoted by those who drew the greatest benefit from the free operation of merchant relations. They had the necessary economic conditions to emerge as winners from the free market struggle. The laws of the market therefore enabled them to perpetuate their domination.[12] Politically, their aim was to use power to extend the freedom of the market as far as possible. The more successful they were in doing so, the more firmly established the dependence of others on their hegemonic power. This dependence became and continues to be a structural phenomenon.[13] It developed within an international structure governed by the laws of the market which enabled particular social classes or regions of the world to emerge as dominant classes or regions, while other classes or regions were dominated.[14]

In its regional aspect, dependence should not be confused with colonialism. Colonialism was simply one of the means by which the law of the market was enforced and certain regions were made dependent. Dependence of classes should not be confused with the relationship of dependence of hired labour and capital. Slavery is the worst form of class dependence developed from the free market. It is true that slavery has existed since very ancient times, but the slave trade reached its height with the evolution of the free market, at least in the seventeenth, eighteenth and nineteenth centuries. It should not be forgotten that it was this "liberalism" which built the greatest slave empire in human history.[15]

The different stages followed through in the creation of this system of domination must be seen as moments in the evolution of an international system. Two principal stages can be distinguished: one from the industrial revolution to the war of 1914-1918; the other from the end of that war to the present time.

From the industrial revolution to the war of 1914-1918

While England and later western Europe, the USA and Japan, rapidly developed the forces of production, in the rest of the world existing productive forces were destroyed. India is the most striking case. At the beginning of the industrial revolution, India was the biggest producer and exporter of textiles in the world. Colonization and the free movement of market prices soon reduced it to a producer of raw materials for the British textile industry.[16] This destruction of traditional forces of production throughout the world was a corollary to the development of the forces of production in dominant countries. It went hand in hand with a systematic policy designed to hinder the industrialization of the other countries:

The quick expansion of exchanges had its cause in the increase of physical productivity taking place in those areas where the capitalist mode of production was penetrating. The new products, emerging from changes in the form of production, were used as instruments to open new lines of trade. From this contact between a culture oriented towards innovation and expansion, and others oriented towards respect of tradition, emerged a strong relationship of domination of the former on the latter, which tried to reproduce the consumption patterns of the dominating one. The explanation of this process can be sought in many places, but no matter which it could be, it should be kept in mind that the culture which based itself first in the capitalist mode of production was rooted in a process of accumulation, which meant *inter alia* that it could impose itself by force or through exchange of its products. To put it briefly: the formation of a system of international division of work was not only a problem related to the openness of new lines of trade, but also and mainly, the imposition of cultural patterns, which would consequently condition first the process of accumulation, and later of industrialization in these regions . . .[17]

As stated in the quotation from Celso Furtado, two main methods were used: on the one hand, direct destruction of the native forces of production through colonization; on the other, the establishment of free trade in politically sovereign countries.[18] This is what happened mainly in China and Latin America: refusal of free trade during this period was considered, by hegemonistic countries, a sufficient reason to declare war. The diplomacy of these countries did not achieve the expected results, war was declared, as was the case with the Opium Wars in China (1839-1842) and the war of the "Triple Alliance" (Brazil, Argentina and Uruguay, supported by European powers, mainly Great Britain) against Paraguay (1865-1870). Where there was a colonial relationship, or at least a submission to the hegemonistic centres, freedom of trade was always assured between the powerful and the powerless, or less powerful. If, notwithstanding freedom of trade and commerce, competitive industries developed in the colonies, they were destroyed.[19]

The destruction of traditional industry throughout the world and the direct or indirect hindrance to the development of modern industries in dependent countries compelled the latter to convert into suppliers of raw materials for the industries in the hegemonistic countries. *This brought impoverishment on a vast scale in those countries and a corresponding willingness to devote themselves to whatever type of activity the free-market system might require of them.*[20]

With the conversion of the dependent world into producers of raw materials, large sectors of the population in the highly populated dependent countries became superfluous. These people were former workers in traditional industries that had been destroyed, only a very small proportion of them being required in the production of raw materials which replaced industrial activity. They became the new poor of the dependent societies.

At the same time, in dependent countries with low density of population, opportunities for the production of raw materials developed, which could not be exploited to the full with only the existing population as a working force. This brought slavery in the Americas and the Caribbean to new heights. Although the slave-based empires already existed in the Americas a few years after the conquest, they reached their zenith between the end of the industrial revolution and about the middle of the nineteenth century.[21] Present patterns of poverty in the Americas and the Caribbean have been strongly determined by the fact of slavery.

Parallel to the impoverishment of the peoples of dependent countries and colonized regions of the world, important sectors of the population of the hegemonistic countries themselves also became poorer. Although production standards in those countries rose quickly following the industrial revolution, the living standards of the poor dropped considerably from what they had been prior to the beginning of the process of industrialization after the middle of the eighteenth century.[22] Only towards the end of the nineteenth century did the situation of the workers in the hegemonistic centres begin to improve, resulting in higher consumption which helped improve economic growth in industrialized countries. However, the dependent countries continued to be poor. It is clear that while absolute poverty continues to exist throughout the world, it has become a phenomenon affecting only a minority in the economic centres, whereas in Africa, Asia and Latin America it continues to be a condition of life of the majority of the population. Only ruling minorities and related social groups of the dependent countries have benefited from the economic changes there.[23]

From the war of 1914-1918 to the present

Around the time of the 1914-1918 war, a decisive change took place in the system of domination. Through the so-called second industrial revolution, the technological monopoly of the industrialized countries where power was concentrated developed in a very clear way. Accumulated in their industries are the elements of one and a half centuries of technical progress.[24] Their technologies have been perfected to a degree which makes it impossible for anyone who has not gone through the same process to use them independently.[25] Since their own traditional industries have been destroyed and their industrial development obstructed and delayed, the dependent countries cannot now become industrialized without using the technical knowledge of the industrialized countries or acquiring machinery, know-how and the assistance of technicians from the industrialized countries.[26] However, there is no market where such technologies can be bought. The situation is different from the sale of merchandise in the previous stage. Since the industrialized countries hold the monopoly of technology, they give access to it on one condition only, which is that their own capital must be the agent of the transfer of this technology. One result is the increasing integration of national economies into a single unified economic space, which means that we are living now a "process of increasing integration of national economic systems".[27]

A decisive change has taken place in international relationships. The "free-market diplomacy" of the nineteenth century concentrated on the policy of free trading, not shrinking from war in the case of the countries which refused it. The "free-market" diplomacy of the twentieth century centres on the free movement of capital and becomes threatening to those countries who refuse it.

This linking of the sale of technology with freedom of capital has made possible the emergence of modern transnational capital, unthinkable without the industrialized countries' technological monopoly.[28] Economic growth of dependent countries can now be controlled by making acceptance of the agency of transnational capital a condition of transfer.[29] Foreign capital operates according to rules related to the "law of the market", which is to obtain the maximum possible profits.

Transnational corporations are now pursuing profit on an international scale. Dependent countries, on the other hand, are competing with one another to attract foreign capital. To do so, they must create the conditions which will attract it: low wages, unemployment and strong governments (very often of a military type) capable of suppressing any attempts by the dominated peoples to assert their economic and social claims.[30]

At present, transnational capital generally does not transfer capital or surpluses in a continuous way from industrialized countries to the dependent ones. Transnational capital in the dependent countries is largely a result of those countries' own resources appropriated through loans and reinvestment of profits. Since transnational capital has the monopoly of technology, it also has access to the financial channels of the dependent countries, which enables it to build up transnational empires throughout the dependent world.[31]

The industrialization of the dependent countries being thus entrusted to transnational capital, transfer of technology is determined by maximum profit. The result of this policy is industrialization directed towards the demands of the economically most powerful, which marginalizes production of goods necessary for the basic needs of the population. As industrialization advances, the gap between high and low income groups widens, unless structures for the redistribution of income are reformulated to the benefit of the poor.[32] Alongside this rapid increase in the disparity between incomes, a still more destructive phenomenon has appeared. Given the technological monopoly of the already industrialized countries, the emergence of new industries is very severely limited, and management also is being progressively transnationalized.[33] In the last instance, the capacity of the dependent countries to import determines their capacity to industrialize. The more capital-intensive modern technology becomes, the less employment the industrialization process brings with it.[34]

Even in developing countries where the industrialization process is most dynamic, industrial development has been stagnating in recent decades. In many countries the proportion of work force employed in industry has diminished against the total. This is the case, for example, in Brazil[35] and Mexico.[36] However, no non-industrial jobs have been created in really important numbers. In the meantime, small industries using tra-

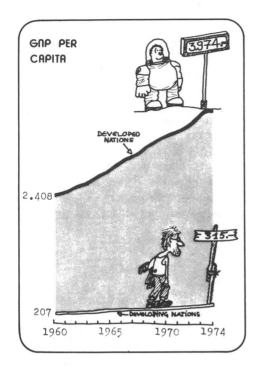

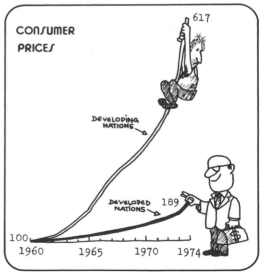

ditional methods of production have severe survival difficulties. The efficiency of more modern industry is killing them little by little, but without making any kind of provisions to absorb the work force being put out of jobs.the result, as already stated, is galloping unemployment.[37]

To conclude, prevailing patterns of industrialization in dependent countries, where economies are functioning according to "the laws of the market", do not help change the situation of impoverishment inherited from the nineteenth century, and in many cases they aggravate it still further. This process does not hold out big hopes for the future; it simply ignores the deprived masses of the dependent world. Within the structures, as developed, there is no room for action. If they are to function, they have to use the poor, keeping them in their desperate situation. The poor are then condemned to perish in poverty, or challenged to struggle if they want a better life.

NOTES

[1] DAVID M. PATON (ed.): *Breaking Barriers: Nairobi 1975*, p. 122. Grand Rapids, Mich.: Wm. B. Eerdmans, & London: SPCK, 1976.

[2] As stated by the well-known Brazilian economist CELSO FURTADO, in *Prefacio a nova economia política*, p. 29: "Consequently the composition of the (economic) surplus is to a large extent a reflection of the system of social domination, which means that unless we know the power structure we cannot advance in the study of the development of productive forces." Rio de Janeiro: Editoria Paz e Terra, 1976.

[3] SISMONDE DE SISMONDI, observing how this process was being consolidated at the beginning of the nineteenth century, wrote in his *Nouveaux principes d'économie politique*, p. 188: "... an abyss divides the day labourer from any manufacturing, commercial or tenant farming undertaking, and the lower class has lost the hope that sustained it in the preceding period of civilization ... they can scarcely preserve the feeling of human dignity, or love of freedom".

[4] CELSO FURTADO, following the analysis of Fernand Brandel, Werner Sombart and Max Weber, says in *op. cit.*, pp. 36-37: "... if we look closely at one or another form of social organization, then we can prove without difficulties that in capitalism there are hidden co-active forces fulfilling a fundamental role, because the use of the surplus for the production of another surplus or for its transformation into capital, presupposes the imposition of given social relationships. So, capitalism must be understood as a socio-political organization, that is, as a power structure which imposes a certain kind of social relationship in which the surplus is more easily transformed into capital."

[5] Cf. LIONEL ROBBINS: *The Theory of Economic Policy in English Classical Political Economy*, p. 19: "The system of economic freedom was not just a detached recommendation not to interfere: it was an urgent demand that what were thought to be

hampering and anti-social impediments should be removed and that the immense potential of free pioneering individual initiative should be released. And, of course, it was in this spirit that, in the world of practice, its proponents addressed themselves to agitation against the main forms of these impediments: against the privileges of regulated companies and corporations, against the law of apprenticeship, against restrictions on movement, against restraints on importation. The sense of a crusade which emerged in the free trade movement owed some of its force to other, extraneous, influences. But, up to a point, it is typical of the atmosphere of the general movement for freeing spontaneous enterprise and energies of which, without doubt, the classical economists were the intellectual spearhead." London: Macmillan, 2nd ed., 1978.

[6] Cf. THOMAS HOBBES: *Leviathan*, p. 151ff. London: Everyman's Library, 1924. Adam Smith, based on Hobbes's ideas, developed this conception further.

[7] Cf. in JULIO DE SANTA ANA (ed.): *Separation Without Hope?*, the chapter by Mario Miegge. Geneva: WCC, 1978. CELSO FURTADO, in *op. cit.*, p. 39 says: "The economists looked to this process only from outside, as the multiplication of a market economy, when really it is about the evolution at the level of power structures which control the appropriation of the surplus."

[8] FRANZ HINKELAMMERT: *Las armas ideológicas de la muerte*, p. 33: "From this not only a theory of values is derived but also a theory of the interiorization of values. Behind money is the infinity which it promises to attain. From this, the values which have to be realized in order to pursue the goal can be derived. But since the goal is of infinite value, religious illusion permits it to be given a sacred character as an object of piety. The pursuit of money is transformed into an object of piety, *ad maiorem Dei gloriam*." S. José: Educa, 1977 and Salamanca: Sígueme, 1978.

[9] J. J. ROUSSEAU: *Discours sur les sciences et les arts*, 1750: "What is the source of these abuses, if not the fatal inequality between men brought by the honour paid to talents and the depreciation of virtues? ... We have physicians, geometers, chemists, astronomers, poets, musicians, painters; we no longer have citizens."

[10] Economists have played an important role in this process. As CELSO FURTADO puts it, in *op. cit.*, p. 30: "The great ideological achievement of economic science, in the sense that it helped to facilitate the development of productive forces in the framework of capitalism, comes from the fact that economic science has contributed a lot to hide the element of power which is always present in economic decisions, presenting it as 'automatisms' or 'mechanisms' whose laws should be discovered and carefully respected. ... The evolution of the anonymous corporation, the main institution of the capitalist economy, allows us to see with clarity this masking of that element of power."

[11] S. RADAKRISHNAN, the great Indian thinker of our century, has described this situation very well, but from the other side, in *Religion and Society*, p. 16: "With the centralized machinery of the state, with the modern instruments of technical progress and mass propaganda, total mobilization of the subjects, their bodies, minds and souls are affected. The absolute state and the totalitarian community become identical. ... We seem to be in the grip of demonic forces which degrade mankind to the semblance of the lower animals. The god-man becomes the herd animal. The creed of the great Leviathan compels us to lead lives of effort and emptiness, heart-

less, vulgar, trivial and coarse in spirit. Our humanness is destroyed by regimentation." London: George Allen & Unwin Ltd., 1947.

[12] Cf. CELSO FURTADO, *op. cit.*, p. 43: "It was not the evolution of the productive forces which expulsed the population of the rural areas, and which destroyed the professional corporations; all this was related to the ascension of bourgeoisie in the structure of power. . . . The control of the production system passed from the hands of owners, who became receivers of rents, to the hands of the merchant bourgeoisie. Those rights that tradition and habits granted to workers, disappeared in front of the new system which tried to impose its legitimacy from the 'laws of the market'."

[13] Cf. RICHARD D. N. DICKINSON: *To Set at Liberty the Oppressed*, pp. 64 ff. Also *To Break the Chains of Oppression*, pp. 16-18. Geneva: WCC, 1975.

[14] Cf. CELSO FURTADO, *op. cit.*, p. 43: "To summarize, the capitalist mode of production — that is, the merchant way of appropriating the surplus, applied to the direct control of all productive activities — resulted in being a much more efficient power system than other authoritarian ways of appropriation of the surplus, which till the seventeenth century have prevailed in other social organizations."

[15] Cf. ERIC WILLIAMS: *From Columbus to Castro: 1492-1969*, pp. 136-155. London: André Deutsch, 1970.

[16] Cf. VERA ANSTEY: *The Economic Development of India*, p. 5: "Till the eighteenth century the economic conditions of India were relatively good; production methods, industrial and trade organization, could resist well the comparison with those existing everywhere in the world at the same time . . . That country, which has manufactured and exported precious silks and other luxurious articles at a time when the English still lived in a very primitive way, could not take part in the economic revolution, whose beginners were precisely the children of those same barbarians." London: Longmans Green, 4th ed., 1952. PAUL BARAN remarks that such breakdown was not accidental: it was the result of the terrible exploitation exercised by British entrepreneurs since the beginning of British domination of India: cf. *Economie politique de la croissance*, p. 188. Paris: Maspero, 1967. Cf. also ROMESH DUTT: *The Economic History of India*, pp. VII ff. London: Kegan Paul, 1950, 7th ed.

[17] CELSO FURTADO, *op. cit.*, pp. 54-55.

[18] Cf. CESAR ESPIRITU: "Economic Dependence and Independence: As Seen from Southeast Asia," in DENYS MUNBY (ed.): *Economic Growth in World Perspective*, pp. 196-197. New York and London: WCC, Association Press and SCM Press, 1966.

[19] The case of India, already mentioned in note 16, is again an example of this affirmation: even in the last decade of the nineteenth century, emerging textile industries in that country were dismantled with the help of the military.

[20] In Chile, becoming aware of the influence and threat of external interests, the Minister Luis Aldunate wrote in 1894 that foreign capital *"loin de nous être utiles et profitables, nous épuisent, nous affaiblissent, nous mènent à la ruine sans nous apporter ni nous apprendre quoi que ce soit . . ."*. Quoted by H. RAMÍREZ NECOCHEA: *Historia del imperialismo en Chile*, p. 254. Santiago de Chile: Ed. Austral, 1960.

[21] Cf. ERIC WILLIAMS, *op. cit.*, pp. 255-279. Cf. also by the same author: *Capitalism and Slavery*. London: Putnam, 1966.

22 CELSO FURTADO, in *op. cit.*, p. 48, says something which explains this situation: "A technical innovation can place a producer in a privileged position, in the same way as the building of a highway can favour a given region. However, the price system progressively reduces the emerging discrepancies, because accumulation tends to be less in those activities which occasionally are becoming less profitable."

23 *Ibid.*, p. 60: "In those economies which were penetrated by the capitalist mode of production in a framework of external dependency, the phenomenon of social insecurity becomes aggravated. This problem has been deeply studied under the topics of *under-employment, masked unemployment* and *social marginality*, and there is a general consensus that it is a structural characteristic of the so-called underdeveloped economies. If to this insecurity the fact of increasing social inequalities is added, than the need for more expensive repressive systems and the risk of revolutionary explosions is understandable."

24 *Ibid.*, p. 135: "When an economy is more developed, it is more important for it to have access to technical innovations. If the country does not produce such innovations . . . it is necessary to import them. This explains why the accelerated development which took place in the last quarter of a century in industrialized countries, assumed also the form of intensification of interdependence among them. . . . The fundamental problem is, who controls this technique, who exercises the power which in our civilization is generated by technology, and who pays, in order to have access to such technology, with resources which certainly are less powerful, particularly with that despicable money which is the cheap labour force of third world peoples."

25 *Ibid.*, pp. 92-93: "Since the industrialization of a country, whatever the epoch at which it takes place, is shaped by the great accumulation realized in the countries that have taken the lead in technical progress, the effort required to take the first steps tends to increase with time. It is understandable, therefore, that after a certain point, the possibility of opting for the project of a national economic system becomes practically nil. And from that moment one has to speak of a qualitative difference between central capitalism and peripheral capitalism. . . . It is therefore less a case of a problem of level of development than of qualitative difference in the process of development."

26 In *Scanning our Future*, a report from the NGO Forum on the World Economic Order organized in support of the Seventh Special Session of the United Nations General Assembly on Development and International Economic Cooperation, Marcelo Alonso stated: "The development plans of the developing countries depend on the flow of technology from the developed countries. No less important is the capacity of the importing countries to correctly identify their technological needs. An importing country which has not developed this capacity may only succeed in multiplying its development problems." New York: Carnegie Endowment for International Peace, 1976.

27 CELSO FURTADO, *op. cit.*, p. 77.

28 *Ibid.*, p. 58: "Everything points to the fact that the transnationalization of production is geared towards its own transformation into a decisive element in the struggle for the preservation of systems of social domination based on the capitalist

mode of production, particularly in the countries most advanced in the process of accumulation."

[29] JACQUES ATTALI: *La parole et l'outil*, pp. 40-41: "All one can see is that the dominant system develops, ramifies, assumes a structure, becomes more complex and to what end if not the abstract and anonymous increase of capital? ... On a purely theoretical level there is in fact no conceivable limit to the financial growth of the prevailing system, which could control everything within a century. Investment, marketing, export, worldwide spread of production are then the phases in the growth of a product and of the inevitable extension of the control of the prevailing system over the explosive process ... Ultimately, worldwide quasi-monopolies of production and technology appear in certain sectors, They are then in a position to determine quality and carry out price extortion in the same way as certain producers of raw materials, holders of rent. They determine in particular at will the length of life of products. The prevailing system is above all a financial system, and it is hard to say it is concentrated more particularly in certain branches of industry." Paris: PUF, 1975.

[30] On transnational corporations and their relationships with states of dependent countries there is an extensive literature. Among it we call attention to the following: WCC *Report of a Consultation on a Proposed Action/Reflection Programme on Transnational Corporations*, Geneva, June 1977. PAUL GREGORIOS (ed.): *Burning Issues*. Kottayam: Sophia Centre Publications, 1978. *Multinational Corporations in World Development*, New York: UN, 1973. *The Impact of Multinational Corporations on Development and on International Relations*. New York: UN, 1974. DIMITRI GERMIDIS (ed.): *Transfer of Technology by Multinational Corporations*, 2 vols. Paris: Ed. OCDE, 1977. JON P. GUNEMANN (ed.): *The Nation-State and Transnational Corporations in Conflict*. New York: Praeger Publishers, 1975. RICHARD J. BARNET and RONALD E. MUELLER: *The Global Rich*. New York: Simon & Schuster, 1974. CEDAL: *Multinationales et travailleurs au Brésil*. Paris: Ed. Maspero, 1977. XAVIER GOROSTIAGA: *Los banqueros del Imperio*. San José de Costa Rica: Ed. Educa, 1978.

[31] ECLA: *Report of the Cartagena Conference*. Santiago de Chile, 1968.

[32] HANS SINGER, in *Scanning our Future, op. cit.*, p. 96: "When you start off with an unequal income distribution to begin with, the 'free market mechanism' will inevitably tend to support, perpetuate and indeed accentuate the unequal income distribution. When the richest 20% of the population have 75% of the GNP while the poorest 20% have only 5% of the GNP, then in the free market an increase in the purchasing power of the richest 20% by a given proportion, say by 10%, will weigh fifteen times more heavily than the same proportionate increase of 10% in the incomes of the poorest 20%. Yet from a development as well as a welfare point of view, it should be exactly the other way around. To bring the poorest 20% above the poverty line, or at least nearer the poverty line, is a much more important objective rather than to increase further the wellbeing of those who are already well above the poverty line."

[33] CELSO FURTADO, *op. cit.*, p. 95: "... the industrial activities of peripheral capitalist countries are increasingly controlled by big transnational corporations. The internal scarcity of resources has been used in many countries to justify the offering of additional advantages to these corporations, which aimed to occupy the sectors

in which the technological control provides greater advantages. Occupying strategic positions, they aim to appropriate the increasing part of the expanded surplus of production. This explains why the transformation of the process of industrialization has generally been accompanied by another transformation in the control system of industrial activity, that is, the quick substitution of the local capitalist class by agents of big corporations of transnational action."

34 R. BARNET and R. MUELLER, *op. cit.*, pp. 166-167: "The one characteristic of global corporate technology with the most devastating consequences for poor countries is that it destroys jobs... The expansion of the global corporation has contributed to the expansion of world unemployment."

35 MARC NERFIN (Ed.): *Another Development: Approaches and Strategies*, cf. the chapter by PAUL SINGER and BOLIVAR LAMOUNIER: "Brazil: Growth through Inequality," pp. 125-151. Uppsala: Dag Hammarskjöld Foundation, 1977.

36 *Ibid*, cf. the chapter by CYNTHIA HEWETT DE ALCANTARA: "Mexico: A Commentary on the Satisfaction of Basic Needs," pp. 152-207.

37 ECLA: *Report of the Guatemala Conference 1976*. Mexico, 1976. Estimates there indicate that 38% of the active labour force in Latin America was unemployed in 1976.

IV · Religion and Popular Culture in Relation to Poverty

For a more global interpretation of these situations of extreme poverty and oppression endured by millions of human beings today, we have to understand that forms of domination are present in all spheres of people's lives, not only in the economic one.

Although one may say that the growth and perpetuation of poverty are mainly due to the way in which economic relationships are organized, there are other forces at work, such as cultural and ideological mechanisms which exert their influence on the people or try to dominate them. It is important to keep this in mind in discussing popular culture and religiosity. Though the people's system of values, their artistic expressions, or their social organizations are influenced and shaped by powerful economic and ideological mechanisms, it is equally true that popular culture resists, survives and in some cases even grows strong, in spite of those very mechanisms of the dominant groups. This survival of popular culture demonstrates that popular wisdom and philosophy develop remarkable forms of resistance to manipulation and destruction. The dominant groups are not always able to grasp or control these mechanisms of resistance and survival.

If we wish to understand the struggle of the poor and consciously decide to stand by them, we have to go beyond a mere economic appraisal and grasp the deeper meaning of their expressions, their way of thinking and standpoint in order to interpret their actions. We should not do this from the viewpoint of the ruler but from the perspective of the poor. We must be able to read their language and symbols in their own terms, and strive to understand their rationale and the dynamics of their social organizations.

This is certainly not an easy task; for the dominant group it will almost always be impossible. Generally, popular culture is disqualified through simplistic attitudes or tendentious and ideologically biased interpretations, leaving it in an inferior position so as to justify and legitimize the ideological tools the dominators use to manipulate and alienate popular culture in their own interests. These mechanisms are present in different spheres of life, such as the mass media or incentives to consumerist attitudes.

The ways of expressing popular culture are quite varied and cover all aspects of the life of the poor. They can be found in the workplace, in art, in feasting, in family life, in their homes, food, education of children, in dressmaking, ornaments and especially in their religious expressions. Because of the main thrust of this book we will confine ourselves to indicating some of the elements necessary for interpreting popular religiosity. Although the forces which created and sustain injustices are powerful, history teaches us that social change is possible and that social justice has been achieved in increasing measure in many parts of the world in the last two centuries. Industrial workers and peasants are much better off now in the western world than a century ago. Similarly, it is possible to say that in some countries of Asia, Africa and the Caribbean, people have struggled and continue to strive to overcome poverty, that is, in order to achieve more justice and a greater sense of freedom which they did not have some decades ago.

The culture of the poor indicates a situation of deprivation of life and a subordinated social condition. Their habits and customs, their traditions and values, their social feelings, their social, economic and ideological expressions, all mirror that situation and that condition. The same happens with the religion of the people:[1] it cannot evade the social and economic structures which characterize the existence of poverty. The relationship between material conditions of life and the ideological expression, including religion, of social groups always has to be taken into consideration. Both culture and religion give evidence of the submission and the resistance of the poor, at the same time, to the situation that is theirs and to the elements which cause them. This explains why we look at the reality of popular religion and popular culture, not from a perspective of domination, but from the persistent effort of the poor for equity and liberation. There is at present a reaction against the very widespread sentiment which only esteems these phenomena for their interest as folklore or their esthetic characteristics.[2] As a result of better observation of these expressions of people's life, their more significant and deeper aspects have become apparent, thus demonstrating the baselessness and the superficiality of the conclusions which had dominated earlier writings on the subject. The Church, too, which is seriously confronted with the problems raised in this way, especially in third world countries, faces the challenge of overcoming its over-simplified attitude, pervaded by elitist assumptions of an ideology of domination which condemns these expressions of the people, rating them as manifestations of inferior and backward groups.

Without adopting an idealistic or naive attitude, it seems important to indicate briefly some aspects of popular culture and religiosity which regularly recur.

It is worth emphasizing that we are conscious of the precariousness, and of the double risk one runs, in making generalizations or drawing conclusions about social phenomena, which go to the very roots of the life of the peoples with different histories and systems and which have their ground and significance in whole cultural patterns which we do not fully share or understand.

Some positive elements of popular religions

1. In the search for meaningful answers to the various levels of needs in a social practice, people build up a *whole system of symbols and concrete practices* which enable them to give deep meaning to their life of suffering and conquests. This system very profoundly expresses moments of struggle and liberation. It is rooted in the actual views of the world that the people hold and which are an integral part of the historical course their formation has followed. These forms of popular strength and organization cannot simply be despised or changed as it were by magic for another conception of life. The people's values are important components of their own life and their annihilation means violence and death. The people's *common sense* forms part of their world and is present in its religious forms.[3]

2. A relevant characteristic of popular religious sensibility very common, for instance, in Africa and Latin America, is its *close connection with the dynamic aspects of life.* It is not simply a concern for individual life but for all dynamic elements of the natural and social process in which life is involved. In African and much of Latin American religiosity, religious elements are bound up with very concrete communal practices, such as the harvest, hunting, fishing, war, the choice of chiefs, and so on.[4] It is not a matter of a few relics cut off from the material aspects of life, but on the contrary it assumes force and meaning because it is in the centre of the vital interests of the community's existence.[5]

Gramsci affirms that this constitutes perhaps the chief characteristic of the religion of the people; it is materialistic and concrete, quite different in this respect, therefore, from the idealistic and abstract speculations of some religious thinkers.[6]

3. This being so, the expressions of religious worship demand intense practical participation. There are no merely passive spectators. The whole community forms part of the religious expression because it is clearly significant. It is not a matter of individual options, but rather something built up in common. This aspect, *the rich sense of community*, often perplexes the defenders of religious individualism who cannot understand how deeply social the creation of these religious practices is.[7]

4. Naturally, these expressions call for very *concrete means or representation*. The thought of the people is manifested through very concrete examples linked to their own life. Food, clothes, drinks, animals, ornaments, the sun, the moon, are elements present in worship; they are offered to God or represent the deity. Religion is not cut off from life; it is an important component of the whole social process, not extraneous to its formation. In the Umbanda cults which have grown tremendously in the last few years in Brazil, the religious entities come down to earth, are incarnated in the believers, concretely take possession of them as their own, and those who receive them take on the attitudes and deeds of the entities which are present in their bodies.[8] It is a religion where the sense of incarnation is not reduced to an ideal expression but is a real God with them (according to their beliefs).

5. Some of the deeper studies of popular religious sensibility have recently brought out a very abundant element: its *dynamic sense of process*. It is not a static religiosity which is completed and exhausted in the present. Its close contact with the concrete facts of life does not suppress the sense of process. It can even be compared to the biblical concept of "pilgrimage".[9] Nor is it reduced to a cult of the past or the nostalgic cultural manifestations. Its outlook takes into account that important elements present in the life of the poor cannot be justified simply by the observed facts of the moment. Popular religiosity builds a necessary bridge with the past through its heroes, its dead, its peoples. It reconstructs its history out of different elements than those employed by western thought. However, the connection is not only with the past, but also with the future. And this future is thought of in very material images — a place where there is food, water, houses, joy; where there is no more war nor struggle, where the peoples will be without sufferings.[10]

6. The *sense of solidarity* and of the relevance of the communal elements in popular religious feeling and worship leads to the formation of a conception of salvation and liberty which is very difficult for certain sectors of Christian theology to understand and interpret. The sacrifices, the liturgy, the offerings, in short, all the manifestations of religion are related

to collective communal concerns. It is the nation, the tribe, or the people which is thought of as the object of liberation, hardly the individual. The sense of salvation is collective. God saves and protects his people, God blesses the harvest, the fishing, the hunting, warlike struggle, which are in the interest of all; He does not watch over and protect individuals in isolation.

7. Another positive perspective in the religion of the people is the *conception of totality that it involves.*[11] There is no artificial separation of two essential elements — there is a close inter-relation between God, nature and humanity. Woods, water, sea, stars, animals, children, old people, work, festivities, etc., are integral parts of one universe. They are not antagonistic elements, but complementary; they form part of the same reality, synthesized by the religious vision.

Some negative uses of popular religions

1. The social organizations in which the elements of popular religions took shape were not immune to the process of industrialization, technology, social modernization and new forms of social structuration.

Structures of power have used the elements of popular religion to preserve their privileges and the mechanisms which maintain them. They prevent the people from realizing that, in present circumstances, their struggles require different instruments and that the explanatory terms used for present problems are scarcely to be found in religion. In this way, they contrive to use the significant elements of culture and religion to maintain privileged situations (the castes in Nepal and India[12]), to suggest religious explanations for economic and social problems (poverty, illnesses, deaths[13]), to support those in power (people called by God) and thus popular religion loses its force of endurance and unity and becomes a powerful factor of alienation.[14] Modern means of propaganda and social communication are effective weapons for manipulating popular values.

2. *The control of the means of socialization by dominant groups has made it possible to introduce into popular culture the ideological elements of their class.* Many social institutions have served as an apparatus for propagating the dominant ideology, for instance school, family and the churches.[15] The power of interiorization which these instruments possess should not, however, be either under-rated or exaggerated. It is always good to be alive to the fact that the people possess and maintain a wisdom of their own and that they escape from views which form no part of their experience.

It is not possible, however, to think today of pure popular religion, devoid of any presence of class ideology, as though it were immune from any ideological infiltration. It is worth recalling the statements of Henri Mottu in his article "Critique théologique de la religion populaire" based on the propositions of Gramsci:

However, recent researches on pentecostalism, methodism, charismatic revival movements, etc., show that there is no, as it were, mechanical link, no "elective affinity" between these movements and the lower classes of society. On the contrary, "popular religion" is popular only in appearance or, at least, only in the first stage of this history. It never exists in the pure state. As soon as long duration enters in, one realizes that it is the ideal religious type, not of the lower classes, but of the intermediate classes, notably those who have come from the "petite bourgeoisie" (middle class), *threatened with proletarization*, thrust aside, politically and socially traditional, not yet possessing or having already lost their chances of socio-professional betterment.[16]

3. With the infiltration and domination of the capitalist system, principally by the western world in underdeveloped countries, all the elements of society came to be seen as objects of consumption and profit. The "law of the market" also affected the expressions of popular religious sentiment which came to be commercialized and exploited. The values of the people, their cults, their worship, their festivities, and even sufferings came to be an object of commercial exploitation. In Latin America, religious leaders enriched themselves through the "industry" of religious healing, industries were set up to produce and sell objects of popular piety, pilgrimages were organized and religious festivals and ceremonies were used for tourist and economic purposes.[17] Many traditional religious organizations also made use of popular values to maintain their structures for their economic advantage and to alienate the people.[18]

4. In recent years, especially in African countries, the colonizing nations or their representatives have very often used the values of popular culture as a means of sowing division among peoples. In this way, the national values are falsified and nationalism is exacerbated to create disputes between tribes and divide the forces of liberation. Signs of strength of popular culture and its potential for liberation are manipulated to make continued domination and injustice possible. This rather well-known strategy is based on putting the most deeply-rooted sentiments of the people at the service of injustice.[19]

The appropriation and perversion of popular values and expressions, whether religious or not, by the power structures or by the most privileged sectors of society is a phenomenon which is not restricted to the Third World, but can also be found in Europe or North America. One can point to several examples of this type of manipulation and cooptation of the cultural values by society as a whole, including the Christian churches.

Apart from coopting and distorting elements of popular expressions of other religions, the Christmas feasts, so much valued by affluent sectors of society, serve as handy instruments for promoting consumption of commercial products. Naturally this corresponds to the interests of strong economic groups, and also alienates ideological messages.

Another example is the cooptation by dominant sectors of society of the North American black liberation songs, using them as mere artistic expressions of a sentimental and individualistic kind, obliterating their original meaning as manifestations of a collective popular struggle.

Christianity and popular religion

Besides Christianity, other religious movements too have become tools for the devaluation or the ideological manipulation of popular culture and religiosity. However, due to the specific nature of this book, this is not the place for further discussion.

The coming of Christianity to Africa, the Americas and Asia was always linked with the spread of the colonial system. Therefore, it was not simply a question of introducing a new expression of faith and religious ideas.

Consciously or unconsciously, a new view of the world and a new style of life were introduced. It was not by chance that the arrival of Christianity was followed by the foundation of a large number of schools and other forms of ideological penetration.[20] This process transformed not only religious conceptions, which were regarded as pagan and backward, but also customs and social organization. It was as if the model to be followed were that of the society from which the representatives of Christianity themselves originated. It logically followed that popular values were sure to be under-rated. The music of the people, popular traditions and cults, were considered inferior, the product of traditions which do not know "the true sense of life". In many cases, they were regarded as expressions of sin and even as infestations of the devil.[21] In many countries, there were confrontations and aspects of popular culture were destroyed.[22] The music of the people was replaced by western hymns, local clothes were considered not fully appropriate, and even the national language was exchanged for western languages.[23] Worship that was musical, colourful, joyous, participatory, was replaced by a liturgy that was aseptic, demanding, rational, extremely organized and vertical. The word, the sermon became the centre of the worship service, and the participation by the congregation lost the dynamism of the people's tradition. National elites were formed who received privileges for associating more closely with the missionaries, acquired prestige and little by little put a distance between themselves and the people. Their children were sent to study abroad, and since the language of the colonizers almost always was dominant, many of them became effective local instruments of domination. In some cases it is necessary to qualify these statements. For individuals of prevailing social groups, the ideology of domination and all the effects it entailed was not always very clear. Many, by a sincere desire to do good (as they conceived it), did not perceive the nature of the whole process of which they formed part. Many sacrificed their lives, sought individual improvement of the poor, gave proof of renunciation, but were not able to grasp the full significance of their mission and the fact that they were tools of an aggressive colonizing policy with plain economic and political purposes.[24]

Another significant element was the replacement of the religious concepts of the people by a different religious outlook. As we have already said, popular religion presents very marked features of materiality, communal solidarity, practical participation, application of common sense, a very effective sense of incarnation, and a holistic conception of life, including God, nature and human beings. Most of the Christian missionary enterprises replaced this pattern with an ethical and abstract religion; it emphasizes the individual (salvation as a personal option), puts special stress on aspects of life after death, attaches great importance to souls ("to win souls for Christ" is its slogan), separates the material from the spiritual, promotes rationality and order in accordance with its own models, considers the rejoicings of the popular festivities as manifestations of "the world and the flesh", cuts off the Church from society, uproots believers from their effective communities and keeps them away from the struggles of their people.[25] However, there are other Christian groups who do not wholly reject the people's values and make use of them in their own world, so that they serve as a means of strengthening their own religious project.[26]

In recent decades, these attitudes have been criticized and reconsidered. Some church sectors have perceived the equivocal nature of a mere rejection of popular culture and values. Confrontation and destruction of this religion and culture are not necessary and do not represent an appropriate Christian standpoint.[27] The havoc wreaked on the native populations of Latin America, the attempt to replace the religious values and practices of the African and Asian populations, are seen to have been like a deviation of the missionary spirit which emerges from the Gospel. It is not possible to attach a label to God or classify his manifestations according to our own particular criteria. The Holy Spirit has complete freedom from those that dominant groups regard as genuine.[28] God cannot be imprisoned in our models and the parametres of western culture. *The attitude which regards the people's values as inferior has repelled the poor from certain Christian churches which compromised themselves with the interests and values of the dominant groups.*

It is felt that in the present sociological and theological formation of pastors and leaders of the churches, there is a perceptible lack of understanding of the value, strength and characteristics of the religion and culture of the people. They are either not studied at all or are presented from the point of view of the dominant sectors of society. It would therefore be very difficult for these pastors to realize that the people's culture contains manifest signs of liberation and endurance and that the Spirit of God and his message of liberation can be present also in these religious practices.[29] It is not a question of having "a bad conscience" or seeking a recompense for the centuries of exploitation and domination in which we took part. A sense of humility and confession of sins is prompted by the realization that our religious formation is pervaded by an ideological world view and that our reading of the Gospel is influenced by our position in life and the social class or stratum to which we belong.

Hostility to the religion of the people is a phenomenon also found in the so-called developed countries. It can be observed in western history. The Crusades, the Inquisition, the racial discrimination in the USA show that the problem challenges everyone to be concerned.[30]

Another aspect which we can only refer to is the complex phenomenon of the so-called religious syncretism and the challenge it represents to Christian faith.[31]

The danger of idealizing popular religion

In the course of this chapter, we have shown that it is not possible to take these religious phenomena as pure and ideal manifestations, consisting solely of liberating elements. Such a view would be oversimplified, naive, and irresponsible.

The values of popular religion have appeared at certain historical moments, in concrete social formations and are the fruits of given types of social relations. These values helped to legitimize distinct social organizations and were accepted and interiorized as significant for those historical moments. Their strength and relevance were well founded because they were the social products shared and built up by all people as meaningful and liberating instruments.

Meanwhile, we have to consider that there is a vast historical distance between their origins and the present moment in which we live. It is a striking fact that these values and these social practices have passed through setbacks, endured powerful dominant movements down to the present day.

These cultural values were not influenced by other social structures, some completely authoritarian and oppressive, which modified in some respects their original liberating force.[32] So, we must not take an idealistic view of popular religion and then say that statements that come from the people are good, that popular religiosity is always a symbol of liberation, or that the culture of the people is exempt from tendencies towards domination. It should be replaced by a more historical, political and realistic outlook.

The political potential of popular religion

The Church and social scientists have been impressed by the capacity shown by popular religion to survive and even to grow. Despite the determined attacks, despite the advance of technology and of the means of social communication, it endures and revives even in unfavourable conditions. In what does the strength of these movements of the weak and the poor consist?

In it, there exists undoubtedly a significant reserve of resistance and hope which can never be destroyed by colonial domination, by the process of secularization of the enlightened elites or by the consumer culture of world capitalism. All this makes up the inestimable value of the evangelical presence of the poor.[33]

Popular religion also constitutes a significant ideological expression of people's views; it is a way of resisting the rationale of the "law of the market". It expresses a "wisdom" developed by the people themselves and has an incalculable strength which comes from the people themselves, based on values of great significance in the struggle for that people's very survival.

To despise these forms of popular organization, to regard them as expressions of inferiority, to use them for the maintenance of power indicates both a failure to realize their importance and a downright elitist and imperialist mentality.

Comparison of Health and Education Resources Available in Developed and Developing Countries, 1974

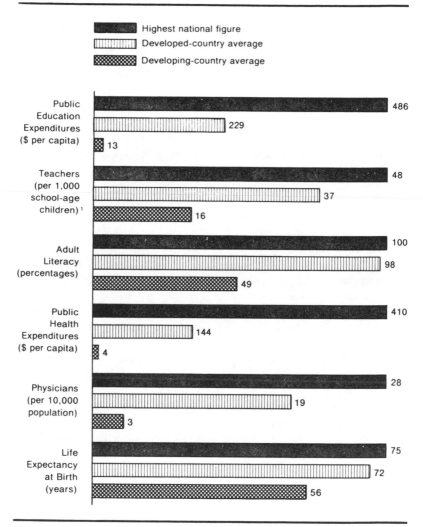

¹School-age children are those 5-19 years of age.

SOURCES: Teachers per 1,000 school-age children based on Ruth Leger Sivard, *World Military and Social Expenditures, 1976;* per capita public health expenditures and physicians per 10,000 population based on Ruth Leger Sivard, *World Military and Social Expenditures, 1977* (WMSE Publications, Box 1003, Leesburg, Virginia 22075); per capita public education expenditures, adult literacy, and life expectancy at birth figures based on this volume, Annex A, Table A-4.

Relative Shares of Selected Resources and Expenditures of Developing and Developed Countries (percentages)

The gap between the developing and the developed countries in both human and capital resources remains substantial. The developing countries—with some 72 per cent of the world's population—have only 20 per cent of world GNP, 27 per cent of world export earnings, and 7 per cent of world public health expenditures. In contrast, the developed countries—with a quarter of the world's population—spend 87 per cent of the amount spent worldwide on public education and have 80 per cent of the world's income.

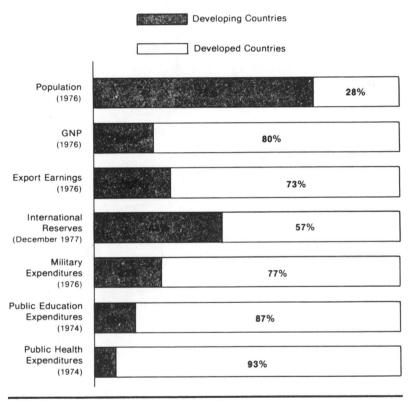

NOTES: World population, 4.0 billion; world GNP, $6.7 trillion; total world export earnings, $1,014.1 billion; world international reserves, $316.2 billion; total world military expenditures, $398.9 billion; total world public education expenditures, $271.0 billion; and total world public health expenditures, $156.5 billion.

SOURCES: Population and GNP figures are based on this volume, Annex A, Table A-8; export earnings and international reserves figures are based on this volume, Annex A, Table A-4; military expenditures are based on this volume, Annex D, Table D-3; public education and public health expenditure figures are based on Ruth Leger Sivard, *World Military and Social Expenditures, 1977* (WMSE Publications, Box 1003, Leesburg, Virginia 22075), p. 21.

Two Measures of the Gap Between Developing and Developed Countries, 1960-1976

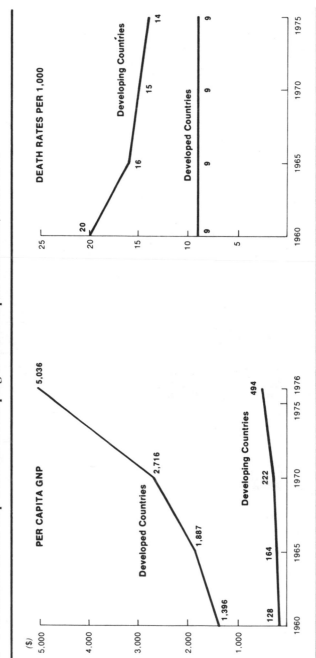

SOURCES: Per capita GNP figures for 1960, 1965, and 1970 are from Ruth Leger Sivard. *World Military and Social Expenditures, 1977* (WMSE Publications. Box 1003. Leesburg, Virginia 22075). p. 20. 1975 and 1976 per capita GNP figures are from this volume, Annex A, Table A-4: death rate figures are from United Nations. Department of Economic and Social Affairs, Population Division. *Selected World Demographic Indicators by Countries, 1950-2000*. Doc. No. ESA/P/WP. 55. May 28, 1975.

Income Distribution Within Selected Developing and Developed Countries (percentages)

	Share of National Income of Population Groups				
	Richest 20%	2nd 20%	3rd 20%	4th 20%	Poorest 20%
Developing Countries					
Argentina (1961)	52.0	17.6	13.1	10.3	7.0
Ecuador (1970)	73.5	14.5	5.6	3.9	2.5
Egypt (1964-65)	47.0	23.5	15.5	9.8	4.2
India (1963-64)	52.0	19.0	13.0	11.0	5.0
Kenya (1969)	68.0	13.5	8.5	6.2	3.8
Korea, Rep. of (1970)	45.0	22.0	15.0	11.0	7.0
Mexico (1969)	64.0	16.0	9.5	6.5	4.0
Sri Lanka (1969-70)	46.0	20.5	16.5	11.0	6.0
Tanzania (1967)	57.0	17.0	12.0	9.0	5.0
Developed Countries					
Australia (1967-68)	38.7	23.4	17.8	13.5	6.6
France (1962)	53.7	22.8	14.0	7.6	1.9
Germany, Dem. Rep. (1970)	30.7	23.3	19.8	15.8	10.4
Germany, Fed. Rep. (1970)	45.6	22.5	15.6	10.4	5.9
Hungary (1967)	33.5	23.5	19.0	15.5	8.5
Japan (1968)	43.8	23.4	16.8	11.3	4.6
Sweden (1970)	42.5	24.6	17.6	9.9	5.4
United Kingdom (1968)	39.2	23.8	18.2	12.8	6.0
United States (1970)	38.8	24.1	17.4	13.0	6.7

NOTES: Income distribution data are incomplete and deficient, and inter-country comparisons should be made with caution. A completely equal distribution of national income would show the richest 20 per cent and the poorest 20 per cent of the population (as well as all other quintiles) each receiving 20 per cent of that country's income.

SOURCE: Montek S. Ahluwalia, "Inequality, Poverty and Development," *Journal of Development Economics* 3 (1976).

The four graphs reproduced here have been taken from *The United States and World Development: Agenda 1979*, by Martin M. McLaughlin and the staff of the Overseas Development Council. New York : Praeger Publishers, 1979.

NOTES

[1] We understand religion in the sense that P. BOURDIEN gives it: "A symbolic medium, at once structured and structuring, in so far as it is the condition of the possibility of an agreement on the meaning of signs and the meaning of the world." "Genèse et structure du champ religieux". *Revue française de sociologie*, XII, 1971,

pp. 295-296. FRANÇOIS HOUTART, commenting this definition in *Religion and Ideology in Sri Lanka*, p. 7, says that it is necessary to "add a further element by saying that religion is a symbolic medium referring to supernatural forces, personified or not". St Peter's Seminary, Bangalore: TPI, 1974.

² The starting point of the current interest in popular religion is related to MAX WEBER's views that religion contributes simultaneously to the legitimation of power of the privileged groups and at the same time to the subservience of the underprivileged, promising them better conditions in an after-life as a compensation for their present position. Cf. his *The Sociology of Religion*, pp. 80-118. Boston: Beacon Press, 1963. The fact that the underprivileged accept the official religious views on the one hand, while on the other hand correct these views according to their own interests, has challenged sociologists and theologians to improve research in the field of popular religion.

³ HENRI MOTTU has underlined the importance of common sense as an essential characteristic of popular religion. Cf. "Theologische Kritik der Religion und Religion des Volkes," in *Ein Bonhoeffer-Symposium*, ed. HANS PFEIFER, pp. 75-78. Munich: Chr. Kaiser, 1976. This concept is very well developed in Gramsci's *Quaderni del Carcere*, II, pp. 1045, 1396-1397, 1401, 1410, etc. Torino: Einaudi, 1975.

⁴ JOHN MBITI: *Introduction to African Religion*, pp. 19-30. New York: Praeger, 1975. Cf. also E. BOLAJI IDOWU *African Traditional Religion*, pp. 165-173. London: SCM Press Ltd., 1973.

⁵ The community is rooted in the past. The role of the memory of the ancestors is particularly important for the cohesion of the community. As stated by E. BOLAJI IDOWU, *op.cit.*, p. 185: "The ancestors are a factor of cohesion in African society. This is a fact well illustrated in the sacred stools which are the ancestral symbols of the Ashanti, especially the Golden Stool . . . It is the supreme genius of the nation and is thus that which gives the nation a sense of cohesion."

⁶ Cf. HENRI MOTTU, *op. cit.*, pp. 74-75.

⁷ G. VAN DER LEEUW notes in *La religion dans son essence et ses manifestations*, p. 187: "In relation to power, human life is not primarily individual life, but that of the *community* . . . It is life simplified and reduced to its essential features, life as it is lived by all . . ." Paris: Payot, 1955.

⁸ Cf. ALFRED MÉTRAUX: *Vodei*. Buenos Aires: Ed. Sur, 1963. Cf. also CANDIDO PROCEPIO DE CAMARGO: *Aspectos sociológicos del espiritismo en São Paulo*. Friburgo and Bogota: Ed. Feres, 1961. ROGER BASTIDE: *Les religions africaines au Brésil*, pp. 412-414. Paris: Ed. PUF, 1960. VAN DER LEEUW, in another context, talks about possession in a similar way in *op. cit.*, pp. 282-283.

⁹ MARCELO PINTO CAVALHEIRA, Bishop of Paraiba, Brazil: "A Caminhada do Povo de Deus na America Latina", *Revista Eclesiastica Brasileira*, Vol. 38, fasc. 150, 1978, pp. 300-309.

¹⁰ G. VAN DER LEEUW, *op. cit.*, pp. 313-314, and especially 320-321.

¹¹ H. H. PRESLER: *Primitive Religions in India*, p. 301: "Primitive (popular) religion is nature religion. Its truth is derived from the facts of biological nature; its certitude is confirmed by the mystery of nature; its absolution is realized by involvement with nature." Bangalore: Christian Literature Society, 1971.

[12] CHRISTOPH VON FÜRER-HAIMENDORF: *Caste and Kin in Nepal, India, and Ceylon*, pp. 22-23. Bombay: Asia Publishing House, 1966. Cf. also for the case of Sri Lanka, FRANÇOIS HOUTART, *op. cit.*, pp. 197-200; 320-328; 347-351, etc.

[13] JOHN MBITI, *op. cit.*, pp. 110-125.

[14] FRANÇOIS HOUTART, *op. cit.*, p. 487: "The functional needs experienced in social living, particularly the need to justify power, will likewise exert an influence on the way religious rites are organized and performed."

[15] Cf. what PAULO FREIRE states about "manipulation" and "cultural invasion" in *Pedagogy of the Oppressed*, pp. 144-167. New York: Herder & Herder, 1970.

[16] HENRI MOTTU, *op. cit.*

[17] ALFRED MÉTRAUX, in *op. cit.*, pp. 11-12, recognizes how Vodei is used for commercial purposes. Something similar happens in other Afro-Brazilian cults.

[18] The best known case in Latin America is "Patria, Familia y Propriedad". Cf. JAIME ROJAS and FRANZ VANDESCHUEREN: *Chiesa e Golpe Cileno*. Torino: Claudiana, 1975.

[19] FRANÇOIS HOUTART, *op. cit.*, p. 475: "To view the belonging to a caste as a fact of nature may give it legitimation, but not explanation. And this is where the religious symbolic system comes into play. By rendering meaningful the natural origin of social position (social function of the *Karma* law in the Buddhist system), it explains the social order. Besides, by symbolically turning the social scale into a moral scale, it stands as guarantor of power. Such recourse to religion, that is, to a supernatural referent supplying an *ipso facto* sanction, appears to be a necessary condition for transference from the social to the natural. The object of this transference may be the origin of a group's social location or an individual's position of power. In any case, its need will be felt when institutionalization has made social actors oblivious of the man-made beginnings of social structures."

[20] Cf. in JULIO DE SANTA ANA (Ed.): *Separation without Hope?*, the chapters by C. I. ITTY: "The Church and the Poor in Asian History", pp. 137-154; and by SAMUEL KOBIA: "The Christian Mission and the African Peoples in the 19th Century," pp. 155-170. Geneva: WCC, 1978.

[21] For example, VICTOR E. W. HAYWARD, reporting about a WCC consultation on African Independent Church Movements, held in Mindolo, September 1962, wrote in relation to the problem of monogamy in Africa: "Members of the consultation were themselves clear that monogamy is the Christian ideal! The hesitation related to its imposition as a kind of law. There was general agreement that early missionaries' insistence that a man who had contracted polygamous marriages must put away all wives but one, had failed to show a truly Christian attitude towards the wives so divorced or towards their children. The fundamental Christian concern should have been, and should still be, for the personal values of a stable Christian home life, founded upon mutual love and respect. Independent churches have often with good reason charged the older churches with hypocrisy in this matter . . . However it has been preached, Christianity has all too often in Africa, as elsewhere, been heard in terms of law and not of Gospel; as a burden to be borne instead of a liberating and life-giving power." *African Independent Church Movements*, pp. 10-11. London: Edinburgh House, 1963.

[22] This attempt was opposed by Fr Bartolomé de las Casas, the Spanish Bishop at the beginning of the colonization process in Central America and Peru. Cf. ANDRÉ

CASTALDO: "Les questions péruviennes de Bartolomé de las Casas (1564)", *Foi et Vie*, 77th year, No. 1-2, January-April 1978, pp. 65-124. Also ENRIQUE DUSSEL: *Historia de la Iglesia en América Latina*, pp. 92-99. Barcelona: Nova Terra, 1974.

23 *Guinea-Bissau, Reinventing Education*, p. 19. Geneva: Institut d'Action culturelle, 1977.

24 As C. I. ITTY, in *op. cit.*, p. 141, points out rightly about some missionaries who saw the struggle for Indian independence as a Christian duty: "Most missionaries did not see that way. They continued to be loyal supporters of British rule and were generally critical of the independence movement."

25 Cf. P. D. DEVANANDAN: *The Gospel and Renascent Hinduism*, pp. 23-24, who strongly reacts against this dualism. London: SCM Press Ltd., 1959.

26 See D. T. NILES: *Upon the Earth*, pp. 139 ff. London: Lutterworth Press, 1962.

27 Fortunately, through the WCC's Sub-unit on Dialogue with People of Other Faiths and Ideologies, a different approach is being developed. Cf. STANLEY J. SAMARTHA (Ed.): *Towards World Community*. Geneva: WCC, 1975.

28 Cf. JÜRGEN MOLTMANN: *The Church in the Power of the Spirit*, p. 293. London: SCM Press Ltd., 1977.

29 GUSTAVO GUTIÉRREZ: *La fuerza histórica de los pobres*, extract from *Signos de lucha y esperanza*, p. xxxiv: "The believing dimension in the life of the peoples also implies, as it is demonstrated through their praxis, that they have an immense potentiality of liberating faith." Lima: Ed. CEP, 1978.

30 That was the case of the persecution during the late middle ages in Europe, of the Waldensians, the poor of Lombardy and the Hussites. Cf. AMÉDÉE MOHIAR and JEAN GOMET: *Les Vaudois au Moyen Age*, 2 vols. Torino: Claudiana, 1974.

31 Cf. DAVID M. PATON (ed.): *Breaking Barriers: Nairobi 1975*, p. 75: "What kind of community are Christians committed to seek? ... the community with people of other faiths and convictions, and, in the widest sense, the community of all humanity. Some felt that this could be described as 'wider ecumenism' ... For the time being, the term 'ecumenical' should perhaps be used of inter-Christian dialogue, while the wider dialogue should be referred to as 'inter-religious'." Grand Rapids, Mich.: Wm B. Eerdmans, and London: SPCK, 1976. Also see M. M. THOMAS: *Towards a Theology of Contemporary Ecumenism*, pp. 225-237. Madras and Geneva: Christian Literature Society and WCC, 1978.

32 This is what happened with the institution of monarchy in the history of Israel. Its liberating role (cf. Psalm 72) was abandoned many times. Jeremiah criticized Joachim precisely because of this distortion (cf. Jer. 22 : 13-17). Things of this kind happen very often in the history of religions. They are not justifiable at all.

33 MARCELO PINTO CAVALHEIRA, *op. cit.*, p. 309.

V · The Poor in the Church

The history of the Church helps us to understand beyond any doubt that there has always been a real concern for the poor among Christians. The assistance given to the underprivileged by ecclesiastical institutions, private Christian groups and individual believers does not need to be proven.[1] The problem has not been the assistance, but rather the way in which such aid was provided to the poor, and the paternalism shown in providing such help.[2] Poor industrial workers during the nineteenth century, the poor peasants in most Christian societies, as well as the real poor of Africa, Asia, the Americas, the Middle East and the Pacific, do not find their spiritual home in Christian circles.

This does not mean that the poor are not in the churches. They attend Christian celebrations, some of them participate in the Christian liturgy, some share their religious concerns with Christian communities. However, the problem for them is *not* whether they are in the Church or not, but rather if churches represent the poor, or at least if the churches can become representatives of this kind, standing for the fulfilment of the aspirations and hopes of the poor.

Of course, it is not appropriate to generalize about the poor. Nevertheless, it is possible to say, following the line of thought developed in these pages, that "the poor, before being a social class for the Church, whose interests are opposed to those of other classes, are mainly all the people who are defenceless and who suffer injustice because they cannot achieve their valid rights because of laws controlled by those in power and who exercise it according to their own interests. Because of that, the poor are 'subjugated, those who are underneath, humiliated' *(anawim)* in an unjust way by the powerful."[3] These are the people in regard to whom it is asked whether the churches represent them or not.

Similarly, it is also necessary to say that no institutional ecclesiastical body can be analysed as if it were a monolithic block. It cannot be other-

wise, because since it forms part of a divided society with different social
classes and strata, shaken by conflicts and crises, containing differing
ideological views, the contradictions and tensions of society are also
apparent and arise inside the Christian community itself. Consequently, it
is possible to speak of sectors and segments of the churches which have
particular standpoints, act in a dominating way in the decision-making
process and influence the definition of the Church structures. At the same
time, there are other social sectors and segments in church constituencies
which play a more passive and marginalized role in ecclesiastical life.[4]

Challenging questions have recently been put to the more historical
Christian ecclesiastical institutions, calling them into question and placing
them in a position in which it is no longer possible to evade the issues
involved. For example, why are the majority of industrial workers, the
working classes, and the poor no longer much in evidence in the
churches? Is this perhaps due to there no longer being any place for them
in a significant way in the decision-making structures of local Christian
congregations? Has the Christian message lost its meaning for the victims
of injustice and exploitation? Have the urgent problems of the scandal of
poverty and destitution not succeeded in making sufficient impact among
Christians and ecclesiastical structures to make them commit themselves
seriously to the struggle against the causes of this scandalous situation?[5]

Obviously these questions call for answers which cannot be given in
simple terms, and which would require profoundly radical attitudes and
decisions. Nevertheless, the simple fact that these questions are asked and
the insistence with which they have been raised in the ecumenical movement, in the national churches and even in local congregations, are signs
that the situation and present position of the Church are being called into
question, and that they should be open to renewal and commitment to
more faithfulness to the action of Jesus Christ and the Spirit of God.[6]

The inadequacy of present structures

We can say that many structural forms of ecclesiastical institutions are
representative, or tend to reproduce the kind of structures, of the societies
to which they belong. Some of them were transplanted from metropolitan
centres to colonized regions, and then imposed there. Some of these structures still reflect hierarchical and authoritarian patterns. Others are open
to social groups who have prestige; they mirror a petit bourgeois world
view, with the values and ethical standards of the middle strata of society.

At the same time, and in principle, they have to be open to people's participation, as in some churches in Africa.[7] However, in many cases their orientation and functioning have their centre in a power structure, the legitimacy of which is based on the actual economic and social position of the membership.[8] This helps to explain why in some situations the liturgical forms and message are attuned to the social outlook of the leading side of their membership, and correspond to the questions and interests of these sectors of society.

This is not a gratuitous assertion or an arbitrary description. It is only necessary to visit the established churches, especially in Asia and Latin America, check the social strata from which their members come, and try to understand how the churches are structured and what the criteria are by which the members of their directing bodies are chosen, to be able to say that the actual social composition of the governing structures of the ecclesiastical institutions in most cases is *not* really appropriate for active participation and meaningful presence of the poor when they seek to give concrete form to their religious practice.

The ability to produce "middle-class" respectability which the ecclesiastical bodies have shown to possess often justifies the remark that they *can* become effective means for spreading the traditions, the values, the world views and ideas of the social groups in power. Then how can the poor effectively participate in the life of Christian communities (parishes and others) not radically concerned about their problems? If from time to time the poor begin to frequent local congregations and even become recipients of Christian charity, then they are encouraged to adopt the "middle-class" values of the leading people of the congregation, to the extent of being coopted by its dominant structure. In an individualistic perspective they can even come to acquire a certain social mobility and as a result end up by abandoning the interests and expectations of their fellows from the same social group to which they belong.[9]

The scandal of poverty in today's world is a challenge to the Church and requires answers which go beyond declarations of principles and reaffirmations of faith. If the cause of the poor is not the focus of attention of the Church in the social domain, and if the struggle for justice does not concern it or affect it deeply, how can the local congregation cope with the presence and the participation of the poor? Only concrete commitment to the poor can help the Christian groups to move ahead in their social involvement. This implies a clear decision for social justice, with all its political, social and economic implications.

Search for new options

Fortunately there are very positive signs, in churches throughout the world, that a genuine decision in favour of the poor is being made. These signs are multiplying and the rich new experiences demonstrate that the ecclesiastical institutions are again becoming — as happened sometimes in the past — the voice of those whose cries of suffering rise up to God.[10]

There is one point which must be brought out very clearly: the church of the poor is not becoming possible simply because the rich are open to it. The church of the poor is also a result of the work of the Holy Spirit through a process in which the people themselves are taking a leading role. The poor, who for a long time have suffered, within official ecclesiastical bodies, the same process of marginalization to which they were submitted in society, are seeing that churches are not (or, at least, should not be) foreign to them. It is the poor themselves with their presence and participation in the body of Christ, with their problems and struggles, who make possible the transformation of ecclesiastical institutions. The people of God, in these cases, feel they belong to the Church and it is not foreign to them. This kind of situation, the pilgrimage of the people of God through history, is opening ways of freedom to all humanity.[11] An example of this is the struggle in which some sectors of the people of God are participating for the rights of women (who, in many cases, are the most oppressed persons among the poor).[12]

The Church is renewed when people participate decisively in its process of transformation: ecclesiastical institutions will not attempt changes in Church structures, unless they are called to do so by the people of God. However, in many places, because of their social positions, leaders of ecclesiastical institutions find it almost impossible to understand the full intensity of the suffering and problems of the poor. Nobody can doubt their good will and good intentions. Perhaps they may come to be effective supporters and allies in the attempts to transform society (which involve a process of renewal for the churches), but the main agents of that achievement will be the poor themselves.[13] Much humility is needed on the part of those who are not poor to grasp this harsh truth. It is necessary to overcome the sense of superiority and pride which sometimes prevails among those who belong to Christian establishments, going beyond present intellectual attainments, trying not to be caught and kept in the captivity of the power system, which neglects the potential of the poor. The really dynamic element of transformation, sought by those struggling for justice and liberation, is the presence of Christ and the Holy Spirit, especially and by preference, in the poor and the oppressed.[14] Only through the renewal that they can bring will the Christian community (in each place) be freed from many of the captivities which at present bind it.[15]

The fact that its liberation (since ecclesiastical institutions can also be captive of the structures of domination of this world) is through the Christian community's placing itself at the service of the poor and for the sake of justice has a deep evangelical meaning for the Church.[16] In this sense, once again, it is necessary to remember that Christ became poor and put aside his glory so that God might raise him as Lord and liberator (Phil. 2 : 5-11).

At decisive moments in history the collusion between church leaders and the powerful led the ecclesiastical institutions to withdraw from one of the aims of the evangelizing mission of the Church: "To preach the Good News to the poor" (Luke 7 : 22-23; Matthew 11 : 4-6). This is what motivated the strong protest of Bartolomé de las Casas at the beginning of the evangelization of the Americas.[17] When ecclesiastical bodies, governed by those who share the views of the rich and the powerful, maintain relations and dialogue with the rich and powerful in society, then they are bearers of the same values, they preserve similar traditions and express the same interests. "Only a church of the poor, which has opted for the poor, can loyally talk with the poor."[18]

The people of God are a pilgrim people. They are a people on the move. They *have* to be. That movement has a sense, an orientation: it is movement towards love and justice. It is a movement which takes its dynamism from the hope in the Kingdom of God. In the meantime, the cry of the poor and the destitute of the world is rising in loud tones that sound frightening to the ears of the rich and the powerful. The churches are challenged by the poor's claim: they can no longer close their ears.

Signs of renewal in the Church in our time

We must not be pessimists. There is no reason to be, for when we consider the pilgrimage of the people of God in the course of the last decade, the presence and force of the Spirit of God must be acknowledged to have been operative in it. In the midst of the challenging historical contradictions which our society is passing through, that Spirit will know how to guide the Christian community in fidelity to Jesus Christ and his Gospel. These signs are already evident in churches that have opened themselves to the poor and above all in those that have actually made a radical decision in favour of combating the causes of want and injustice.

1. GROWTH OF PENTECOSTAL MOVEMENTS

We are not concerned about discussing doctrine or interpretation of the biblical texts which form the basis of the pentecostal phenomenon. We must emphasize, nevertheless, that in almost every part of our world the majority of members of the pentecostal churches are poor and that their structures make participation possible.[19] Popular music with its ordinary instruments infuses joy into their religious services. Speech is not monopolized by those who are considered the best interpreters of truth. All can share their experiences and expound the concrete problems of their lives. The Bible is interpreted freely and though some texts, it is true, may not be understood very well, it is also true to say that the Bible occupies the central place in the life of every believer. The church endeavours to solve very vital problems of the poor, such as illness, unemployment, lack of resources, housing, travel, etc. It is also undoubtedly true that this kind of church may become the cause of alienation of the people,[20] but it is undeniable that the poor find a place in it, and that the structures of the local congregations are sufficiently flexible to allow them to be present and play an active part. The leaders come from the congregation itself and belong to the same social class as other members. In some countries of Africa and Latin America the pentecostal congregations are challenging and questioning the traditional churches and are fast coming to form the majority of the evangelicals in many countries.[21]

It is clear that the dangers already referred to, such as the alienation that can result from the practice of popular religiosity, are also found in the pentecostal movements. They are a challenge to historic churches, but in many situations they are not representative of the poor.

2. THE BASIC ECCLESIAL COMMUNITIES

In many countries of Latin America, in the Philippines, in Italy, and so on, a new church born of the people is growing.[22] Small groups meet around common problems — very concrete ones connected with the daily life of the people; they read and reflect on the Bible, celebrate and sing hymns, and share in all efforts of the community. They are essentially groups of poor people, located in rural zones and in the marginal districts of the cities. They discuss problems of the neighbourhood and of work, take decisions collectively, organize themselves to struggle for their rights, face their difficulties together, adopt attitudes of solidarity, create fuller democratic and participatory structures. All can speak, decisions are always taken jointly and the outlook and problems of the poor are the parameters in terms of which action is defined. In Brazil alone there are more than 50,000, and they undoubtedly constitute the chief expression of vitality and renewal of the Church in that country.[23] It is a church of the poor, which emerges as an evident sign of the action of the Holy Spirit who — through the poor — is purifying a Church which for centuries has been operating mainly in the service of the rich and powerful. It throws down a clear challenge to the schemas of classical ecclesiology; it has totally transformed the traditional forms of liturgy; it has created its own hymns, and shattered the traditional dichotomy between faith and life.[24] It has come to be a real ecumenical experience, because it has opened itself to the problems of the community, sharing with everyone the endeavour to find solutions to common problems. Nevertheless since it is a recent experience, it is not yet possible to draw definitive conclusions from what is going on. But at least it is possible to say it means that the poor are once again finding a place and a voice in official ecclesiastical structures and they feel that the Church is becoming their representative.

3. OTHER FORMS OF SOLIDARITY WITH THE POOR AND OPPRESSED

The strong movement of solidarity between the blacks and ethnic minorities in the USA has enormous importance and significance. The struggle against forms of racial oppression did not end with the movement for the civil rights of the black population. Now it is finding expression in the struggles of the American Indians for the right to their land, the right to be recognized as a nation with its values, traditions and institutions. Numerous social contingents of Latin and Hispanic American origin are involved in this movement of solidarity, for instance Chicanos, Puerto Ricans, Dominicans, and others. In the development of the movements which express their claims, sectors of the churches play an important part, providing a place where activities can be coordinated, making the connection more fluid between these groups, as well as improving the attempts to create bonds of solidarity with the white majority of the population of North America. This expression of solidarity is not limited to the USA and Canada, but is also found in other developed countries in which active sectors of Christian communities try to create a union of wills in the struggle for international justice. We must understand the churches' participation in programmes of education for development in this context.[25]

The testimony of solidarity expressed by the churches with the Palestinian refugees in the Middle East is also impressive. In the Lebanon, for example, where it must be admitted there are Christians who have compromised with oppression and injustice, there are also Christian communities which have become places of solidarity and understanding, open to the most persecuted and suffering sectors of the population such as the Palestinian refugees. There, too, the decision was made to be the church of the poor, a place of refuge and liberation for the oppressed.[26]

4. THE RE-DISCOVERY OF THE LIBERATING FORCE OF THE BIBLE

This is an important sign of the renewal of the Church. The growth of the number of groups in which the people are beginning "to read the Gospel in the Bible" from a perspective of the poor is a distinctive feature of the Church of the poor.[27] The Bible and life are linked in the people's view. When they open the Bible the poor want to find there the things of life and in life they want to find the things of the Bible. Understanding the Bible as a critical mirror of reality awakens a sense of inquiry in the people. The Bible is read and studied with the aim of knowing better, from a perspective other than the dominant one, our present reality and also the calls that God addresses to us to participate in changing that reality. The final purpose of the use of the Bible is not so much to interpret the Bible as to interpret people's own life. Undoubtedly these observations can lead to a less academic interpretation of biblical texts. This is not, however, the most important thing; what stands out and what must be emphasized is that Christ's liberating message, his clear siding with the poor, is being assumed by the people, is met with in the Bible, is effectively serving as an instrument in the struggle for justice and human freedom.

5. THE RE-DEFINITION OF BASIC CONCEPTS OF THE CHRISTIAN FAITH

The actual experience of churches which make an option for the poor forces us to re-think the implications of certain basic concepts of the Christian faith for today. We are now living in a new situation with new challenges. The concepts of evangelization, salvation, reconciliation, church, and so on, as they have traditionally been employed, seem to require re-definition in terms of the outlook of the poor and the oppressed.[28] This task cannot be carried out in comfortable study rooms and libraries. It demands a liberating practice from the theologian, from the Christian believer. It demands a commitment to struggle, a decision from the perspective of the poor and in their own terms. In this way Christians come to understand a new theology and construct a new language based on the significant elements of the life of the people whose expectations and struggles they are sharing. These signs are becoming visible and the presence of the Holy Spirit is transparent in this church of the people which is setting itself free.

NOTES

1 Cf. JULIO DE SANTA ANA: *Good News to the Poor*, chapters 4-7. Geneva: WCC, 1977. Also Julio de Santa Ana (ed.): *Separation Without Hope?* Geneva: WCC, 1978, esp. the chapters by ANDRÉ BIÉLER, RONALD WHITE, Jr., Metropolitan GEORGE KHODR and NICOLAI ZABOLOTSKI. In the context of the Orthodox Church, cf. DEMETRIOS J. CONSTANTENELOS: *Byzantine Philanthropy and Social Welfare*. New Brunswick, NJ: Rutgers University Press, 1968.

2 Cf. JOHN KENT: "The Church and the Trade Union Movement in Britain in the 19th Century," in J. DE SANTA ANA (ed.): *Separation Without Hope?*, *op. cit.*, pp. 36-37.

3 MARCELO PINTO CAVALHEIRA: "A Caminhada do Povo de Deus na América Latina", *Revista Eclesiastica Brasileira*, Vol. 38, fasc 150, 1978, p. 303.

4 In the report of the general secretary to the Fifth Assembly of the WCC, Dr PHILIP POTTER said: "It may well be that despite their profession that the Church means the whole people of God, most churches have not yet learned what this may mean in their life and witness. The same hierarchical and non-participatory structures which exist in society are reflected in our church structures and styles of living — preaching, teaching, decision-making, authority." In DAVID M. PATON (ed.): *Breaking Barriers: Nairobi 1975*, p. 252. Grand Rapids, Mich.: Wm B. Eerdmans, and London: SPCK, 1976.

5 NICOLAS BERDYAEV, already at the end of the twenties, was raising similar questions. Cf. *Christianity and Class War*, pp. 117-118: "The ordinary preaching of Christian virtues, love, humility, mercy, is barren and without effect; it is often even dismissed as conventional rhetoric, hypocrisy, a concealed attempt to weaken and disarm the enemy. ... A very grave responsibility rests with us Christians. Our times call for speech that is charged with freshness, youthful vigour, creative energy — and we have not yet found it; the usual exhortation to humility rings false in this atmosphere of social wrongs. The soul of the worker has been contaminated by the poisons given off by capitalism and class war, and it is extremely difficult to bring it to an understanding of Christian truth. To do this successfully it is needful that Christianity present itself to the mind of the worker associated with social truth, and not with social falsehood. In other words, Christians ought to be on the side of work and the workers". London: Sheed & Ward, 1933.

6 Cf. in this sense the document *Jesuits Today*, Washington, DC, 1975, drawn up by the staff responsible for the preparation of the 32nd General Congregation of the Society of Jesus.

7 Cf. DIANGENDA-KUNTIMA: "The Essence of Kimbanguist Theology", p. 22. *WCC Exchange*, No. 4, July 1978.

8 *Asian Ecumenical Consultation on Development Priorities and Guidelines*, pp. 59-60, and especially p. 69: "To the extent that our churches are themselves sometimes a microcosm of the power structures of the secular society, action is needed to seek structural changes in the churches." Singapore: Christian Conference of Asia, 1974. In a clearer way, N. J. DEMERATH III, in *Social Class in American Protestantism*, p. 4, says: "American religion, especially Protestantism, has been widely held to be an activity of the middle and the upper classes. The argument rests principally on three indicators of involvement: church membership,

attendance at church services, and participation in the church's formal activities. On each of these measures, persons of high status appear to be more deeply involved than those of low status." Chicago: Rand, McNally & Company, 1965.

ROGER MEHL, talking about "the socio-professional" composition of the churches, admits that they have in the West mainly a *bourgeois or rural character* (italics mine). *The Sociology of Protestantism.* London: SCM Press, 1970.

[9] Cf. the study of CHRISTIAN LALIVE D'EPINAY on pentecostalism in Chile, *Haven of the Masses.* London: Lutterworth, 1969.

[10] Cf. CCPD Dossier *Good News to the Poor.* Geneva: CCPD/WCC, 1978. Also BOBBI WELLS HARGLEROAD (ed.): *Struggle to be Human: Stories of Urban Industrial Mission.* Geneva: CWME/WCC, 1973. This volume includes a series of stories of churches which have made an option for the poor and work with them.

[11] MARCELO PINTO CAVALHEIRA, *op. cit.*, especially p. 317.

[12] Cf. *Sexism in the 1970s: Discrimination Against Women*, report of a WCC consultation, West Berlin, 1974. Geneva: WCC, 1975.

[13] This has been clearly stated in the report of the hearing on the WCC programme unit "Justice and Service" at the Fifth Assembly of the WCC, cf. Part III on "Justice and Development".

[14] Cf. JÜRGEN MOLTMANN: *The Church in the Power of the Spirit*, p. 356: "The poor church will therefore have to be understood as the church of the poor — as the fellowship, that is, in which the poor arrive at freedom and become the upholders of the Kingdom. Christian poverty therefore means the fellowship of the poor and fellowship with the poor — but as a fellowship of the messianic mission and the hope for the Kingdom. In this sense Christian poverty [*and here Moltmann makes a quotation of Gutiérrez*], is 'an expression of love and solidarity with the poor and is a protest *against poverty*'." London: SCM Press, 1977.

[15] *Faith and Order Paper No. 85: Church and State*, pp. 158-160, about the captivity of the Church. There it is said: "Where the churches face powers or a state which oppresses the people, or at least certain groups and individuals, resistance becomes part of their mission. The goals, perspectives and means of powers and states which exercise oppression are incompatible with the imperatives of the Gospel." Geneva: WCC, 1978. The churches can hardly resist if this movement of resistance is not based on the people's resistance itself.

[16] J. L. SEGUNDO: *Liberation of Theology*, p. 203: "If the concrete experience of grassroots communities proves anything at all, it proves that taking cognizance of the liberative function of the Church does not lead to liturgical preciosity and merely intra-ecclesiastical reformism. Instead such communities become the fiercest and most effective opponents of the compromise the Church is forced to make when it tries to expropriate the masses as such and thereby impedes the liberation of the latter." New York: Orbis Books, 1976.

[17] ANDRÉ CASTALDO: "Les questions péruviennes de Bartolomé de las Casas (1564)", *Foi et Vie*, 77th year, No. 1-2, January-April 1978. Also GUSTAVO GUTIÉRREZ: *Teologia desde el reverso de la historia*, pp. 35-39. Lima: CEP, 1977.

[18] Cf. A. COUNIN, in the preface to the book by JOSÉ MARÍA GONZALEZ RUIZ: *Pobreza evangélica y promoción humana*, p. 14. Rio de Janeiro: Vozes, Petropolis, 1970.

[19] CHRISTIAN LALIVE D'EPINAY: *op. cit.*, pp. 45ff. Cf. also WALTER HOLLENWEGER: *The Pentecostals*, especially pp. 457ff. London: SCM Press, 1972.

[20] CHRISTIAN LALIVE D'EPINAY, *op. cit.*, pp. 128ff.

[21] WALTER J. HOLLENWEGER, *op. cit.*, pp. 75-175.

[22] Cf. JETHER PEREIRA RAMALHO: "Basic Christian Communities in Brazil". *The Ecumenical Review*, Vol. 29, No. 4, 1977, pp. 394ff. Also MARCELO PINTO CAVAL-HEIRA, *op. cit.*

[23] These figures were reported at the Third National Meeting of "Comunidades Eclesiales de Base", held in João Pessoa, July 1978.

[24] An example of the Church transformed by the Holy Spirit through people's action is given by what is happening in the Philippines. Cf. *Makibaka! Join Us in Struggle! A Documentation of Five Years of Resistance to Martial Law in the Philippines*, pp. 129ff. London: Blackrose Press, 1978.

[25] LAURENS HOGEBRINK gives a good example of this kind of action in "On Communicating the Gospel Today". CCPD Dossier No. 6, *Justice, Rolling like a River.* Geneva: CCPD/WCC, 1975.

[26] Cf. MAKRAM KAZAH: *Le Prado dans les événements du Liban*, preparatory paper for the CCPD consultation in Ayia Napa, Cyprus, on "The Church and the Poor", September 1978.

[27] Cf. GUSTAVO GUTIÉRREZ, *op. cit.*, pp. 41-50. From an affluent context, but trying to assume something like the perspective of the poor in Bible study, cf. the book by RONALD J. SIDER: *Rich Christians in an Age of Hunger.* Downers Grove, Ill.: Intervarsity Press, 1977.

[28] On this "new hermeneutics", cf. the good account of ROBERT MCAFFEE BROWN: *Theology in a New Key*, pp. 85-100. Philadelphia: Westminster Press, 1978.

VI · The Struggle against Poverty

Poverty as defined here is the unfulfilment of basic human needs required to adequately sustain life free from disease, misery, hunger, pain, suffering, hopelessness and fear, on the one hand, and the condition of defenceless people suffering from structural injustice on the other. In either case, such conditions may be summarized as oppression.[1] Therefore the struggle against poverty is described as activities engaged in by the oppressed and those working on behalf of the oppressed to attain a "better life". Such a life would not be limited to the satisfaction of basic human needs, but would include an existence with dignity, based on the exercise of justice, participation and freedom.[2]

In most human societies, unceasing attempts have been made by individuals, groups, governments, churches and institutions to ease or eliminate poverty. Too often, these attempts have failed because efforts were focused on working "for" rather than "with" the poor, without attacking the oppressive causes of impoverishment.[3]

"Give a man a fish and you only feed him once; but if a man is taught to fish, he can eat forever." The thesis here is: if complete liberation is to be achieved, the struggle must be implemented by the poor and oppressed. The catalyst in the liberation movement need not be of the oppressed, but must be identified with and committed to the struggles of the poor.[4] If the churches are serious about their desire to become involved in the liberation of oppression, then they must clearly and boldly identify with and dedicate themselves to the elimination of oppression wherever it exists. *There is just no other way.*

The human being was not created as an oppressed organism; therefore, it is necessary to place oppression in historical perspective.

The Bible reveals that oppression was manifested when powerless and powerful cultures met. Eventually, the powerful dominated the powerless (Gen. 12 : 10-15). Therefore, oppression probably emerged with the development of civilized cultures where barter and trade were commonplace. Human beings discovered that they could increase their productivity with improved tools and technology (improvements on their own hands and inventions), and by exploiting other human beings.

According to Celso Furtado: "Two basic forms of appropriation of the surplus seem to have coexisted in history. On the one hand, there is what can be called the *authorization* form, which consists in the appropriation of a surplus through coaction. On the other hand, there is the *merchant* form, that is, the appropriation of the surplus in the framework of barter and exchange . . . As diverse social formations as they could be, those of the Pharaonic Egypt, or imperial China, or the Luca empire, had an important element in common: the sharing of the surplus was strictly administered and controlled by a central power which monopolized the use of coaction . . . Feudal processes seem to be linked with the disintegration of imperial socio-political formations. The authoritarian appropriation of the surplus passes to the hands of local groups and the use of this surplus tends to be effective in the same region where it is appropriated. At the same time as this process of deconcentration of appropriation and utilization of the surplus, there is a decline of urbanization and exchange. This does not mean that exchange no longer plays a role in society, even if it is a lesser role, in the transformation of the surplus in furnishing indispensable goods for the reproduction of society. The predominance of one or the other basic forms of appropriation of the surplus historically belongs to a given socio-political formation: the imperial type or the urban-merchant one . . . The nation-state of modern Europe is more than a compromise between both systems of domination. At its base, there is an effective integration of both cultural systems." [5]

Although the use of force could have played a role, it is likely that early exploitation was based on psychological persuasion whereby a person, in an effort to "do a good deed", did not recognize domination and exploitation. This early form evolved into oppression by demand, force and finally law.

History reveals that human beings have always opposed oppression: frontally, passively, indirectly or by active resistance. Thus the "weak" and "unfortunate" became the oppressed while the "strong" and "fortunate" became the oppressors. The point here is that a conditioning process occurs before oppression becomes law. Sometimes imposed by force, the conditioning process may be described sociologically as "practices" which later become "habits". These habits then evolve into social mores, traditions, customs, and finally laws. The resulting system receives the confidence of the "strong" and the "weak" because it guarantees order, ensuring domination for the strong and mere survival for the weak. As Charles Elliott states: "The main feature of this is that a relatively small group . . . control much of the production and all the fiscal redistribution in such a way that their interests and their level of living are not seriously threatened. They are sufficiently sophisticated to realize that there are conflicts between the short-term and the long-term: short-term costs have to be paid by long-term stability. They make errors in the assessment of those costs and of the long-run benefits that they accrue from them. As a group, they may be ignorant of those benefits, or a significant minority (or even a majority) may believe, or want to believe, that they cannot change the system in such a way that will enduringly alter the distribution of benefits. Further, we do not discount completely the altruism or humanitarian interest in the poor, particularly the visible and non-threatening poor. Nonetheless, the elites maintain a system in which function, as hierarchically ordered by them, is differentially rewarded. Despite the huge weight of evidence that suggests that the incentives for progress up this hierarchy are grossly exaggerated or, to put it into more neo-classical terms, that income differentials work in the wrong direction . . . the system is kept in being."[6]

Both the oppressor and the oppressed must accept each phase in the conditioning process before oppression is possible. The oppressor must believe that oppression is "right", while the oppressed must accept it as a "way of life".[7] History also reveals that every conceivable tactic has been used to create an acceptance of oppression; the Bible and the Church are no exception.[8]

History further reveals that many of the oppressed and the oppressors never accepted oppression; nevertheless, it continues to exist because it is accepted by the majority. As a case in point, many decades passed before American blacks accepted slavery and segregation. Some never did. Thousands chose death for themselves and their children rather than submit to the shackles of slavery. Unfortunately, many decades may pass before oppression is eliminated. The hope for liberation, though, lies in the social and political actions of the oppressed. Fortunately, not all of them accept the prevailing order; some are prepared to fight against injustice and oppression and their militancy is the main force in the struggle for liberation.

Liberation and the liberation process require planned strategies which must originate with the poor; organization is the process through which the poor community is unified to implement group action.[9] Therefore the concept of organization as an instrument of struggle against factors generating poverty are discussed here.

Three major organizational strategies are noted as effective tools in the struggle against oppression and injustice. These are: (1) organization for liberation and justice; (2) organization for liberation and acceptance; and (3) organization for liberation and participation. These organizational strategies may not be universally applicable, nor do they exist in any particular order, but they were successfully employed by American blacks in the struggle for social change. Although alternative strategies may be necessary in other situations, these can be viewed as practicable approaches to the attainment of justice and liberation.[10]

1. Organization for liberation and justice

The main goal of organization for liberation and justice is the removal of laws which legitimize oppression. Depending on the status of the oppressed, this strategy may include these steps: (a) awareness, (b) readiness and planning, and (c) action.

a) AWARENESS

When oppression is accepted as a way of life, it promotes itself. Thus, after several generations of poverty, the poor do not view poverty and its concomitant ills as a problem; they believe poverty is God's will and that there is no hope for anything different.[11]

An example: During the mid-1960s, a civil rights worker in America was speaking to a group of black residents in a typical farming town in south-east Alabama. By all standards, the town was poor and blacks suffered the brunt of oppression. They earned an average annual income of less than $1,400, while for whites, the average was over $4,000. No street in the black communities was paved; there was no running water or indoor bath facilities and, in many instances, no electricity (electricity had been cut off because of failure to pay utility bills). The white community not only enjoyed all modern conveniences, but many streets were being resurfaced, sewer lines were being expanded, and job conditions were being improved.

At the end of the civil rights worker's speech in which such inequities were stated, a bitter protest was voiced by an indigenous black leader. He exclaimed: "We ain't got no problems here. De niggers and de white folk, de git along fine. Y'all ain't gon do nothing but git us in trouble talking dat kind of mess."

After this statement, a two-hour discussion ensued between the young and old, clearly revealing that the latter accepted poverty as a way of life while the former demanded change. Three months after this initial meeting, several civil rights workers were jailed and the church which had served as a meeting place was burned to the ground.

b) READINESS AND PLANNING

Readiness and planning entail a carefully planned strategy which the poor must understand and accept. This process is crucial because failure to develop a common strategy may result in irrecoverable setbacks.[12] The basic questions which must be resolved in the readiness and planning process are:

1. What is the most effective plan of action under existing conditions?

2. Should passive or active resistance be used?
   — If passive, what does this involve?
   — If active, what does this involve?[13]

3. What are the anticipated outcomes of the approach chosen?

4. What alternatives are available?

When these questions have been resolved, the oppressed group is prepared for *action*.

c) ACTION

The action phase of organization for liberation and justice involves the implementation of carefully designed plans. Recent history reveals that liberation for justice can be accomplished by both passive and active resistance. From the Christian perspective, passive resistance is perhaps the best approach and both Gandhi and Martin Luther King successfully utilized it. Once liberation for justice has been accomplished, laws which legalized oppression are removed; however, this does not end oppression. Before liberation is possible, radical changes in the relationships, social status and personal identity of oppressors and oppressed must occur.

2. Organization for liberation and acceptance

Once radical political and social changes have occurred, too often oppression continues in reverse, with the oppressed assuming the role of the oppressor, and former oppressive laws are replaced with new ones.[14] To avoid this, organization for acceptance is necessary. This strategy is a conscious attempt by the liberator to encourage the oppressed to take advantage of opportunities provided under the new laws. As an example: after the passage of Civil Rights Legislation in the United States, blacks and sympathetic whites were organized and encouraged to come into the south-east and physically integrate formerly segregated facilities. This was a deliberate attempt to visibly demonstrate the reality of the equal facilities law. Though initially there was strong resistance by "die-hard" racists, repeated visible actions finally resulted in acceptance of the Civil Rights Legislation by both the oppressed and oppressor.

Liberation is not accomplished by merely acquiring legal justice through forced acceptance; therefore, the struggle must progress to the final strategy of organization for participation.

3. Organization for liberation and participation

Organization for liberation and participation involves the oppressed in all aspects of the new society — culturally, socially, politically and economically. This aspect of liberation is extremely difficult to attain, especially if the former oppressor remains omnipotent. This is evidenced by the struggles of blacks in the United States and the working classes of western Europe, societies with recent histories of oppression, where full participation by the formerly oppressed is absent. Therefore, the "struggle must move on". This need certainly becomes clear for many countries in Africa, Asia, Latin America, the Middle East and the Pacific.

Particularly important is the role that ideologies and political movements play in the people's organization. On the one hand, ideologies — despite their limitations, over-simplifications and schematisms — help people to identify easily the aims of the struggle for liberation. In this sense, ideologies fulfil a clarifying function. On the other hand, political parties provide a framework at the organizational level for people's actions. The contribution that progressive ideologies and popular political parties have made in combating oppression and fostering liberation cannot be overestimated. However, it must be noted that these instruments have not always been utilized for the service of the poor. When ideological goals are defined without direct and wide consultation with the people, and when political parties do not base policy-making on people's participation, then they can betray, or do not give priority to, the struggle for justice and liberation.

NOTES

1 *Docet*, Series 6, No. 8, pp. 3-24. Lima: Ed. CELADEC, June 1973. There, Thomas Hanks develops the topic "Oppression and Poverty in the Bible", showing through linguistic analysis and biblical exegesis that for the Scriptures the condition of poverty is basically created by oppression. For example, the way Old Testament writers talk about oppression (*ashaq* = the injustice of oppression; *yanah* = enslaving oppression; *nagas* = dehumanizing oppression; *lahats* = the pain of the oppressed; *ratsats* = the brutality of oppression; *daka* = the crushing consequences of oppression; *anah* = the humiliation of the oppressed; *tok* = the tyranny of the oppressor, etc.) is always related to the situation of the poor. In the New Testament, other than the explicit texts of James and Luke-Acts, the analysis shows that "according to biblical theology, the main cause of poverty is oppression", p. 22.

2 In a similar line, the report of Section VI of the Fifth Assembly of the World Council of Churches on "Human Development: Ambiguities of Power, Technology and Quality of Life", states in paragraph 11: ". . . Poverty, we are learning, is caused primarily by unjust structures that leave resources and the power to make decisions about the utilization of resources in the hands of a few within nations and among nations . . . Unjust structures are often the consequence of wrong or misdirected goals and values." Cf. DAVID M. PATON (ed.): *Breaking Barriers: Nairobi 1975*, p. 123. Grand Rapids, Mich.: Wm B. Eerdmans, and London: SPCK, 1976.

3 This has been the case, for example, in Latin America, with the programme called "Alliance for Progress". In the USA, something similar happened with welfare programmes during the 60's. President Marcos's policies of this sort are failing like the others, and maybe the same will happen with present efforts of the World Bank, unless they put more emphasis on structural change than on quantitative growth.

4 Cf. *To Break the Chains of Oppression*, p. 52: "The struggle for justice is essentially the struggle of the people themselves. However, the question has often been raised whether the people take up struggle by themselves, or whether it is precipitated by a catalyst, the 'agents of change'. The question in itself may be irrelevant in the final analysis. In the historical perspective, it can be said that all popular movements of any significance resulted not from spontaneous acts of banding together, but from a process, often precipitated by 'agents of change' . . . The question is not who stimulated a process, but who propels it. Similarly, the basic question to be asked of the agent of change is not what is his social class, but where his commitment lies." Geneva: CCPD/WCC, 1975.

5 CELSO FURTADO: *Prefacio a nova economia política*, pp. 32-36. Rio de Janeiro: Editoria Paz e Terra, 1976.

6 CHARLES ELLIOTT and FRANÇOISE DE MORSIER: *Patterns of Poverty in the Third World*, pp. 13-14. New York, Washington, London: Praeger Publishers, 1975.

7 Cf. A. MEMMI: *The Colonizer and the Colonized*. Boston: Beacon Press, 1967.

8 Cf. especially the advice of Paul to the slaves: Col. 3 : 22. What St Paul says to the masters is not comparable with what he asks of the servants.

9 Cf. the chapter by JULIO DE SANTA ANA in the book: *Pueblo oprimido, señor de la historia*, on "Teoría revolucionaria, reflexión a nivel estratégico, táctico y reflexión

sobre la fe como praxis de liberación", pp. 229-232. Montevideo: Ed. Tierra Nueva, 1972.

[10] Other organizational strategies, not very different from the one recorded here, can be found in the book by BOBBI WELLS HARGLEROAD (ed.): *Struggle to Be Human, Stories of Urban Industrial Mission*. Geneva: CWME/WCC, 1973.

[11] PAULO FREIRE has analysed wonderfully these mechanisms of internalization of oppression. Cf. his *Pedagogy of the Oppressed*. New York: Herder and Herder, 1970. Cf. also *Cultural Action for Freedom*. Cambridge, Mass.: Centre for the Study of Development and Social Change, 1970.

[12] Cf. HIBER CONTERIS, JULIO BARREIRO, JULIO DE SANTA ANA, RICARDO CETRULO, *et al.*: *Conciencia y revolución*. Montevideo: Ed. Tierra Nueva, 1969.

[13] More on this topic can be found in the Report on "Violence, Non-Violence and the Struggle for Social Justice" to the WCC Central Committee meeting, Geneva, August 1973. Cf. also *The Ecumenical Review*, Vol. 30, No. 4, October 1978.

[14] The concept of "reconciliation" expressed by St Paul in II Cor. 5: 14-21, is not an agreement between beings who keep the same relationships that they had before. It is an act which follows the *Cross*, that is the radical judgment of those who were antagonists (v. 14) of God. In this sense, reconciliation is not opposed to liberation, but is rather complementary to it.

VII · Aims of the Struggle against Poverty

The primary intention of the struggle against destitution and misery is to eradicate hunger, illiteracy, needless illness, inadequate housing and to satisfy other basic human needs.[1] However, the ultimate goal of the struggle against poverty is the elimination of all forms of oppression: racial, social, economic, political, cultural, sexist, and so on. Though this may sound Utopian, it is, nevertheless, the goal of those who strive for a more just, participatory and sustainable society.[2]

From the Christian point of view, the process of liberation is an ongoing one and lasts as long as life itself. The ultimate goal of the struggle against poverty is to create a human society where there is neither oppressor nor oppressed, but where all are struggling to be truly human.

Overcoming the law of the market: socialization of the means of production

The root of poverty in the modern world is manifested in the inability of the prevailing "free-market" patterns to provide jobs and participation in decision-making in the economic processes for the majority of the world's population. Nearly a billion human beings have no regular work and cannot, therefore, count on a minimum income to meet their most basic needs. This is a fact that challenges churches and Christians to be deeply committed in action for change.

Oppression around the world has been reinforced during the last century by the expansion of capitalism and the development of the free enterprise system. This system of private ownership of land, resources from the land, means of production and technology has provided for some the necessary power to own and control even the lives of other human beings; it has resulted in every conceivable kind of oppression and dehumanization (slavery, racism, casteism, economic exploitation, etc.);[3] it has also given some nations the right to cross geographical boundaries and, under the name of "civilization", to impose colonialism, government control on other peoples while exploiting human and natural resources at the same time.[4] This has probably, in one way or another, influenced almost every political, social and economic system and institution around the world, the ecclesiastical being no exception. The so-called free enterprise system has given the few almost unlimited right not only to control but to dominate the lives of the many.[5]

It is the purpose of this chapter to discuss alternative means of ownership and production as a way to overcome the enormous number of human problems which have resulted from systems dominated, influenced and/or conditioned by "the laws of the market". Then we shall focus attention on the kind of guidelines for action and thought needed in order to improve people's condition and overcome poverty and oppression, aiming at the transformation of the current free market and free trade system.

There are three types of decisions which a socio-economic system has to control if the economic marginalization of the poor is to be avoided.

First, employment of the whole labour force, whether in industrial work or using simple, traditional means of production. One of the most serious fantasies of the free enterprise system is that anyone can go "from rags to riches". The hard fact is that any system that creates the "bloody" rich also creates the "dirt" poor. The aim, therefore, of collective ownership of land and the means of production is to create a system whereby a community of people jointly owns the land, the means of production, and the distribution of goods and services. This implies controlling the application of modern technology in order to avoid the destruction of the simple and traditional production groups. As contemporary historical examples prove, it is possible substantially to decrease unemployment, and even to achieve full employment in a rather short period of time, if means of production are socialized, if the use of technology is consistently controlled, and if the aim of the process is not economic growth at no matter what price, but *self-reliance*.[6]

Second, control of income distribution to ensure that everyone is able to satisfy his/her deepest expectations and needs. This implies a corresponding limitation of the disparities at the income level.[7]

Third, the essential and unavoidable integration into the international division of labour must be organized in such a way that economic development can fulfil the two conditions already mentioned, that is, full employment (with participation in decision-making processes) of the labour force, linked to the control of technology and organization of distribution in a way which satisfies the deepest expectations and the basic needs of all human beings. This could mean the possibility to reject foreign and transnational capital as the means by which this integration into the international division of labour is achieved.[8]

Only when the liberty of the dependent countries to take such decisions is assured can the laws of the market be considered under adequate control. Without this freedom it is impossible to imagine the liberation of the poor. Decisions of this nature presuppose the restructuring of the socio-economic system which has led to the institutionalization of structural poverty. This implies, on the one hand, that commercial decisions be subject to an adequate system of planning, and on the other that there be a corresponding socialization of the means of production.[9] Planning and socialization of the means of production are essential if countries are to have the possibility of taking these basic decisions, although the degree of centralization of planning and the level of socialization of the means of production will depend on the actual situation in each country.

The three types of decisions mentioned above are those which today can effectively assure success in the struggle of the poor against poverty. This is an inescapable conclusion. It states the political implication of commitment to the poor, giving it the highest value in social relationships.[10]

This conviction is the outcome of reflection on two levels: the first is that of commitment to the cause of the poor, based on the Bible, which in its texts and its intentions requires us to choose this option. The second level, however, is analytical and involves reflection on the political implications of opting for the poor. It is based on reflection of social experiences and on the results of certain theories.[11]

The prevailing conditions which create unemployment, hinder participation and consolidate poverty, are not effects of natural causes, nor of technology. They are the end effects of a social and economic system which created them, and which cannot exist unless it keeps on creating them.[12] It is a system whose fundamental character is manifested through domination and oppression, and which has to sustain oppression in more or less overt forms in order to exist. In this context, human liberation, especially the social liberation of the poor, is the opposite of the action of free enterprise, which manipulates the free movement of prices and capital which underlie the law of the market. This is not a question of good or evil intentions, nor of the so-called social responsibility of private property. The marginalization of the poor is brought about by the very functioning of the laws of the "free market economy", which liberate prices and oppress human beings. The liberation of the poor is not compatible with the liberation of prices.[13] Both the private ownership of the means of production and the control of the price mechanism according to the premises of the law of the market imply the oppression of the poor and the consolidation of structural poverty.

The decision to take action for the liberation of the poor therefore leads to a head-on collision with the prevailing socio-economic structures. At the basis of this confrontation is the economic problem of satisfying the basic needs of all equally. However, this economic demand can only be solved practically by a change of socio-economic structures, which can be brought about only by political means which can be realized only through a change of values. It is strongly felt that value changes create changes in political systems which in turn create changes in economic systems.[14]

The alternative to the current situation cannot be simple abolition of the laws of the market by the suppression of the market itself. It is not at all realistic to think of a current economy functioning without employing commercial relations, trade mechanisms and financial resources. Nevertheless, an adequate alternative can be a socio-economic system which is capable of effectively overcoming present poverty in the world: such a system would have to exercise control of the market laws and not simply remedy their effects. Fundamental economic decisions cannot therefore be left to the arbitrariness of the laws of the market.

Guidelines for achievement

The point to be made here is that the poor and those working on their behalf must not become complacent in their efforts to create self-development alternatives. Such efforts call for exercise at three levels at least: on values, on institutions and on systems, for which some guidelines are emerging on current people's struggles.

First, at the level of *values*, the need to overcome prevailing patterns of economy and society which result from the application of the law of the market implies standing for collective aims rather than for individualistic ones. The search for community, for sharing, for assuming others' burdens and especially those of the weakest, has to receive high priority. This will certainly imply the affirmation of social responsibility and underline collectiveness, rather than following a model based on selfishness which prevails among wealthy sectors of society. New life-styles, rooted in social responsibility and "life together", need to be developed. This presupposes a radical change of utilitarian trends that shape current value systems in "free market" societies.[15]

Second, at the level of institutions, there is an increasing claim for participatory structures in decision-making processes at all levels. When participatory structures exist, enabling the creation of conditions of solidarity between those who have and those who have not, then it is possible to expect some development of feelings of identification from the privileged to the unprivileged. As Jan Pronk, the former Minister of Development of the Netherlands, stated: "But identification is possible only if in the rich countries one identifies oneself also with the needs of the poor in these countries themselves. After all, inequality within rich countries is due to the same capitalist economic process which leads to inequality between states, and to inequality within developing countries. Moreover, only through such identification will it be possible for the masses of the rich countries to identify themselves with the poor of the Third World. This reasoning has far-reaching consequences. It implies that a policy aimed at equality within the rich industrialized countries themselves is a pre-condition for an effective policy for promoting international equality. Giving first priority to an economic and social equality policy within the so-called rich countries is my ... proposal. In my view, it can be carried out only within a socialist framework."[16] Participatory institutions, when they are built-up, lead to fundamental corrections of the mechanisms of domination imposed by the application of the law of the market.

Third, the results of new values and new institutions are new systems, in which the law has not to be the rules of the market game, but the imperatives of self-reliance: new systems in which oppression will not be the fate of the poor, but in which human beings will know existentially and structurally what liberation means. This could be considered as Utopia, but without such aim, such motivation, it is impossible to conceive social, economic and political change in the world. These systems, though grounded in ideas, will not be primarily the results of theories, but of people's action. To quote Jan Pronk again: "Self-reliance means that the aims and instruments of development policies have to be adapted to the specific situation of the developing countries and to the future economic, social and political structures as desired by them. This may be a structure entirely different from capitalism, socialism or communism, entirely different from systems chosen by East or West. Self-reliance also means that the choice of aims and instruments should be made freely, without being influenced by the interests of foreign economic, political and military powers. But at present multinational corporations and powerful, rich nations still influence and dominate many decisions and choices to be made by people of the Third World, and therefore we have to admit that in 1974 self-reliance still means 'liberation'."[17] What the poor are aiming at is precisely a world liberated from oppression and injustice.

It is therefore the responsibility of the poor and those working on their behalf constantly to apply pressure for change. The poor in almost all societies where severe oppression occurs constitute the majority. This means that the poor through mass and unified action have means to struggle for change. Recognizing this potential, the poor and those working on their behalf should continue to plan and improve strategies for:

a) collective ownership of the means of production, technology and knowledge;

b) creation of participatory structures aiming at a democratic control of political decision-making related also to production, consumption and appropriation of the surplus; a combination of central planning and self-management of workers' enterprises would be necessary for this purpose; the end result should be an increase in self-reliance;

c) development of people's power, necessary to balance the trend of domination which generally evolves from influential apparatus, like bureaucracies;

d) change and repeal of tax and other laws which were designed specifically to make the rich richer and the poor poorer; for example, transnational corporations in many countries enjoy tax advantages and concessions which shift the burden of the necessary taxes to support "greedy" governments from the rich to the poor; this being true, the poor have no choice other than to demand tax advantages that favour equity; tax reforms are needed in order to eradicate poverty and its causes;

e) limiting the amount of land and wealth that can be held by one person (physical or juridical); this can be done in most western cultures by simply enforcing tax laws that are already on the book; as an example, taxpayers in America are required to pay taxes in proportion to their family income; however, the "loop-holes" designed to avoid this law are too numerous to mention here;

f) redistribution of the land and wealth on a more equitable basis; this probably sounds preposterous to many; however, the Christian assumption is that "the earth is the Lord's, and the fullness thereof"; if the Church still believes this to be true it could, for example, advocate a "Year of Jubilee" as described in the 25th chapter of Leviticus;

g) establishment of new values, not based on the ownership of private material wealth, but on collective human wealth and dignity.

Two examples

An example from the rich countries is the new surge of cooperative development in the south-eastern United States. The basic principle of cooperative development is that ownership of land, the means of production, and the distribution of goods and services must be controlled by the people. The principle of "one man-one vote" is practised.

One such cooperative, the South East Alabama Self-Help Association, Inc. (SEASHA) will be discussed in detail. It can be seen how this cooperative fits into a network of poor people's cooperatives across the southeast — covering 14 states — to form a process whereby the poor can liberate themselves from poverty.

SEASHA, conforming to cooperative principles, is an organization which covers a 12-county area in south-east Alabama. It is governed by a board of directors of 24 people, two from each of the twelve counties. The board is responsible for establishing policies, setting goals and implementing plans for the accomplishment of these goals. It is also responsible for hiring a president and assisting him in hiring a staff. President and staff are in turn responsible for implementing, on a day-to-day basis, those goals established by the board of directors. The major goal of SEASHA is: "To eliminate the paradox of poverty in the midst of plenty in the counties of Barbour, Bullock, Coosa, Grenshaw, Elmore, Lee, Lowndes, Macon, Montgomery, Pike, Russell and Tallapoosa, and to join with other areas of Alabama and the nation in a concerted effort to eliminate poverty by opening to everyone the opportunity to work, and the opportunity to live in decency and integrity."

SEASHA's approach to this goal is to create a number of self-perpetuating economic projects, which can generate the necessary income for their own sustenance while, at the same time, generating surplus capital for continued growth and development.

In keeping with this approach, SEASHA currently operates five major components, most of which have sub-components. These are:

1. The *SEASHA agricultural cooperative* which provides production assistance, marketing, livestock feed production, credit and financial services for member farmers throughout the twelve countries.
2. *SEASHA homes*, aiming at furnishing decent housing for its members.
3. *Credit and finance* provides small, short-term loans for the personal use of members.

4. *Business development* is concerned with improvement, planning and development of new business components of the cooperative enterprise.
5. *Community services* whose major goal is to organize the poor around issues which concern them. It assists the poor to secure existing public services and, at the same time, helps establish community facilities owned by the poor themselves. In this connection, health, child care, community and other facilities have been set up.[18]

Another example, this time from a socialist country, is the process of collectivization which took place in the rural sector of the Soviet Union. The form of production cooperation most profitable for the peasant has been the collective farm *(kolkhoz)*, where the poor and middle income peasants were admitted on an equal basis and where the basic means of production were socialized: the land, part of the livestock and implements. The collective element prevailed and the individual holding began to play a subsidiary role. The distribution of income was carried out according to the quantity and quality of work done on the collective farm.

Peasant cooperatives were easier to establish in areas growing marketable industrial crops, especially cotton, the bulk of which was marketed or bought up by the state. The process was not so easy in nomadic and semi-nomadic areas where a subsistence type of economy still prevailed. With irrigation and technical re-equipment of agriculture, the peasant cooperatives were able to transform the countryside and eradicate poverty.[19]

NOTES

[1] Cf. *Employment, Growth and Basic Needs*. Geneva: International Labour Office, 1976. Document drafted in connection with the ILO Conference on Employment, Geneva, 1976.

[2] Cf. the report of the Advisory Committee of the WCC Central Committee on: "A Just, Participatory and Sustainable Society", to the WCC Central Committee meeting in Kingston, Jamaica, January 1979, especially the chapter on justice as the main goal.

[3] Cf. chapters I and II of this book.

[4] Cf. what Tissa Balasuriya says in *The Development of the Poor through the Civilizing of the Rich*, p. 25: "The causes of the underdevelopment of the colonized peoples of Asia, Africa and Latin America must be also understood historically. Their underdevelopment coincides with the rise of the present world establishment. The present unjust world order historically arose out of the expansion of the European

peoples during the past four and a half centuries. From the point of view of the western man, they were a period of great expansion, triumph and growth. For others they were centuries of defeat, colonization, pillage and exploitation. Western man systematically plundered our lands, subjugated our peoples, exterminated some, colonized others and marginalized all. Our economies were made to serve his needs and this position still continues among those open to them." Colombo: Centre for Society and Religion, 1973.

[5] As stated in the report of Section VI on "Human Development: the Ambiguities of Power, Technology and Quality of Life", of the WCC's Fifth Assembly, paras 41-42: "The desire for control over resources all over the world has always been and still is a basic reason for the exercise of economic power and the establishment of exploitative structures of domination and dependence. Colonialism was the classic form of such domination. Overt forms of colonialism are rather rare today, but there are many subtle forms of neo-colonialism which result in the rich countries exploiting the poor countries. Transnational and State corporations are one of these patterns. They represent a concentration of economic and technological power in the hands of a few. .... These corporations (the so-called transnationals) claim to bring capital and technology to the countries where they operate and thereby to create employment and income. But, essentially, their aim is to take advantage of the cheap labour that is available in the host countries and to draw out profits from them, making use of immense control they exercise over world trade and prices. ... Transnational corporations are a typical example of the ways in which capitalist forces in the international and national spheres join together to oppress the poor and to keep them under domination. Measures to check the activities of the transnational corporations are now under discussion, but because of the immense control they exercise over the channels of the 'free-market' international economy, it is very difficult to envisage any effective measures which will eradicate their innate exploitative patterns." See DAVID M. PATON (ed.): *Breaking Barriers: Nairobi 1975*, pp. 130-131. Grand Rapids, Mich.: Wm B. Eerdmans, and London: SPCK, 1976.

[6] Cf. the 1975 Dag Hammarskjöld Report: *What Now*, pp. 58-59: "Tanzanians do not claim to have achieved participatory, self-reliant, socialist development, but to have begun the long transition to it. They do not claim that the *ujamaa* village core of another rural development is complete but that it has begun to emerge. The participatory nature of the transition forbids laying down detailed patterns for the year 2000 as opposed to evolving sequences and programmes within the strategic framework. The 1967-1975 record is one of significant change towards another development. Basic needs — food, habitat, water, mass education, health, the utilization of surpluses to increase provision of essentials — are central to economic strategy. The quest for self-reliance informs major village, regional, national and international policies. *Inequality of income and access to basic services has been reduced rapidly both by redistribution and increased production. Participation and decentralization have moved very far from the colonial, authoritarian, bureaucratic starting-point, with an increasingly socialist and mass-party in control of strategic and basic policy matters.*" (italics mine). Uppsala: Dag Hammarskjöld Foundation, 1975. Concerning similar processes in Cuba, see the report of a CCPD-Unit II/WCC Team Visit to Cuba (20 February-6 March 1978) to the CCPD Commission Meeting, Sofia, June 1978.

[7] Cf. SAMUEL PARMAR's statement at the "Ecumenical Consultation on Ecumenical Assistance to Development Projects" (26-31 January 1970, Montreux): "... a high rate of growth which alone can lead to self-reliance is dependent on distributive justice. Today, in all parts of the world, not only in developing countries, there is a revolt of the disinherited. Unless society gives them their due the productive process will be constantly disrupted. Pursuit of policies based on social justice is the only way to overcome the dissatisfaction of the masses and ensure their full support to development programmes." PAMELA GRUBER (ed.): *Fetters of Injustice*, p. 51. Geneva: WCC, 1970.

[8] Cf. the report of the Colloquium on "Self-Reliance and International Justice", held at the Ecumenical Institute, Bossey, April 1976. Geneva: WCC, 1976.

[9] Cf. *To Break the Chains of Oppression*, p. 79. Geneva: CCPD/WCC, 1975.

[10] Cf. REGINALD HERBOLD GREEN: "Accumulation, Distribution, Efficiency, Equity and Basic Human Needs Strategies: Some Political Economic Implications and Conditions." Paper presented at the meeting of the International Economist Association and Political Economist Association, June 1978, pp. 41-42, and especially p. 46. "Because BHN is a revolutionary strategy based on an egalitarian and communitarian view of society, it is unlikely to be accepted without struggle.... Its success therefore is dependent on whether the present context (historic, political, economic, intellectual) is one in which mobilization in support of BHN is necessary and possible in a substantial number of politics."

[11] Dag Hammarskjöld Foundation, *op. cit.*, pp. 13-14.

[12] Cf. CELSO FURTADO: *Prefacio a nova economia politica*, pp. 44-51, on the measurement of the social product and the price system. Rio de Janeiro: Editoria Paz e Terra, 1976. About the role of the monopoly that TNCs have on technology in this process, see Constantine Vaitsos' affirmation: "The technology developed and employed by transnational enterprises in their worldwide operations stems from research and development (R and D) activities in the industrialized world and is concentrated mainly in the home countries of such firms. (For example, in 1966, US-based transnationals undertook about 97% of their global R and D activities in the United States.) As a result of (a) high absolute saving levels, (b) accumulated capital stock, (c) relative high labour costs, and (d) large-scale production of goods and services, technological development in high-income countries has been directed towards increased-biased production processes. The application of these largely unadapted processes by foreign-owned subsidiaries and national firms in developing countries can lead not only to inappropriate relative factor utilization *but also to absolute direct labour displacement. Such labour displacement can and does take place even under conditions of expanding production. Thus the resulting technological orientation accentuates existing problems of unequal income distribution — both within a country and internationally — and counteracts basic developmental needs related to the enhancement of employment opportunities in the Third World.*" GUY F. ERB and VALERIANA KALLAB (eds.): *Beyond Dependency*, p. 87. Washington: Overseas Development Council, 1975.

[13] CELSO FURTADO, *op. cit.*, p. 48: "Measurement of the product of work in a particular branch of business, whether it be complex like a car factory or simple like a barber's shop, can only be made on the basis of a price system. Since the worker's remuneration acts as an exogenous factor, the result of the forces which determine

the cost of reproduction, the price system has to fulfil the function of regulator of the distribution of the surplus (excluding the part appropriated by institutional means) in proportion to the accumulation realized in the productive units (perequation of the rate of profit)."

[14] Cf. REGINALD HERBOLD GREEN, *op. cit.*, p. 30: "BHN (Basic Human Needs) admittedly does not posit the same specific content of growth or technology or sub-modes of production as most present decision-takers choose. That, however, is a question as to *its political feasibility conditions* not as to the plausibility of viewing growth in disaggregated terms and as means rather than an end."

[15] Here the whole theme of "new life-styles" comes under discussion. On this, cf. CCPD Dossiers Nos. 10 and 11: *In Search of the New*, I-II. Geneva: WCC/CCPD, 1976 and 1977.

[16] Cf. JAN PRONK: "Development in the 70's: Seven Proposals." *The Ecumenical Review*, Vol.XXVII, No. 1, January 1975, p. 22.

[17] *Ibid.*, p. 17.

[18] Prospectus of the South-East Alabama Self-Help Association, Inc. (SEASHA).

[19] YURI IVANOV: *The Road of Progress*, pp. 30-33. Moscow: Novostny Press Agency, 1977.

2.
The Challenge
and the Relevance
of the Poor
to the Church

VIII · How the Poor Challenge the Church

A seminary student studying pastoral counselling was assigned as interim associate pastor to a rural local church. One morning he saw a blind woman being led by her husband into his church office. While they were yet a little way off, the student pastor said to himself: "Now, here is a chance to put into practice my theory of pastoral counselling." As the blind woman and her husband came into the office and sat down, ready to explain their condition to the young pastor, he began to talk. And he talked and talked and talked, until the woman could stand it no longer. Then she said: "Wait a minute, who are you?" The student pastor replied: "I am the assistant," and before he could say "pastor", the lady said: "Boy, looka here man, I ain't got time to play. I don't want to speak to an assistant or anybody, I want to speak to someone who can minister to my needs. I have come here because I am hurt, because I am troubled. I have come here because I believe the Church can help solve my problems. I ain't got time to play; show me the real person who can minister to my needs."

A call to the apathetic church

It is in these same terms that the poor inside as well as outside the institutional Church are addressing it today — with these words of challenge. They are calling the Church back to a redefinition of its original goals in Christian commitment to Jesus Christ. The poor are challenging the Church to rethink its mission and reorder its priorities in the light of its redemptive role in human history as proclaimed in the Gospel. The poor are challenging the Church about its real identity in the world. What is the self-understanding of the Church which is called to preach the message of the Good News to the poor? Has the Church really chosen to be the servant to the one who said: "The Spirit of the Lord is upon me because he has anointed me to preach good news to the poor. He has sent me to proclaim release to the captives and to recover the sight of the blind, to set at liberty those who are oppressed, to proclaim the acceptable year of the Lord" (Luke 4 : 18-19).

Who is considered the poor? "The 'poor' person today is the oppressed one, the one marginalized from society, the member of the proletariat struggling for his most basic rights; he is the exploited and plundered social class, the country struggling for its liberation."[1] This poor can be found both in as well as outside the Church.

The challenge is, *will the Church identify with this community of the poor in their struggle for liberation or will it choose the option of being neutral towards the problems of the poor?* Take sides it must. What side it takes depends upon its understanding of the Jesus of history and the Christ of faith involved in human history not only for Israel's redemption but for the redemption of the whole world. It has the option to side with the poor or with the forces of society that create oppression, dehumanization and poverty.

The Church can never be neutral in society, it is either for or against — its silence on vital issues of poverty and human anguish is a clear indication of its preoccupation with the oppressive system which impoverishes over three fourths of the world's population. Silence is acquiescence, and acceptance is collaboration.

The Church has tried in some instances to "play safe" by adopting policies of neutrality, or ally itself with the powerful when dealing with the problems of the poor.[2] But the Church is being challenged by the poor to identify with them if it is truly to become a viable and vibrant agent of God in human liberation. The Church is challenged to participate in the suffering of the community of the poor, the disinherited, the victimized, the outcast and the broken-hearted. The Church is challenged to join hands in solidarity in the struggle for justice with those who live in poverty, hunger, and with their backs against the wall; the second class citizens, the slaves, the wretched of the earth.[3]

"If the proclamation of the Gospel is to be meaningful in our time, it must be closely related to the present struggles for justice, because that is the arena where the people find themselves today. In other words, the Gospel should be proclaimed to men and women, not in isolation, but in their social solidarity."[4]

The other dimension of the challenge, the poor are saying, is that the Church has not been very sensitive to their needs and problems. It has failed to identify or stand in solidarity with the poor. The Church has not only been mouthing empty theological and ecclesiastical rhetoric about participation and involvement; it has been listening to itself alone, doing very little in terms of social action. It has had little time for critical self-examination or a real dialectical encounter with the poor, hurt and torn by oppressive societies.

The poor are saying: "We ain't got time to play. We don't want a *communiqué* from the Church, we want communication. If the Church fails to engage in dialogue, we will explore new ways of communication with other organizations or institutions that are willing to minister to our needs. We will join institutions that address themselves concretely to the existential problem of our impoverishment and degradation."

Is the Church ready to respond?

Can the Church provide this kind of forum for dialogue with the poor? Is the Church willing and ready to respond to the demands of this challenge of the poor or should the poor look outside of the institutional Church for different options in their struggle for liberation? The Church needs more than ever before an objective and critical reflection upon the level of its involvement and participation in the struggle of and for the poor. And this reflection can best be done from the perspective of the poor.[5]

Historically the Church has frequently identified itself with oppressive systems of society involving social, political, economic and racial oppression and domination, but it has become evident that in many instances (not invalidating the other contributions it has made) it has provided channels for the legitimization of oppressive structures and groups in power. It has accommodated itself with the structure and even tried to coopt it for its own survival and growth.

To help us understand this, José Miguez Bonino draws out a significant point from the work of Benoît Dumas, a French Dominican. Referring to Dumas's *The Two Alienated Faces of the One Church*, Bonino suggests: "Dumas's basic thesis is that the poor belong to the understanding of the mystery of the Church, or if you wish to use other language, that the poor belong to the understanding of the very nature of the Church. He says that if the identity of the Church is found in Jesus Christ, *ubi Christus ibi ecclesia*, then we must pay attention to the fact that Christ said that He would be present when his words were remembered and the meal was shared, and that He would be present in the poor and the oppressed. Father Dumas uses, of course, Matthew 25 as the basic text. I will not fight here for a sacramental interpretation because I do not think that his point rests on the interpretation of this text. You may refer to many other texts throughout the Bible. I think that the point he establishes is valid in any case. And therefore, he says, in our present situation as churches the Church does not recognize itself in the poor. It may recognize the poor as a very important part of the world, but the Church does not recognize itself in the poor, and the poor do not recognize Christ in the Church. But this situation is one of lost identity, of self-alienation for the Church, a situation in which the Church is not altogether the Church. The Church which is not the Church of the poor puts in serious jeopardy its churchly character. Therefore this becomes an ecclesiological criterion."[6]

The message of the pulpit with its heavy other-worldly emphasis, its abstract and unrelated theological reflection and most of all its handout paternalistic welfare programmes has largely benefited the dominant structures of societies. The Church has supported prevailing institutions of injustice and baptized with religious sanctions those who manipulate the system for vested class, socio-political and economic interest.

In North America, for example, certain churches supported slavery for a long time. It was a common conviction among many white Christians that there was nothing wrong with slavery.[7] Certain passages of Scriptures were frequently quoted to justify the claim (Eph. 6 : 5-8, 1 Cor. 7 : 17-24), as well as from other sources. Some whites even tried to prove through Scripture that the non-white race, particularly the black people, were the cursed sons of Ham and therefore the Church had the right to join hands with colonial forces to exploit such races.

Another example of the Church preoccupation with the prevailing institution of injustice can be seen when we look at the role of the Church during pre- and post-colonial eras in Africa.[8] In colonial times, the European and American missionaries worked hand in hand with the colonizers in administering colonial policies which were anathema to the African, so that he could not tell the difference between the Church and the state. Mbiti writes: ". . . Christian missionaries from Europe and America penetrated into the interior of Africa either shortly before, or simultaneously with colonial occupation. The image that Africans received and to a great extent still hold of Christianity, was much coloured by colonial rule and all that was involved in it. We are still too close to that period to dissociate one from the other. A Gikuzu proverb summarizes this fact very well: 'There is no Roman Catholic priest and a European — both are the same!'"[9]

Under colonial regimes the Church lost its universality. Frantz Fanon, referring to this, said: "The Church became the white people's church, the foreigner's church. She does not call the native to God's ways but to the ways of the white man, of the master, of the oppressor."[10]

In South Africa where there is blatant exploitation of millions of Africans, the Church has done very little in terms of solidarity with or struggling on the side of the poor for the liberation of an oppressed community.[11] Cosmas Desmond, a priest formerly working in South Africa, has pointed out that the apartheid policy is not only backed by the colonial political power but also by some churches that have failed to exercise their prophetic role in pronouncing the judgment of God upon the oppressors. The Church is not called to be a silent supporter of oppression, but to adopt a revolutionary option under the mandate of the Gospel.[12]

Is Christ still the Church?

The message and actions of the Church today do not always reflect the presence of Christ amongst us. The poor are asking: "Is Jesus still in the Church?" Some have suggested that it is the Church that is dead, not God or Jesus Christ. God in Jesus Christ is alive and actively involved in human history reconciling the world unto himself; but his presence is no longer clearly manifested in ecclesiastical institutions. The reason is that many elements of the language, liturgies, songs, message and the interpretation of Christianity have become obsolete and irrelevant for our changing societies. Ecclesiastical bodies are not always moving in pace with the signs of the time, and they continue to employ mission methodologies two or three decades behind enormously complex contemporary societies.

For example, in Africa, the Americas, Asia and other poverty-stricken parts of the world, one sees a growing proliferation of new churches emerging among the poor.[13] The poor are coming of age, the age of awareness and consciousness that the established ecclesiastical structures have not been always faithful to their calling and to the world of the poor to whom Christ sent the Church. The poor, on the other hand, feel that they are separated, even alienated, from many ecclesiastical institutions. They organize their own religious structures, searching for a place to feel at home. They are looking for the creation of new social structures which could offer hope and newness of life as opposed to existing structures that are closed and controlled. There is emerging a prophetic ministry of the community of the poor.

After many centuries of missionary activities in India, Africa, Asia and Latin America, Christianity has not won the entire heart of the indigenous people. It is still regarded by some as an alien religion with western trappings. It did not incarnate itself in the culture of the people. It has failed to come into harmony with the people's spirit.

The challenge to actually become poor

Another challenge of the poor to the Church is that, while the message of the poor is becoming incarnated and rooted in the culture and experiences of the people, numerical growth outside of the historical churches' structures is threatening the Church of the status quo. The poor now know that traditional Christian institutions have resulted in an overly westernized, overly materialized and overly institutionalized Christianity. Along with the poor's demand for a critical approach to the gospel message, there is an equal call for a "decolonization of Christianity". The effectiveness of the poor's involvement in this decolonization challenges the Church. The rediscovery of the functionality of popular religions defies Christian institutions. They must first liberate themselves before they can truly participate in the liberation of the poor.

A question of equal importance is whether "the Church finds Christ in the poor".[14] The Church, in the beginning of its missionary work in the colonial period, did not associate the poor with Christ because its concept of Christ had been partly distorted by the West European baggage with which its proclamation was in many ways bedevilled from the start. But when it began to see more clearly a new life-style of love, *koinonia* or community sharing, participation, involvement, and *diakonia*, a community characterized by love and service, all existing among the poor, it began to feel the impact of the challenge. The Church started to re-evaluate its own position in the light of its Christian commitment to the world and to the poor.[15]

The challenge is not only to identify with the poor, but to become poor and above all else to become the Church it ought to be. The Church must see itself as the church of the poor and create a new structure supportive of the poor's struggle in their liberating praxis. It is important for the Church to join with the poor in the creation of this new fellowship of sharing and participation.

"Only by rejecting poverty and by making itself poor in order to protest against it", says Gutiérrez, "can the Church preach something that is unique to its own: 'spiritual poverty', that is, the openness of man and history to the future promised by God. Only in this way will the Church be able to fulfil authentically ... its prophetic function of denouncing every injustice to man. And only in this way will it be able to preach the word which liberates, the word of genuine brotherhood."[16]

The reinterpretation of the biblical message which views God as the liberator who manifests himself through the poor in society to liberate the oppressed and the oppressors puts a new challenge to the Church.[17] The poor are engaged, however falteringly, in a new theological and ethical quest to give meaning and dignity to their lives, until now marginalized and domesticated.[18]

The poor seek a place where they can feel free to share their tears, voice their sorrows, present their spiritual and physical needs, respond to the world in which they live and empty themselves before God.

Present patterns of poverty are a scandal for the Christian faith. In Liberia, for example (as is also true of other countries), the distribution of wealth is deplorable. The people have not learned to share what they have. The land is rich with mineral resources, fertile soil, rich forest filled with lumber being cut by foreign and local companies and shipped abroad. Yet nearly all of Liberia's 1.6 million people are poor. Nine out of every ten persons are poor. Only 4% of the population controlled 60% of the income in 1971. By 1976, 2.1% of the population were in control of 60% of the nation's income. In 1976, the situation in the country had deteriorated to the point where the government had to declare a "war on poverty".[19]

Much of the world is plagued with mass unemployment, under-employment, poor health facilities, lack of decent education, poor standard of living. Degradation and death loom over the heads of both children and adults.

Poverty is a scandalous situation for the Church. When one man's life is made cheap, all of life is cheapened. Christ came that we might have life in its fullness. *But the prevalence of hunger, sickness, death and disease challenges the Church. Misery among the people for whom Christ died poses a problem of faith and praxis for ecclesiastical structures which live in wealth and affluence.*[20]

In wealthy churches, sharing is not easily accepted by the congregation. It is a difficult situation to subscribe to, but one must give of what one has in order to understand costly discipleship. This is part of the challenge. This challenge requires sacrifice and stewardship. In these words the challenge comes to the rich churches: "Christ Jesus, though He was by nature God ... emptied himself, taking the nature of a slave (Phil. 2:6), and being rich, he became poor (II Cor. 8:9) for our sakes. Thus, although the Church needs human resources to carry out its mission, it was not established to seek earthly glory, but to proclaim humility and self-sacrifice."[21] "For you know how generous our Lord Jesus Christ has been: He was rich, yet for your sake He became poor, so that through his poverty you might become rich" (II Cor. 8:9).

Finally, the poor are challenging the Church because most of the poor of the world are non-Christian; Christians are in most cases people who have wealth and can satisfy their needs. Christians not only control the wealth of the nations, they also control dominant political, economic and educational systems. And because they have the control mechanism to manipulate the system to their advantage, they swing the pendulum in their own direction, leaving the rest of humankind in destitution and starvation. This they do as Christians, captives in the operational framework where the "laws of the market" prevail.

The rich are getting richer, the poor poorer. The growing gap between the rich and the poor is not only a challenge to the Church; it is a scandalous situation for the Christian faith.[22] Unfortunately, the Church has not always been able to act responsibly in the context of its Christian vocation. The poor therefore see the Church as indifferent and uncommitted to their own claim — this, too, is a challenge.

In the light of these challenges, what is the Church's response? Maybe it will have to answer once more the question raised by Jesus when He asked his disciples: "Who do men say that the Son of Man is?" They answer: "Some say John the Baptist, others Elijah, others Jeremiah, or one of the prophets." "And you," He asked, "who do you say I am?" (Matt. 16 : 13-16).

The Church's self-understanding depends on its own understanding of Jesus Christ. That would be the first step in knowing how to respond to the challenge of the poor.

How are they relevant to the Church?

"In spite of these obstacles, however, the outcasts, the poor and the orphans saw the Christian faith as the source of a new humanizing influence and the foundation of a human community. Where conversion was genuine, whether of individuals or groups, the converts saw salvation in Christ not only in terms of individual salvation or heaven after death, but also as the spiritual source of a new community on earth in which their human dignity and status were recognized. It was the promise of humanization inherent in the Gospel of salvation that led to the influx of the oppressed into the Church."[23]

Christian individuals, groups and ecclesiastical institutions, challenged by the unprivileged of the world, are looking with new perspectives at the situation of the poor and oppressed. More and more it is apparent that charitable actions and policies can alleviate the misery of some, but are not enough to eradicate structural poverty and to attack effectively its root causes. More and more it is becoming a conviction that to combat the agents of deprivation, misery and domination, a comprehensive effort must include political action and people's mobilization.

Communities of Christian believers are becoming aware of the blatant material poverty of millions and millions of human beings in the world. At the same time a minority of people live in abundance and waste. The contradiction has become so clear that people in the churches are looking for patterns to curb consumption and to practise solidarity with people who do not have enough to live. The poor, in the meantime, emotionally and rationally, are becoming aware of their misery, know their frustrations, and naturally show their irritation when they compare their own situation with that of others.

Ecclesiastical bodies are responding to injustice and inequality. During the last two decades, renewal in churches has been expressed through the discovery of the poor, their challenges, and their potential for the renewal of society, including the churches. In all parts of the world, East and West, North and South, sections of the Christian community are taking up much clearer positions of solidarity with the poor, and are trying to remedy the separation which emerged during the last two centuries of world history between the poor and oppressed who were aware of the situation and the ecclesiastical institutions.[24]

A new dynamism, a new vitality is experienced by Christians and ecclesiastical bodies in sharing the struggle of the poor and oppressed for justice and liberation. New ways are being opened for the life of the Christian community. One of the most important experiences being developed is the new understanding provided by the poor of Christian symbols and the Scriptures. As in other times the Bible came to the hands of people (when it was translated into local languages), now the interpretation of biblical texts is being appropriated by the poor. It is the sign of a new age: the Good News is given to the needy and destitute (Matt. 11 : 2-6; Luke 7 : 18-23).

This reaction reveals the depth of the challenge of the poor: they are like agents of God's judgment, calling the Church to repentance. ". . . we must consider the poor as of central significance in our understanding of our society and of our way of life. The 'poor' here are all those whom society is effectively treating as less than human because they are being used (that is, exploited) for the production of its enjoyments which they do not have, are being left outside the operation of the benefits of society, are being positively driven outside what the more well-off and powerful take for granted. The way the poor are treated as less than human reveals the essentially dehumanizing trends at work throughout society. Thus the poor (in the extended sense to take in the marginals and the excluded and not just the physically grossly underprivileged) are not just *a* problem of society. Focused in them in their flesh and blood and their deprivations, is *the* problem of society. It is in this sense that they are signs of the judgment of the Kingdom. Hence the poor and the marginals are not primarily objects of charity and compassion but rather subjects and agents of the judgment of God and pointing to the ways of the Kingdom." [25] This challenge shows at the same time the relevance of the poor to the Church.

In the face of this challenge the churches could adopt a cavalier position, as they have often done, and say: "Poverty is of no concern to us." But even in the most elemental sense, poverty is indeed our concern, for while certain churches may correctly say that the world's poverty does not immediately affect them, many churches, particularly those in the Third World, cannot remain aloof. For in these instances the people of the churches are themselves poor.

This *is the first area of the relevance of the poor to the churches.* (Our brothers and sisters are poor.) The New Testament sets this as the minimum for social concern.

The Apostolic Council at Jerusalem, which is described in chapter 15 of Acts, sought to resolve the question of the catholicity of the Church. [26] Did being baptized into Christ mean that one first had to enter the cult of Judaism? Or had the Lord so radically revealed himself in this new age that the older cult practice as a sign of obedience to him might be set aside? Could Christians whose national origin was outside Judaism be fully-fledged members of the Church by simply believing the Gospel and living with others in the discipline of the Holy Spirit?

The Jerusalem Council resolved the matter in freedom. [27] Because of the experience surrounding Paul and Barnabas in their preaching to the Gentiles, the Council elected to eliminate the Jewish cult practice as essential to Church participation. The few exceptions to this freedom are a minimum of ethical prescriptions to prevent the Gentile Christians' practice of liberty in the Gospel from being grossly insulting to Jewish Christians, and thus divisive. Luke records these minimal ethical standards as: abstaining from what has been offered to idols; abstaining from eating blood or that which has been strangled; and practising sexual chastity (Acts 15 : 20-21).

In this Epistle to the Galatians Paul mentions a fourth reservation which the Jerusalem fathers gave to Barnabas and him at the conclusion of the Council at Jerusalem. He writes: "And when they had perceived the grace that was given to me, (they) gave to me and Barnabas the right hand of fellowship, that we should go to the Gentiles and they to the circumcized; *only they would have us remember the poor, which very thing I was eager to do*" (Gal. 2 : 9, 10). Such an admonition to remember the poor comes logically from a Church whose experience embraces not only prayers and miracles, but also sharing food from house to house and holding property in common (Acts 2 : 43-47).

This challenge to a practice of concern for the poor in the Church issued in at least two major collections for poor Christians for which Paul took responsibility (Acts 12 : 29-30 and I Cor. 16 : 3). His insistence on delivering the second collection to Jerusalem resulted in his arrest and imprisonment.

But poor Christians challenge the Church by more than what they lack. To the churches they give not only their pressing physical need but an experience as well. They offer the rest of the Church an understanding of the way the world is, not the way it should be. It is a world of oppression and misery. To persons of faith in this situation the apostolic Church offers a view of life that does not allow them to be lost in despair, and to that Church these poor offer a view of life that prevents the Church from losing touch with history.

In this regard poor Christians are no different from poor non-Christians. The first revelation to the Church is not the poor man's faith but the poor man's poverty. *But now there comes a second revelation for the Church out of poverty.* The first revelation is specific and may be measured with the tools of economics and sociology. *The second revelation is a statement about faith in the face of poverty and oppression.* As a theological statement about eternal life becomes more relevant when we or someone we love dearly must die, so a theological statement about poverty is most relevant when spoken from the experience of impoverishment.

Today such statements, and a host of actions consistent with these statements, are challenging the Church. The list of new theologies is rather long. Some of them are serious and comprehensive, while others appear more as "fads". The one commanding the most attention is called the "theology of liberation".[28] More will be said later of this kind of theology and of the practice of the Church flowing from it. What is important here is that there is a great ferment of ideas and mission in the churches.[29] It has the character of freedom and spontaneity, even inconsistency. It is emerging, springing up. To the Church, with its creed and its historic mission to witness to the Lord Jesus Christ, this new thought and new way of mission emerging within that part of the Church gathered around the poor is highly relevant.

The conflict of the new theology with the old theology drives the Church back to something more basic than theology. For most of the Church this more basic thing is the Bible, or an event or events which underlie the Bible. The recognition of the condition of the poor as an issue in the Church has been relevant in the call for a new look at the Bible.[30]

This return to the Bible to understand life when the old way was being challenged was true of the Reformers in the sixteenth century and true of the radical Protestants, the so-called Anabaptists, in that same century. It is apparent in the fresh attention to the scriptures current among Roman Catholics. There does not yet appear a similar fundamental return to Scripture among Protestants, but it may be anticipated as the Church among the poor increasingly finds its present existence described and defined in Scripture.

Thus far in this discussion of the relevance of the situation and struggle of the poor to the Church, we have dealt with those elements which are more or less concrete and tangible. Poor Christians are visible. They make poverty visible and they interpret it. Theology about liberation and in reaction to liberation is written down. The practice of solidarity with the poor in struggle has a strategy and tactics. The Bible is the Word of God, but it is in our language and presupposes our comprehension.

Now there emerges out of the struggle of the poor something intangible. It is perhaps best seen in considering how the Bible is read. *If there is a classic interpretation of Scripture challenged by a new interpretation, which is correct? And what is meant by "correct"?* Here we may seek understanding from the historical context; and that is helpful, but Christians also have a doctrine of illumination. In that doctrine there is the belief that God himself will give the right understanding of Scripture by his Holy Spirit directing the understanding and interpretation. Such a practice may seem anarchic but is an essential historical element in the use of Scripture as well as an important and vital function of present-day piety.

The Holy Spirit is at work, however, not only in the Church's understanding of the Word of God, but in its practice of mission as well. Acts 16 describes very clearly how the Holy Spirit redirected well-made plans for the work of the missionaries, Paul and Silas. The missionaries were "forbidden" to preach in the region of Asia; they revised their plan and attempted then to preach in Bithynia, but now the "Spirit of Jesus did not allow them" to do so. Finally the Holy Spirit gave a vision, whose implications provided the new direction for the mission.

That part of the Church which has sided with the poor would say the Holy Spirit has called and driven it there. For those who believe this, as well as for those who see this claim as a sacrilege, it is important to be humble. It is easiest to claim that which cannot be materially measured, but despite that warning an entirely predictable Church, without surprises and enigma, has little claim to being the temple of the Spirit of God.

The line of thinking followed thus far presupposes that the poor have a saving function for the Church, that their existence, and especially their sensitive awareness of life, serve to call a proud Church back to right practice, to repentance. Thus far we have seen the poor as being a positive, corrective, creative force as their situation of poverty impinges upon the thought and mission of the Church. *But there is a sense in which the relevance of the poor in the Church and in the world is more negative, or even a negation.* It is the sense in which the poor do not bring repentance and right practice, but serve only as human signs of the coming wrath of God.[31] It is to the prophets of the eighth to sixth centuries BC that we turn for such an understanding of the poor (Amos 5 : 10-24).

Why must we turn to the prophets? Do we not have the scriptures of the New Testament to prescribe faith and practice? We can indeed confine ourselves to the New Testament if we will; Jesus and James are ready to give us texts (James 5 : 1-6, Mark 10 : 23-25) but the situations of the churches that are identified with the culture of the western nations and wealthy social classes more directly correspond to Israel's situation in the age of the Old Testament prophets.[32]

The New Testament church was a church of the poor. No one will seriously challenge this. For example, Paul clearly described the church at Corinth as being made up mostly of the poor (I Cor. 1 : 26).[33] Had the Church through history remained aligned with the poor and powerless, there would remain a correct view of life today through a simple and direct application of the New Testament ethical teaching. But the churches in the West, for the most part, and those in eastern Europe before the advent of socialism, have been identified with the dominant powers in society.[34] Thus their position is inverted from that of the New Testament community. The Old Testament community of the eighth to sixth centuries BC offers a more direct parallel.

What do the prophets tell us? For this discussion we limit ourselves to Amos, Isaiah, and Jeremiah.[35] All three prophets see two principal causes for a forthcoming judgment of God to be meted out to Israel and Judah.

On the one hand, the people have abandoned the ritual worship of Yahweh and substituted in its place a host of foreign cult practices (cf. Amos chapters 3-4; Isaiah 28 : 7-22; Jeremiah 2 : 26-37, for example); on the other, they have abandoned the moral law of justice to one's neighbour and instead practise oppression, greed, lying, robbery and the violation of the rights of the fatherless, the widow, the poor, and the stranger (see especially Jer. 22).

The prophet's function in the face of apostasy is to call the people to repentance. Christian churches have preached on these scriptures with the expectation that repentance would come if the people were warned. But the prophets were not so optimistic! Perhaps it is most succinctly put in the Lord's call to Isaiah (Isaiah 6), but all three prophets expect that there will be no serious repentance. The Lord commands Isaiah: "Make the heart of this people fat, and their ears heavy, and shut their eyes; lest they see with their eyes, and hear with their ears, and understand with their hearts, and turn and be healed." And the prophet said: "How long, O Lord?" And the Lord said: "Until cities lie waste ... and the land lies utterly desolate." It is striking that Jesus and Paul picked up this word of doom from Isaiah and applied it in their day (Matt. 13 : 14-15; Acts 28 : 25-27).

The scriptures say that the Lord hears the cries of the poor (Ex. 2 : 23-25; Ps. 12 : 5; James 5 : 4). They do not say that the powerful or those linked with power, hear and heed that cry. The prophets' experience was that injustices to the poor were unnoticed, unheard and unfelt by others. But God knew, and God enabled the prophet to know. God used the prophet to make the situation of injustice clear. The final, chilling fact of the relevance of the poor to the churches is that while they may evoke a prophetic cry in the Church, the majority of the Church may never hear that cry.

NOTES

[1] GUSTAVO GUTIÉRREZ: *Theology of Liberation*, p. 301. Maryknoll, NY: Orbis Books, 1973.

[2] ANDRÉ BIÉLER: "Gradual Awareness of Social, Economic Problems (1750-1900)", in JULIO DE SANTA ANA (ed.): *Separation Without Hope?*, pp. 3-29, especially pp. 26-28 on "The majority of Christians indifferent, conservative and often reactionary". Geneva: WCC, 1975. Cf. also in the same volume the chapters by JOHN KENT: "The Church and the Trade Union Movement in Britain in the 19th Century", and by GÜNTER BRACKELMANN: "German Protestantism and the Social Question in the 19th Century".

[3] Bishops of Western-Central Brazil: *Marginalization of a People: a Cry of the Churches*, pp. 41-42: "Our Church denounces marginalization and supports workers' organization." Goiânia, May 1973.

[4] PAULOSE MAR PAULOSE: *Church's Mission: 1: Struggle for Justice. 2: Involvement in Political Struggles*, p. 9. Bombay: Build, 1978.

[5] GUSTAVO GUTIÉRREZ: *Teología desde el reverso de la historia*, pp. 24, 28-32, 35, and especially 43: "The other (central) perception (in theology of liberation) is the perspective of the poor: exploited classes, marginalized races, despised cultures. This led us to take the subject of poverty and the poor in the Bible. In this context the poor appeared as the key to understand the meaning of liberation and the revelation of the liberating God. . . . Theology understood in this way starts from popular classes and from their world: theological line that becomes truth is *verified*, in a real and fruitful involvement in the process of liberation". Lima: CEP, 1977.

[6] BENOÎT DUMAS: *The Two Alienated Faces of the One Church*, mentioned by JOSÉ MIGUEZ BONINO in "The Struggle of the Poor and the Church." *The Ecumenical Review*, Vol. XXVII, No. 1, 1975, p. 40-41.

[7] ROGER BASTIDE: *African Civilisations in the New World*. New York: Harper & Row, 1971.

[8] JACK WODDIS: *Introduction to Neo-Colonialism*. New York: International Publishers Co., 1968.

[9] JOHN MBITI: *African Religions and Philosophy*, p. 231. London: Heinemann, 1967.

[10] FRANTZ FANON: *The Wretched of the Earth*, p. 42. New York: Grove Press, 1968.

[11] COSMAS DESMOND: *Christians or Capitalists?: Christianity and Politics in South Africa*. London: Bowerdean Press, 1978.

[12] *Ibid*.

[13] JULIO DE SANTA ANA (ed.), *op. cit.*, André Biéler's and Nikolai Zabolotski's contributions.

[14] Cf., among others, WALTER J. HOLLENWEGER: *The Pentecostals*. London: SCM Press, 1972.

[15] Cf. note 5 above.

[16] Declaration by the Conference of Theologians of the Third World, Dar-es-Salaam, 5-12 August 1976.

[17] GUSTAVO GUTIÉRREZ, *op. cit.*, pp. 301-302.

[18] ROBERT MCAFEE BROWN: *Theology in a New Key*, pp. 96-100 on "A Hermeneutic of Engagement". Philadelphia: Westminster Press, 1978.

[19] *Susukuu Bulletin*: A Response to Mass Poverty in Liberia. Original source: *Annual Report of the Ministry of Planning & Economic Affairs to the Second Session of the Forty Eighth Legislature of Liberia for the Period January 1, 1976 to December 31, 1976*. Monrovia, Liberia: 22 December 1976. Also see the following: *1974 Census of Population and Housing: Population Bulletin Nos. 1 and 2*. Ministry of Planning and Economic Affairs, Monrovia, Liberia, 26 December 1975 and 27 September 1976 respectively. See also *Indicative Manpower Plan of Liberia for the Period 1972-1982*.

[20] Cf. the statement on "Structures of Captivity and Lines of Liberation: Some Theological Reflections", adopted by the CCPD-CICARWS Joint Consultation at Montreux, December 1974: "We are captives in a world where even the Word of God is not easily or everywhere heard. The Church itself seems to be in captivity wherever it has become allied or compromised with the powers of the old age, and there the Word of God too is bound. Liberation has to begin in the household of God." *The Ecumenical Review*, Vol. XXVII, No. 1, January 1975, p. 45.

[21] GUSTAVO GUTIÉRREZ, *op. cit.*, p. 300.

[22] DAVID M. PATON (ed.): *Breaking Barriers: Nairobi 1975*, pp. 122-123. Report of Section VI of the Fifth Assembly of the WCC on "Human Development: Ambiguities of Power, Technology and Quality of Life", paras 9, 11 and 13. Grand Rapids, Mich.: Wm B. Eerdmans, and London: SPCK, 1976.

[23] M. M. THOMAS: "Salvation and Humanization". *Salvation Today: a Contemporary Experience*, p. 59. Geneva: WCC, 1972.

[24] Cf. in this sense the statements of Latin American Roman Catholic Bishops in the *Second General Conference of the Latin American Roman Catholic Episcopate*, Medellin, 1968. Also the *Speech from the Dock* by Mgr Donal Lamont. London: Catholic Institute for International Relations.

[25] DAVID E. JENKINS: *The Contradiction of Christianity*, p. 49. London: SCM Press, 1976.

[26] Acts 15:4-29. St Paul, mentioning in his Epistle to the Galatians (2:6-10) what happened there, states (v. 9-10): "And when they perceived the grace that was given to me, James and Cephas and John, who were reputed to be pillars, gave to me and Barnabas the right hand of fellowship, that we should go to the Gentiles and they to the circumcised, only they would have us remember the poor, which very thing I was eager to do." Cf. MARTIN DIBELIUS: *Studies in the Acts of the Apostles*, chapter 5, "The Apostolic Council." London: SCM Press, 1956.

[27] GÜNTER BORNKAMM: *El nuevo testamento y la historia del Cristianismo primitivo*, p. 102: "The result of the convention was an unrestricted concession of freedom for the proclamation of the message of salvation among the gentiles." Salamanca: Sigueme, 1975. Original edition: *Das Neue Testament Bibel*. Stuttgart: Kreuz-Verlag, 1971.

[28] There is a very extensive bibliography on the theology of liberation. Among those theologians who develop this line are Gustavo Gutiérrez, Hugo Assmann, Leonardo Boff, José Miguez Bonino, Jon Sobrino, Juan Luis Segundo, Porfirio Miranda, Georges Casalis, M. M. Thomas, Manas Buthelezi, James Cone, etc.

[29] See especially chapters IX, XI, XII and XIII of this book.

[30] GUSTAVO GUTIÉRREZ: *Theology of Liberation*, *op. cit.*, chapter XIII.

[31] DAVID JENKINS, *op. cit.*, pp. 53-54.

[32] N. BERDYAEV: *Christianity and Class War*, pp. 121-122. London: Sheed & Ward, 1933.

[33] Cf. SERGIO ROSTAGUA: *Essays on the New Testament*, pp. 42-55. Geneva: WSCF, 1976.

[34] See PIERRE BURGELIN: "La fin de l'ère constantinienne." *Foi et vie*, 58th year, No. 1, pp. 8-55. Cf. also JULIO DE SANTA ANA (ed.): *Separation Without Hope?*, *op. cit.*

[35] About Amos, see GEORGIO ZOUM: *Amos, il profeta della giustizia*. Turin: Claudiana, 1971. On Isaiah, see especially J. H. BOX: *The Book of Isaiah*. London: Isaac Pitmans & Sons, 1908. Also ELMER A. LESLIE: *Isaiah*. Nashville, Tenn.: Abingdon Press, 1963. On Jeremiah, cf. HAROLD C. CASE: *The Prophet Jeremiah*. Cincinnati, Ohio: Women's Division of Christian Service, Methodist Church, 1953. On prophets and prophetism see MARTIN BUBER: *The Prophetic Faith*. New York: Macmillan, 1949.

IX · Theology from the Perspective of the "Underdogs" of History

The struggle of the poor and theological reflection

It would be wrong to believe that the poor have no theology, that they do not reflect on the experience of being Christian, that their reflection includes no protest of their condition of poverty. Much of their theological thinking takes place in community; it is not individualistic. Much of their reflection is geared to the particular and concrete; it is seldom systematized or expressed in abstractions. Much of their thinking bears on their pressing situation and problems; it is seldom ahistorical.[1]

Much of the theology of the poor would not meet the rigorous tests of some current academic theology, nor is that its pretension.[2] The theology emerging from poor communities has a different starting point, a different agenda, a different raison d'être. This is disconcerting to some theologians, a source of hope for renewal to others.[3]

The primitive Church was poor. The immediacy, concreteness and historical character of much of its reflection makes it particularly accessible to the church of the poor today. The Bible is a unique example of the early Church's testimony to the experience of Christ. The church of the poor reads it from the perspective of poverty, oppression, and the struggle for liberation, and finds its own concerns expressed scripturally.

The transformation of the biblical "people of the way", who confessed that "Jesus is Lord", into members of a hierarchically controlled and doctrinally defined institution is already foreshadowed in the New Testament. In the post-apostolic Church the process continued, and the Church which remained largely poor gradually became more vertically structured. In some instances, structures were created as an immediate response to the poor. In others, structures stifled the expression of concern for the poor and alienated the Church from its historical mission. Organization was necessary and inevitable in a hostile world. Yet in all periods when church spokesmen, groups and institutions forget the poor, prophetic voices arise with a call to faithfulness.

That was already so at the time of the New Testament. James, in the document which is called his "letter", says that those who reject the poor or who discriminate against them among the household of God blaspheme the name of Jesus Christ (James 2 : 7). The author of the book of Revelation praises the church of Smyrna, whose spiritual wealth contrasted with its material poverty; those who were against that church and attacked it did not realize how much the material indigence of that Christian community was related to its spiritual richness (Rev. 2 : 9-11). In recent times, when the black community in the USA was discriminated against and the rights of black people denied by the white majority, Martin Luther King became involved in the struggle for racial justice. His letter from Birmingham jail is a major prophetic voice from the underdogs of history in our century.[4]

From the beginning there were slaves in the Church; there were also slave-holders. There were the poor, but also some who were rich. From the time of Constantine, the Church included all social levels in the empire and through missionary activity had already extended beyond the emperor's military reach. Those who were below frequently bore the name Christian because of the conversion of those above. Christian leaders too intransigent in their position, and thus too divisive, might be deposed or exiled. In the Middle Ages the Church in the West became a state, and a power rivalling the secular rulers. Authoritarian hierarchical structures had emerged in the East. The Church strove to be the Church of all; Christendom had emerged. What of the poor?[5]

Few subjects in Christian history demonstrate a more marked ambivalence than the posture towards the poor. Hermits went into the desert in protest against a rich, morally lax Church. Monastic vows of poverty were taken by those who assumed the "evangelical counsels" were not applicable to the masses of common Christians. On the other hand, the notion of poverty was spiritualized so that those of great material wealth could be considered "the poor in spirit". In the Middle Ages, concepts predominated requiring that there be both rich and poor in the economy of God's plan of salvation, the poor as objects of the rich's charity and thereby facilitating their eternal salvation.[6]

The ambivalence towards the poor existed frequently in the same person. Clement of Alexandria asked: "Who is the rich man who will be saved?" and affirmed that riches by themselves need not pose a threat to salvation[7] — this in reply to the growing number of wealthy Christians in his own congregation. In other writings he could nevertheless affirm that all of creation belongs to God; individual interests must be subordinate to the common good, and all people have the right to sufficient means of living. Justice must prevail.

At different historical moments Christians have made clear options for the poor. Common funds in the primitive Church indicate that it was conscious of being a church of the poor. John Chrysostom suffered exile, and his death was not unrelated to this challenge to imperial power and siding with the poor and the marginalized. Significantly, lay movements of protest against poverty are historical constants.

The misuse of theology

The ambivalence of much theological thought about the poor is itself something of an accomplishment, a reflection of the power of the Gospel despite structural opposition. This opposition is seen in the intimate relationship between Church and society. Churches have tended to adopt organizational patterns reflecting those of their culture in the process of arriving at a fixed policy.[8] The Church might have been expected to defend dominant social structures, to make only hesitant or weak protests against social injustice, to fear appearing to be challenging other classes making up the Church in the interests of the poor. Too often, that is just what happened.

In some instances overt theological oppression has been blatantly combined with socio-economic and political oppression. Theology has thus helped to confirm the poor in their condition, since the theologian writing from the centre of power had internalized the social conditions of his context. In attempting to respond to the community he knew best, he provided a theological rationale for that community's domination of other peoples. Such theologians became agents of oppression in theology, Church and society. Examples are not hard to find: complicity with apartheid in Africa; justification of the colonial notion of the white man's burden in Asia; collusion with the subjection of the indigenous people or the black people in the Americas. Such glaring examples, however, may be the most insidious only in the short run. Theologies which legitimize flagrant oppression become, to most concerned Christians, transparent caricatures of the Gospel of Jesus Christ as their social implications become evident.

Theologies, on the other hand, which simply ignore injustice may not display the partiality of their faithfulness to the biblical witness. Their role in justifying situations of oppression is much more subtle and difficult to unmask. The people made poor by the centre of power to which the theologian belongs may be personally unknown to him. These poor are not present in his university or congregation. The face of the poor is absent, distant, and the voice of the poor is outside the theologian's realm of dialogue and discourse. *De facto*, the theologian has fallen victim to the socio-economic perspective of the dominant socio-economic class.

In such a process, existing socio-economic and political mechanisms are accepted without serious analysis of the way they lead to impoverishment of sectors of the national or world population.[9] The interpretation of Christian symbols is carried on with the expressed or implied presupposition that existing social relationships will continue even if not ordained by God or natural law. The call for greater justice, nearly always present in theological expression, is then compromised by the point of departure. Theology thus unwittingly becomes captive to powerful forces aligned against the poor. It submits to the historical project of dominant sectors of society and has itself been dehistoricized. Today it is possible to talk about the bourgeois captivity of theology.[10] Such theology has not emerged from the struggle of the poor through participation with the poor. It is theology from the upper part of the social pyramid, not from its base.

Authority of theology

All theological thought is related to a context. A supposed contextual "neutrality" confirms existing socio-economic and political relationships, and thus inadvertently identifies with dominant groups. It legitimizes situations of oppression. So-called "neutral theologies" differ only in degree from theologies of order or proponents of the *status quo* in sanctioning structures that produce and perpetuate poverty.

A "neutral" theology does not address the poor in their condition. A "neutral" theology does not bear witness to the God of history who acts in and through history to free the oppressed and proclaim good news to the poor. It is thus faithless to this crucial aspect of the biblical witness. A neutral theology implies that the God of history winks at oppression and suffering, that He does not side with the poor. A neutral theology has no authority.

The contextualization of theological reflection means opting for a particular social context, that which is low, at the base of the social pyramid. Theology is thus done from the perspective of the struggle for liberation carried on by the underdogs of history.[11] Opting for the poor means opposing oppression rather than confirming the powerful in oppressing other social sectors. An option for the poor aims at delivering the oppressor from his alienated condition in the hope that he may turn from Mammon to the true God.

Through direct involvement with marginalized people, conversions to the point of view of the oppressed have occurred in widely disparate callings: missionaries in colonial countries have come to challenge operative structures; businessmen have concluded that the injustice of a situation outweighed the need to pursue profits. In most instances, however, the tendency has been to act *on* the poor, not *with* them.

Theology must take into account the Bible and Church tradition in expressions of solidarity with the poor besides the struggle of the poor themselves — their frustrations and successes, in achieving liberation. It must also recognize the Church's apathy and betrayal of the poor. The authority of theology, however, derives from its faithful account of historical situations in which, before God, liberation is occurring and in which the theological statement is itself liberating.[12] That is not theology's only task, but it is a major undertaking and the neuralgic point on which its authority depends.

Emerging trends

1. THE TRINITARIAN APPROACH

The concept of revelation in theologies that legitimize oppression is in the main a static one. If any room is given at all to the Christ experience of the community of faith, it is considered secondary in contrast to the "full" biblical revelation. This static concept of revelation has serious consequences for basic theological assumptions. Much more attention must be given to the action of the Holy Spirit. The third person of the Trinity should be regarded as a source of a new understanding of revelation. What has been lost is the dynamic concept of God revealing himself to his people ever anew through the power of the Holy Spirit (John 15:26-16:4). By conceptualizing the revelation in Christ and by regarding it as closed, theologies that legitimize oppression tend to create closed theological systems, leaving no room for new manifestations of the Holy Spirit. They thus provide a false security which prevents the Christian disciple from living in the constant expectation of God making all things new.

2. JESUS AND THE PHARISEES: CONFLICTING THEOLOGIES

In Mark 3:1-6 we find a confrontation between Jesus and the Pharisees on the issue of healing on the Sabbath. There is a man with a withered arm in the synagogue and the Pharisees keep an eye on Jesus to see whether He will cure him on the Sabbath, so that they could bring a charge against him. Noting that He is being watched, Jesus heals the man. There is no urgency to cure the man on the Sabbath, but Jesus does it purposely. In doing so Jesus affirms that He is different from the Pharisees. The difference is of both doctrine and approach.

Jesus' position in his conflict with the Pharisees is best summarized in his own words in a previous passage: "The Sabbath was made for man, and not man for the Sabbath" (Mark 2 : 28). Sabbath in this quotation stands for "Torah", the God given law, which is the embodiment of God's revelation to his people. Strict obedience to the law is what makes a Jew a member of the chosen people. And the Pharisees are by far the most faithful ones in this regard.

But Jesus says: the law is made for man, and not man for the law. In other words: the law is a means and not an end in itself. The end is obedience to God which is distinct from obedience to the law. The God of Israel takes no delight in legalistic obedience; He wants his law to be an instrument whereby the human being finds liberation in the covenant relationship with him. Obedience to God according to Jesus is liberation; obedience to the law is slavery.[13] This is what makes Jesus' theology different from that of the Pharisees.

The Pharisees regard the law as the permanent truth revealed by God once and for all. It is the norm from which prescriptions for religious and moral conduct are deduced. This code of conduct set forth in all its casuistic possibilities has validity in all situations and in all ages. Any deviation from these prescriptions is considered a violation of the law.

Jesus refuses to take this theological approach. He does not start from a given norm but from the real human situation. There is a man who needs help, and Jesus gives help in spite of the generally accepted code of not doing anything on the Sabbath. Jesus does not preach the good news of healing to the crippled man. No, He heals. Jesus does not enter into a theological dispute with the Pharisees: He acts. His action is the liberating Gospel for the crippled man; his action is his theological answer to the Pharisees.

3. THEOLOGY OF THE RICH — THEOLOGY OF THE POOR

The alliance of ecclesiastical bodies and Christian leadership with ruling powers throughout history has helped to develop a theological understanding which is acceptable to the powerful, and which has become more and more foreign to the powerless. Established theology has been used and manipulated in order to communicate the ideas and expectations of dominant sectors of society. Critics of this use of established theology say, on the one hand, that it has helped to legitimize unjust structures and mechanisms of oppression, calming the people and leading them to accept with resignation the *status quo* in society. And, on the other hand, they point out that such theology is not helping, and will not help, to resolve the problems of the poor and the oppressed: at most, it can help to elaborate policies *for* the poor, but not to share *with* them their struggles and expectations. This kind of theology, instead of motivating the poor to confront injustice, has rather helped to disarm them.[14] Literalism, inappropriate spiritualization, evasion of the world, and so on, have been some of the emphases of theologies which legitimize oppression.[15]

Here is the great inadequacy of this kind of theology. The poor are not people who like to spiritualize; as we saw previously popular religiosity expresses itself in concrete terms, and in a realm of common sense.[16] Though it manifests alienation, it remains also in the sphere of history. A theology *of* the poor is one which helps the poor effectively to try to overcome the injustice they suffer and the oppression which creates such injustice. That is, it is a theology which develops from facts of history of the poor and their situation. As stated in a document on urban rural mission in Asia: "Theological thinking is truly historical when it deals with the historical transformation of the structures of dehumanization and injustice. The historical movement towards a humane and just society unfolds through structural transformation of a society, rather than through any development. The transformation takes place at all levels — economic, political, social and cultural. The traditional cultural structures and values, as well as the more recent economic and political structures of dehumanization must be transformed in order for the people to be liberated for the future Kingdom."[17]

It is evident that this theological approach will be developed basically by the poor and oppressed themselves. In fact this is what has been happening in the last years: from Asia, Latin America, Africa, from the poor and oppressed people in the industrialized countries as well, a new theology is being developed. The prerequisite is that the people appropriate the Church to themselves. In situations of oppression and injustice, the churches are giving the poor a place to be really human. The poor are renewing the Church, which in many situations is coming to be *"the Church of the poor"*.[18] It is from these communities that new theological developments — with new insights, revealing powerful sources of motivation of the poor for action, sustaining their hopes — are emerging.

Theologies that legitimize oppression

Theologies which legitimize situations of oppression are basically *ahistorical*. This is due in part to the priority given to the systematization and conceptualization of Christian symbols without constant reference to the historical life of the Christian community. Moreover, just as the human being must be viewed as a whole person living in society, whose body and social relationships are no less given by God than his mind and soul, so also the human person lives in one history. Theologies that legitimize oppression lead to a static view of history, a confirmation of existing socio-economic and political relationships, and an implicit (even explicit) acceptance of the given historical context. Movement and change, which are the essence of historical reality, and especially the community's historical thrust towards a more just society, are not of central consideration in these theologies.

The assumption that the social context is peripheral to theological reflection leads ultimately to the negation of social reality. Poverty is consequently viewed as a regrettable condition or even a spiritual virtue rather than the result of a historical world dynamic brought on by prevailing socio-economic and political mechanisms. Christian protest and practice challenging these mechanisms have not been thought to merit serious theological reflection. "Fallen world", "the temporal order", "the secular Kingdom", or other such slogans will not dismiss the daily suffering the poor must bear, the result of an all too concrete exploitation.

The lack of social analysis has blinded traditional theologies to their own social and ideological presuppositions. They claimed to be "neutral" and "objective", not recognizing their unconscious surrender to the norms, attitudes and behaviour patterns of their societies. Their "theologies of order" often reflected authoritarian structures of feudal or other kinds of dominant societies, and consciously or unconsciously served to legitimize prevailing socio-economic and political systems created by the dominant classes. Claiming to be independent of a particular ideological point of view, they succumbed to the ideology of those in power.[19]

APPENDIX

In this appendix are presented two examples of this "theology from the underdogs of history". The first was written by Gustavo Gutiérrez[20] and the second is the report from the Asian Theological Conference held in Sri Lanka, 7-20 January 1979.

THE POOR IN THE CHURCH

by Gustavo Gutiérrez

Perhaps I should make the point at the beginning that *the Church is not involved in the question of poverty by the fact that it is present in a poor country. It is involved primarily and fundamentally by the God of the Bible to whom it wants to, and must, be faithful.* The fact that the Church is present in a poor country can indeed provide the whole Church with the opportunity better to understand its responsibility to be a community bearing witness to God who himself became poor in Jesus Christ. This leads us to a second point. I have mentioned poor countries where the expression is ambiguous. Strictly speaking, I mean countries where the great majority of the population live in poverty caused by an unjust social order. *This means that the question of the poor in the Church involves not only the God we believe in but the social conflict we live in.*

Bearing this in mind I'd like to suggest some of the thoughts on the problem which have arisen in the course of experience and discussions during our daily working lives. *These lead to the conclusion that the poor today, rather than being regarded merely as a "problem for the Church", raise the question of what "being the Church" really means.*

The wretched of the earth

For most of its history, Christendom as it was called, the Church has been working out how it sees itself. From within, so to speak. Supernatural salvation is an absolute value of which the Church is the sole guardian. Western Christianity is constructed pastorally and theologically in relation to the believer, the Christian. In order to understand itself the Church looks inwards. This has been called ecclesio-centrism.

The historical reasons for this attitude are obvious and easily understandable. When new countries were discovered, the task of incorporating them into the Church was seen as a mission of salvation. The Church was historically bound up with western culture, the white race and the ruling class of European society and its extension throughout the world was in these western terms. The missionaries followed in the tracks of the colonialists. *Ecclesio-centrism savoured of westernization.*

It is a cliché to say that Vatican II put an end to the "Christendom" mentality. The time has come for dialogue and service to the world. The Church is to turn *outward* towards the modern world. This world is hostile to the Church, existed centuries before it, and is proud of its own values. Pope John XXIII gave the Council the task of opening the Church to the world, finding an appropriate theological language, and bearing witness to a Church for the poor. After it had overcome its initial difficulties, the Church fulfilled the first of these two demands.

The constitution *The Church in the World* showed the new horizon for the Church's action seen by Vatican II. It offered an optimistic vision of the world and its progress, of modern science and technology, the individual as the subject of history and of freedom, with some reservations about the risks involved in such values. In particular it affirmed that these values cannot be fulfilled outside the context of the Christian message. The constitution appealed for collaboration between believers and non-believers in "the just construction of this world in which they live together". In this world outside, which should not however be hostile to the Church, the Lord is present and active and He also calls the Christian community to greater loyalty to the Gospel. In this world the Church must fulfil its mission as a sign, a universal sacrament of salvation.

The great claims of the modern world are recognized, but with due moderation. On the other hand social conflicts are only mentioned in general terms of the existence of poverty and injustice in the world, and the necessity for the development of the poor countries. The individualistic root of bourgeois society is also maintained to a certain extent. *There is no serious criticism of the effects of domination by monopolistic capitalism on the working classes, particularly in the poor countries. Nor is there any clear realization of the new forms of oppression and exploitation perpetrated in the name of these modern world values.* The Council is concerned with something else: the time has come for dialogue between the Church and modern society. That this society is not homogeneous, but divided into conflicting social classes does not come within the scope of Vatican II. The world to which it is "opening up" is bourgeois society.

The third task given by John XXIII to the Council barely appears in its texts. The theme of poverty, "Schema 14" as it was called in the Council corridors, knocked on the Council's door but only got a glimpse inside.

However, *many Christians have recently been becoming more and more aware that if the Church wants to be faithful to the God of Jesus Christ, it has to rethink itself* from below, *from the position of the poor of the world, the exploited classes, the despised races, the marginal cultures. It must descend into the world's hells and commune with poverty, injustice, the struggles and hopes of the dispossessed because of them is the Kingdom of Heaven.*

Basically it means the Church living as a church the way many of its own members live as human beings. Being reborn as a church means dying to a history of oppression and complicity. Its power to live anew depends on whether it has the courage to die. This is its passover. This sounds like a dream to many people but it is the real challenge confronting the Christian community today. The time will come when any other way of talking by the Church will sound hollow and meaningless.

There are now many people working along these lines, in various and perhaps modest ways (the political dimensions of the Gospel, involvement in the struggle of the poor, defence of human rights, Africanization of the Christian faith, breaking with the colonial past, and so on). The aim is to be faithful to the gospel and the constant renewal of God's call. *Gradually people are realizing that in the last resort it is not a question of the Church being poor, but of the poor of this world being the People of God, the disturbing witness to the God who sets free.*

Subversion of history

Human history is where we encounter the Father of Jesus Christ. And in Jesus Christ we proclaim the Father's love for all human beings. As we have already mentioned, this history is a history of conflict, but we cannot leave it at that. We must also insist that history (in which God reveals himself and we proclaim him) must be *re-read from the viewpoint of the poor.* Human history has been written, as a Brazilian theologian has put it, "with a white hand", by the ruling classes. *The point of view of the "underdogs" of history is quite other. History must be re-read from this viewpoint of their struggles, resistance and hopes.*

Great efforts have been made to blot out the memory of the oppressed. This deprives them of a source of energy, historical will and rebellion. Today the humiliated nations are trying to understand their past in order to build their present on solid bases. The history of Christianity has also been written with a white, western, bourgeois hand. We must recall to mind the "scourged Christs of the Indies", as Bartolomé de las Casas called the Indians of the American continent, and with them all the other poor people who have been victims of the lords of this world. Their memory still lives in cultural expressions, popular religion and the resistance to impositions by the Church bureaucracy. The memory of Christ is present in every hungry, thirsty, oppressed and humiliated person, in the despised races and the exploited classes (cf. Matt. 25), this memory of Christ who "for freedom has set us free" (Gal. 5 : 1).

But the phrase "re-reading history" I have used might sound like a mere intellectual exercise if I did not mean it as a *re-making of history*. It is not possible to re-read history unless we enter into the successes and failures of the fight for freedom. Re-making history means subverting it, that is to say, "turning it upside down", and seeing it from below instead of from above. The established order has taught us to think of subversion as something bad, because it threatens it. But contrariwise it is bad to be and perhaps go on being a "super-versive", supporting the ruling power and seeing history from the standpoint of the great of this world.

This subversive history involves a new experience of faith, a new spirituality and a new proclamation of the Gospel. Understanding the faith in terms of the historical praxis of liberation leads to the proclamation of the Gospel as the very heart of this praxis. This proclamation is a watchguard, an active involvement and solidarity with the interests and struggles of the working classes, the word which becomes effective in action, defines attitudes and is celebrated in thanksgiving.

The Gospel of the poor

The Gospel proclaims liberation in Jesus Christ, liberation which uproots all injustice and exploitation and brings friendship and love. I do not mean a liberation which could be interpreted "spiritually", still so dear to certain Christian circles. Hunger and injustice are not merely economic and social problems but human ones and they challenge the very basis on which we live our Christian faith. *As Berdyaev put it, reinterpreting terms frequently used in such circles: "If I'm hungry, it's a material problem, but if someone else is hungry it's a spiritual problem."*

Love and sin are historical realities which take place in real situations. That is why the Bible speaks of liberation and justice as opposed to the slavery and humiliation of the poor in history. The *gift of sonship* is accomplished in history. By accepting others as our brothers and sisters we accept this gift not in word but in deed. This is living the Father's love and bearing witness to it. The proclamation of a God who loves all human beings equally must be embodied in history, become history. Proclaiming this liberating love in a society ruled by injustice and the exploitation of one social class by another, turns this "becoming history" into an appeal and a conflict.

Within a society where social classes clash, we are true to God when we side with the poor, the working classes, the despised races, the marginal cultures. This is the position whence to live and proclaim the Gospel. Proclaiming it to the oppressed of this world will show them that their situation is against God's will which is enacted in liberating events. This will help them realize the vile injustice of their situation.

The Gospel read from the point of view of the poor and the exploited and militancy in their struggles for freedom requires a people's Church: a Church which arises from the people, a people who wrest the Gospel from the hands of the great ones of this world and thus prevent it being used to justify a situation against the will of the liberating God.

When the poor expropriate the Gospel from the hands of those who now consider it their private property, we shall have what has recently begun to be called "the social appreciation of the Gospel" in certain popular circles in Latin America. The Gospel tells us that the sign of the arrival of the Kingdom is that the poor have the Gospel preached to them. It is the poor who hope and believe in Christ or, strictly speaking, are Christians. Can we turn this around and say that the Christians today are the poor?

Perhaps we should go further and say that the preaching of the Gospel will be truly liberating when the poor themselves are the preachers. Then of course the proclamation of the Gospel will be a stumbling block, it will be a gospel "unacceptable to society" and expressed in the vernacular. Thus the Lord will speak to us. Only by listening to this voice will we recognize him as our saviour. This voice speaks *in ecclesia* with a different tone.

Thus the poor of this world are working out their "historical credo", telling themselves and others why they believe in the Lord who sets people free, because they believe in him in communion with a whole historical past, in the social conditions in which they are living now. In various places many attempts have been made and continue to be made in this direction. It is a mistake to think that Latin America today is totally submerged under repression and fascism. Moreover, for the people of the subcontinent, suffering is not something new; it has always been there, but so too have hope and the will to rebel.

For a long time these people have been exiles in their own land, but also making the exodus to regain it. The workers' power of resistance and creativity are incomprehensible to the defenders of the established order, and also disconcerting to those who have recently regarded themselves as their spokesmen.

A few years ago communication between different Christian communities engaged in the struggle for liberation in Latin America was active and enriching. Today the political and ecclesiastical conditions have changed and the lines have been broken to a great extent. But everywhere new efforts are beginning: let us think, for example, of the groups being formed in Brazil. The increasing hunger and exploitation (especially in the poorer countries), imprisonment (the political arrests in the whole subcontinent, the bishops who met in Riobamba), torture and murder (the Honduran peasants, Argentinian priests), are the price being paid for rebelling against secular oppression and beginning to understand what the Church and being a Christian mean today.

But these lives and this bloodshed are a challenge to the whole Church, not just the church in Latin America, requiring more than mere analysis. Its response to this challenge will decide how faithful it is to its own authentic tradition and thus to the Lord who "establishes justice and right".

How can I sing to God in a foreign land, asked the psalmist in exile. There can be no Christian life without "songs" to God, celebrations of his liberating love. But how can we sing to God in a world full of oppression and repression? This is a painful question for the Christian, involving the whole basis of his faith, requiring something like a new covenant "with us who are all of us here alive this day" (Deut. 5 : 3), breaking the historical covenant made with the ruling culture, race and class.

It requires a covenant with the poor of this world, a new kind of universality. This creates a feeling of panic in some; others lose their old security, but many feel a disturbing sense of hope. As José María Arguedas puts it, it is a journey in which "we feel little knowledge but great hope".

ASIAN THEOLOGICAL CONFERENCE

Sri Lanka, 7-20 January 1979

I. Preamble

We, Christians from Asia, along with fraternal delegates from other continents, gathered in Wennappuwa, Sri Lanka, 7-20 January 1979, motivated by our solidarity with our people in the struggle for full humanity and by our common faith in Jesus Christ. Bringing with us the experience of the struggle in our own countries, we came to share in the life and situations of the masses striving for justice in Sri Lanka, through our four-day "live-ins".

During the days that followed, we became more aware of the commonalities and divergences in our background which sharpened our understanding both of the richness and the anguish of our people in Asia.

As Asians, we recognize the important task before us. Our reflections, already begun in our local realities, helped us to enrich the process of interaction and sharing among us who have committed ourselves to the struggle of the poor in Asia. At the same time, we realize that these reflections are only part of the beginning of a collective and continuous search for a relevant theology in Asia.

II. The Asian context

Asia suffers under the heels of a forced poverty. Its life has been truncated by centuries of colonialism and a more recent neo-colonialism. Its cultures are marginalized, its social relations distorted. The cities with their miserable slums, swollen with the poor peasants driven off the land, constitute a picture of wanton affluence side by side with abject poverty that is common to the majority of Asia's countries. This extreme disparity is the result of a class contradiction, a continuous domination of Asia by internal and external forces. The consequences of this type of capitalist domination is that all things, time and life itself, have become marketable commodities. A small minority of owners dictate the quality of life for the producers (workers, peasants and others) in determining the price of their energy, skills, intelligence as well as the material benefits needed to sustain these. What is produced, how and where it is produced, for whom it is produced, are the decisions of transnational corporations in collusion with the national elites and with the overt or covert support of political and military forces.

The struggle against these forces has been courageously taken up by the advocates of socialism. This socio-political order corresponds to the aspirations of the Asian masses both in the rural and urban areas since it promises to them the right to take their life into their own hands, to determine both the social and economic conditions that govern their well-being. A very large part of Asia has succeeded, after long struggles, in establishing this socialist order. However, it must be added that the socialist transformation in these countries is not yet complete and that these countries must continue to liberate themselves from all distortions in an ongoing self-criticism.

Neither will socialist movements in Asia be thorough in their struggle for full humanity without an inner liberation from self-seeking and exploitative instincts. The rich traditions of the major religions of Asia (Hinduism, Buddhism, Islam and Christianity) offer many an inspiration. The richness is not only expressed in philosophical formulations but also in various art forms such as dance and drama, poems and songs as well as in myths and rites, parables and legends. It is only when we immerse ourselves in the "peoples' cultures" that our struggle acquires an indigenous dimension.

However, it is equally true that the social function of religions or cultural systems is ambiguous. In the past religions and cultural systems have played the role of legitimizing feudal relationships, yet the self-critical principle inherent in them can be a source of liberation today from the domination of capitalist values and ideologies.

Hence we feel that the Asian context which dictates the terms of an Asian theology consists of a struggle for fuller humanity in the socio-political as well as the psycho-spiritual aspects. The liberation of all human beings is both societal and personal.

III. The issues

We realize that if large numbers of men and women find themselves socially deprived and progressively thrown further and further away from the centre of life and meaning, it is not a mere accident or the effect of a national catastrophe. In fact, from Pakistan to Korea, passing through the sub-continent and South-East Asia, practically all parliamentary governments, with the exception of Japan, have at some time given way to military governments or authoritarian regimes of one form or the other. In these countries not only are political rights suppressed, but also the rights of workers to strike in the cities and the rights of peasants to organize themselves in the countryside. Many leaders and people holding political views contrary to the ruling group are condemned to spend several years in prison, often without due process of trial.

Behind the facade of "law and order" are Asia's cheap and docile labour and laws which leave the country open to unrestricted exploitation by foreign capital with the profit going to a small elite. A deeper logic is to be found in the dual economies of these countries. The industrial sector, monopolized by the national elite, has developed along the lines of an export economy that does not correspond to the needs of the local population. It also depends heavily on foreign capital and technology. And as a result of unequal trade relations and the weakness of these countries their indebtedness and dependence grew to an extent beyond their control. International banks and transnational corporations have become the new masters of Asia's politics and economics.

At the same time the rural sector in these countries has remained stagnant. The so-called agrarian reforms did not change the unequal social relations of production in the rural areas. The benefit of the "green revolution" went only to the middle and big landowners who could afford the technology. A great number of peasants were driven off the land in the process and ended in the slums of the swollen cities of Asia. On the other hand, the rural surplus thus accumulated is often reinvested in crops for export or channelled into urban industries, preventing the growth of production for food. As a result Asia, which is potentially rich in agriculture, is importing food from outside and the amount is increasing continually at an alarming rate. Hunger and poverty will be the fate of Asian masses for many years to come.

A hopeful sign is the growing awareness among the oppressed peoples which leads to the growth and increase of people's organizations in both cities and the rural areas. The majority of Asian countries have witnessed peasant uprisings and urban disturbances. Put down by bloody oppression and intimidated by imprisonment and torture, many of these movements have gone underground and turned to a protracted struggle as the only means of changing their societies. While not necessarily condoning the use of violence which is most often unavoidable, we question and object to the enforcement of "law and order" which consolidates the control of the power elites while thwarting the organized conscientious objections of the deprived majorities. When legalized violence leaves no room for peoples to free themselves from their misery, are we surprised that they are so compelled to resort to violence? Have the Christian churches sufficiently understood the message of revolutionary violence in the Asian struggles for political independence, social emancipation and liberation from the built-in violence of the present economic and political structures?

The youth in Asia, who form a large segment of the Asian population, are continuously victimized. They constitute the growing number of the unemployed and underemployed labour force. A lack of proper educational facilities and decreasing employment opportunities in the rural areas where the majority of youth come from lead to the irreversible process of migration to urban centres; while in the urban areas, the youth are the targets of consumer-culture and in turn become vehicles of deculturation. We emphasize also that some students, youth and workers have been playing the important role of a critical and committed force in the struggle for the basic rights of the oppressed people. At the same time, they are also made pawns in the power politics of politicians and other interest groups, thus losing their genuine relevance, and are even sacrificed in abrupt physical violence.

The educational system, linked to the established centres of power, is geared to perpetuate the domination of youth. It serves as a mere channel for the transfer of technical skills and alienated knowledge without reference to humanistic values. The pyramidal elitist structure of education is used to fabricate losers, who are continuously exploited.

We recognized deeply that women were also victims of the same structures of domination and exploitation. In the context of the Asian religions and cultures, the relationship between men and women is still one of domination. This situation is worse in the poorer classes of society. Thus women face an unforgivable double oppression.

At the economic level, a male-dominated society reduces the "price" of woman-labour and limits the scope of women's participation in the process of production at all levels — local, national, regional and consequently the international level. At the political level, women are aware of the political situation in their countries, but here too, their competence and activity are greatly stifled.

Women are sexually and intellectually vulnerable in a society where an interaction of traditional and modern forces (especially tourism) compels them to compromise with consumeristic values of capitalist society. It also compels them to prostitution. Instead of condemning the system which forces women into prostitution, it is the women who are condemned by the men who exploit them.

We recognize the existence of ethnic minorities in every Asian country. They are among the most deprived sector at all levels including the economic, political and cultural. They are struggling for self-determination against heavy odds, yet their authentic struggle is often utilized by the centres of power in playing up racial antagonism to camouflage themselves and disrupt the unity among the marginalized.

Mass media, including the printed word, films, television, etc., are controlled by the ruling elite to propagate their dominant value systems and myths, providing a dehumanizing, individualistic, consumerist culture. Despite this domination, we also witness the emergence of a more creative micro-media that portrays realistically the struggle of the dominated people.

We need to mention also the increasing impact of urbanization and irrational industrialization. Women, children and men together face narrowing opportunities for education, housing and health services as these social needs are determined by market forces. With the transfer of the platforms of production and mechanization from industrialized countries, environmental pollution surfaces in most of the Asian countries, causing ecological imbalances. Here we join with our fishermen in their struggle against the unscrupulous practices of certain countries like Japan, Taiwan and South Korea.

We realize also the legitimizing role of religion in the course of history within the Asian context. Religions form an integral part of the total social reality inseparable from all spheres of action. Much interaction has taken place between religion and politics in Asia down the ages and today there are significant movements of social renewal inspired by religions outside the traditional institutions. We need to stress the critical and transforming element in religion and culture. A serious socio-political analysis of realities and involvement in political and ideological struggles should be seen as vital elements of religion in its role as a critic. Here we realize the creative force of culture in bringing people together and giving them an identity within their struggles. Critical cultural action would destroy old myths and create new symbols in continuity with the cultural treasures of the past.

IV. Towards a relevant theology

We are conscious of the fact that the vital issues of the realities of Asia indicate the ambivalent role of the major religions in Asia and pose serious questions to us, hence challenging the dehumanizing status quo of theology. To be relevant, theology must be radically transformed.

A. LIBERATION: AREA OF CONCERN

In the context of the poverty of the teeming millions of Asia and their situation of domination and exploitation, our theology must have a very definite liberational thrust.

The first act of theology, its very heart, is commitment. This commitment is a response to the challenge of the poor in their struggle for full humanity. We affirm that the poor and the oppressed of Asia are called by God to be the architects and builders of their own destiny. Thus theology starts with the aspirations of the oppressed towards full humanity and counts on their growing consciousness of, and their ever-expanding efforts to overcome, all obstacles to the truth of their history.

B. Subject of theology

To be truly liberating, this theology must arise from the Asian poor with a liberated consciousness. It is articulated and expressed by the oppressed community using the technical skills of biblical scholars, social scientists, psychologists, anthropologists and others. It can be expressed in many ways, in art forms, drama, literature, folk stories and native wisdom as well as in doctrinal-pastoral statements.

Most participants asserted that every theology is conditioned by the class position and class consciousness of the theologian. Hence a truly liberating theology must ultimately be the work of the Asian poor, who are struggling for full humanity. It is they who must reflect on and say what their faith-life experience in the struggle for liberation is. This does not exclude the so-called specialists in theology. With their knowledge they can complement the theologizing of the grassroots people. But their theologizing becomes authentic only when rooted in the history and struggle of the poor and the oppressed.

C. Liberation, culture and religion

Theology, to be authentically Asian, must be immersed in our historic-cultural situation and grow out of it. Theology, which should emerge from the people's struggle for liberation, would spontaneously formulate itself in religio-cultural idioms of the people.

In many parts of Asia, we must integrate into our theology the insights and values of the major religions, but this integration must take place at the level of action and commitment to the people's struggle and not be merely intellectual or elitist. These traditions of Asia's great religions seem to understand liberation in two senses: liberation from selfishness within each person and in society; these religious traditions also contain a strong motivation for personal conversion of life. These religions, together with our indigenous cultures, can provide the Asian sense in our task of generating the new person and the new community. We view them as a potential source of permanent critique of any established order and a pointer towards the building of a truly human society. We are conscious, however, of the domesticating role religions have often played in the past, so we need to subject both our religion and culture to sustained self-criticism. In this context, we questioned the academic preoccupation to work towards the so-called "indigenization" or "inculturation" of theology divorced from participation in the liberational struggle in history. In our countries today, there can be no truly indigenized theology which is not liberational.

Involvement in the history and struggle of the oppressed is the guarantee that our theology is both liberating and indigenous.

D. SOCIAL ANALYSIS

Theology working for the liberation of the poor must approach its task with the tools of social analysis of the realities of Asia. How can it participate in the liberation of the poor if it does not understand the socio-political, economic and cultural structures that enslave the poor? The vision of full humanity and the complexity of the struggle leading to its achievement are continually challenged and distorted by the meshing of mixed motives and interests and by the interweaving of the apparent and the real. This analysis must extend to the whole length and breadth, height and depth of Asian reality, from the family to the village, the city, the nation, the continent and the globe. Economic and socio-political interdependence has shrunk the earth to a global village. The analysis must keep pace with the ongoing historical process to ensure a continuing self-criticism and evaluation of religions, ideologies, institutions, groups and classes of people that by their very nature, run the hazard of a dehumanizing bureaucracy.

E. BIBLICAL PERSPECTIVE

Because theology takes the total human situation seriously, it can be regarded as the articulated reflection, in faith, on the encounter of God by people in their historical situations. For us, Christians, the Bible becomes an important source in the doing of theology. The God encountered in the history of the people is none other than the God who revealed himself in the events of Jesus' life, death and resurrection. We believe that God and Christ continue to be present in the struggles of the people to achieve full humanity as we look forward in hope to the consummation of all things when God will be all in all.

When theology is liberated from its present race, class and sex prejudices, it can place itself at the service of the people and become a powerful motivating force for the mobilization of believers in Jesus to participate in Asia's ongoing struggle for self-identity and human dignity. For this, we need to develop whole new areas of theology such as understanding the revolutionary challenge of the life of Jesus, seeing in Mary the truly liberated woman who participated in the struggle of Jesus and her people, bridging the gaps of our denominational separation, and rewriting the history of the Asian churches from the perspective of the Asian poor.

V. Spirituality and formation

The formation for Christian living and ministry has to be in and through participation in the struggle of the masses of our people. This requires the development of a corresponding spirituality, of opting out of the exploitative system in some way, of being marginalized in the process, of persevering in our commitment, of risk-bearing, of reaching deeper inner peace in the midst of active involvement with the struggling people (Shanti).

Our fellow Christians who have become regular inmates of the Asian prisons bring us new elements of fidelity to our people inspired by Jesus. To them we too send a message of humble solidarity and prayerful hope. May the suffering of today's prisoners in the Asian jails give birth to a genuine renewal of ourselves and our communities of believers.

VI. Future tasks

Coming to the end of this conference, we feel the need to continue the search we have initiated here. To keep alive our efforts towards a theology that speaks to our Asian peoples, we see the following tasks before us.

1. We need to continue deepening our understanding of the Asian reality through *active involvement* in our people's struggle for full humanity. This means struggling side by side with our peasants, fishermen, workers, slum-dwellers, marginalized and minority groups, oppressed youth and women so that together we can discover the Asian face of Christ.

2. Our theology must lead us to transform the society in which we live so that it may increasingly allow the Asian person to experience what it means to be fully alive. This task includes the transformation of our church structures and institutions as well as ourselves.

3. We shall continue to assist in the development of a relevant theology for Asia through constant interaction and mutual respect for the different roles we have in the struggle, as professional theologians, grassroots workers and church people.

4. We seek to build a strong network of alliance by linking groups who are struggling for full humanity nationally and internationally. The following concrete actions taken in the course of the conference show the beginnings of this network:

a) a letter of solidarity with 76 boat people in Hong Kong who were arrested on their way to petition for better housing;

b) a public statement by the Sri Lankan delegation pledging to support the Tamil-speaking people in their struggle for their just rights;

c) a message to Bishop Tji of Korea, supporting the Korean struggle and regretting the absence of the entire Korean delegation at the conference;

d) a letter to the Kawasaki Steel Corporation, Japan, protesting the export of pollution to other Asian countries;

e) a telegram to the Latin American bishops as well as to Pope John Paul II, expressing deep concern for the CELAM conference in Puebla, Mexico;

f) solidarity with the Filipino participants in their protest against the pollution caused by the transfer of high pollutant industries and the erection of nuclear power plants.

5. We are concerned about formation programmes in our training institutions and the life-style of our pastoral leaders. The experiences of the conference make it clear that there must be new emphases in our theological and pastoral policy. We need to evaluate our parish and diocesan structures to assess where they alienate us from the poor masses of Asia and give us the image of might and power. We urge that necessary adjustments be made so that our religious personnel may be more deeply in touch with the problems of our people.

6. In order to facilitate the implementation of our tasks, we have formed the Ecumenical Theological Fellowship of Asia.

For two weeks eight of us, participants at this Asian Theological Conference, have tried to grapple with the contemporary call of the Asian poor and oppressed.

The prayerful silence in worship and the unity in faith helped to keep our communion in dialectical and creative tension.

As Christians we see the urgent tasks of renewing ourselves and the churches in order to serve our people.

To this sacred and historic task we humbly commit ourselves and invite all Christians and people of goodwill everywhere to participate in this ongoing search.

NOTES

[1] This is not to deny the presence of other-worldly or escapist elements in widely divergent Christian expressions among the poor. These elements may be, simultaneously, a protest against a present condition of felt impotence and an appropriation of elements from outside the community. The protest asserts: "This condition will not endure forever."

[2] Cf. for example, ALFREDO FIERRO's criticisms of recent theological developments in Latin America in his book *The Militant Gospel*, pp. 323-329. London: SCM Press, 1977.

[3] Cf. REINHOLD NEIBUHR: *Moral Man and Immoral Society*, p. 255: "The insights of the Christian religion have become the almost exclusive possession of the more comfortable and privileged classes. These have sentimentalized them in such a degree that the disinherited, who ought to avail themselves of their resources, have become so conscious of the moral confusions which are associated with them that the insights are not immediately available for the social struggle in the western world. If they are not made available, western civilization, whether it drifts towards catastrophe or gradually brings its economic life under social control, will suffer from cruelties and be harassed by animosities which destroy the beauty of human life. .... The perennial tragedy of human history is that those who cultivate the spiritual elements usually do so by divorcing themselves from or misunderstanding the problems of collective man, where the brutal elements are most obvious. These problems therefore remain unsolved, and force clashes with force, with nothing to mitigate the brutalities or eliminate the futilities of the social struggle." London: SCM Press, 1963.

[4] Cf. MARTIN LUTHER KING.

[5] Cf. JULIO DE SANTA ANA: *Good News to the Poor*, pp. 65-80. Geneva: WCC, 1978.

[6] *Ibid.*, pp. 81-94.

[7] Cf. LEE BRUMMEL, ROBERTO E. RÍOS and CARLOS A. VALLE: *Los pobres: encuentro y compromiso*, pp. 69-86. Buenos Aires: La Aurora, 1978.

[8] Cf. chapter V of this book.

[9] See JUAN LUIS SEGUNDO: *Liberation of Theology*, chapters 1 and 2. New York: Orbis Books, 1976. Also ROBERT A. MCAFEE BROWN: *Theology in a New Key*, pp. 60-74. Philadelphia: Westminster Press, 1978.

[10] Cf. *Church and State*, Faith and Order Paper No. 85, pp. 158-159. Geneva: WCC, 1978.

[11] GUSTAVO GUTIÉRREZ: *Teologia desde el reverso de la historia*. Lima: CEP, 1977.

[12] Cf. RUBEM ALVES: *Theology of Human Hope*, chapter 1. Washington: Corpus Books, 1969.

[13] Cf. FRANZ HINKELAMMERT: *Las armas ideológicas de la muerte*, pp. 135. S. José: Educa, 1977 and Salamanca: Sigueme, 1978.

[14] As JOSÉ MIGUEZ BONINO says in connection with this kind of criticism to religion (so, theology) in *Christians and Marxists: the Mutual Challenge to Revolution*, pp. 49-50: "The religious element is seen always as an ideological screen, as a false consciousness of a real human need. As an ideology, it hides from man the real nature of his alienation. On the one hand, it offers a false remedy to man's sickness — a future of transcendent heaven of peace and unity in which man alienates his human force and thus is lulled into accepting his present real hell. Marx is caustic in the denunciation of this deleterious function of religion. One need only quote one among many of his penetrating comments: 'The mortgage that the peasant holds on heavenly goods is his guaranty for the mortgage that the bourgeoisie has

on the earthly goods of the peasant.' On the other hand, religion invests the present misery with a sacred character: it is the 'opiate of the people' in the negative sense of putting them to sleep. This is the understanding on which a more militant attitude against religion has found its basis in communist anti-religious propaganda. Lenin leans to this interpretation, as is evident from his adaptation of Marx's famous dictum: Lenin speaks of religion as an 'opiate *for* the people'." London, Sidney, Auckland, Toronto: Hodder & Stoughton, 1976.

[15] Cf. JAMES CONE: *A Black Theology of Liberation*, p. 68: "Literalism always means the removal of doubt in religion, and thus enables the believer to justify all kinds of political oppression in the name of God and country. During slavery black people were encouraged to be obedient slaves because it was the will of God. After all, Paul did say 'slaves, obey your masters'; and because of the 'curse of Ham', blacks have been condemned to be inferior to whites. Even today the same kind of literalism is being used by white scholars to encourage black people to be non-violent, as if in non-violence were the only possible expression of Christian love. It is surprising that it never dawns on these white religionists that oppressors are in no moral position to dictate what a Christian response is. Jesus' exhortations 'turn the other cheek' and 'go the second mile' are no evidence that black people should let white people beat the hell out of them. We cannot use Jesus' behaviour in the first century as a literal guide for our actions in the twentieth century.... Scripture ... is not a guide which makes our decisions for us." Philadelphia: Lippincott, 1970.

[16] Cf. chapter III of this book.

[17] Cf. *Towards a Theology of People*, I, p. 174. Tokyo: CCA-URM, 1977.

[18] Cf. JETHER PEREIRA RAMALHO: "Basic Christian Communities in Brazil." *The Ecumenical Review*, Vol. 29, No. 4, 1977.

[19] Cf. JUAN LUIS SEGUNDO, *op. cit.*, chapter 5.

[20] *Concilium*, 104, 1977, pp. 11-16. New York: Seabury Press. Translated by Dinah Livingstone. Copyright 1977 by Stichting Concilium and Seabury Press. Used by permission.

X · The Role of the Church in the Liberation Process

The object of this chapter is to discuss how, in the context of the socio-politico-economic analysis already made in the first part of this book, Christian groups and churches are rediscovering from the perspective of the poor the meaning of the biblical insights about the role the people of God are called to play in the struggle for freedom and against poverty.

The number of Christians awakening and taking sides with the poor is growing. It is true that the cruelty of the struggle, the savagery sometimes seen in the conflicts, prevent Christians from sharing in the struggle of the poor and oppressed. The use of violence is still an unresolved question in this context. However, an increasing number of believers in Christ realize that conflicts bear in themselves the hopes of tomorrow. The Church is, theologically speaking, the sign of the new humanity that God wants to create through Jesus Christ (cf. Eph. 2 : 19-22).

Because of this, Christian communities active in the struggles of the poor and oppressed, as part of the community or in solidarity with the people, pose questions on the role of the Church in the process of liberation — in the combat against poverty, in the struggle for justice, participation, sustainability and livelihood.

The scandal of poverty and the challenge of the poor

The existence of poverty and poor people on so massive a scale as at present is nevertheless a scandal which challenges the Church and reminds it that the *raison d'être* assigned to it by its Lord and Master is that it should live out the radical incompatibility between the authentic evangelical and prophetic dimension on the one hand, and the increasingly contradictory and inhuman situation existing in this world on the other, and by doing so, introduce into this situation the radical novelty of "the new heaven and a new earth in which righteousness dwells" (II Pet. 3 : 13).

Reduced by modernization to a formal code of private values and general ("generous") principles, Christianity finds itself less and less capable of intervening anywhere at all in the economic sphere, of interfering in any way with the law of maximum profitability in the market processes, in the violation of human rights or the growing marginalization of certain sections of society.[1] Economic life takes its relentless course towards the death of man and nature, while some Christian groups, because of their impotence, silence or compromises, can no longer do anything to save the situation. All that Christianity can do is to lend this reality of death a spurious conscience and a spurious hope.[2]

As long as the scandal of the present situation of the poor continues, so too will our churches continue to be confronted with the following question as one of the main challenges to their credibility: Do they live out the struggle for justice as the practice of their Christian faith, and the proclamation of God and his purpose as the complete victory of this practice in human history — as the disturbing witness to the liberating God who "arises" to set oppressed people on their feet again? What is at stake is the credibility of the Church of Christ as a sign and witness established by God in this world in order to reveal here his glory and to manifest his salvation.[3]

Ecclesiastical bodies cannot be seen as monolithic institutions. If it is true that for centuries the establishment in the churches has been allied with the powers that dominated societies (as the ecclesiastical one among them), it is also true that the people have been active in the churches, and that institutional Christianity has opened itself from time to time to people's expectations.[4] This non-monolithic character has become even clearer in our times, with the plurality of opinions prevailing in the churches.

Twofold conversion of the Church

Hence the need for a twofold conversion of the Church, a twofold baptism, a twofold "immersion".

1. First of all, an indispensable conversion to the Word of God as God's praxis in history for the salvation of mankind.[5] The constant invitation to the Church is "to *continue* in my word" (John 8 : 31), "to *act* in the truth" and "to *walk* in the light as He is in the light". This is the indispensable condition for having "fellowship with one another" and for "the blood of Jesus" to cleanse us "from all sin" (I John 1 : 6f.). Prior to being an ethic, the Word of God is an amazingly efficacious historical praxis which "upholds the universe", just as "my word . . . that goes forth from

my mouth ... shall not return to me empty but ... shall accomplish that which I purpose, and prosper in the thing for which I sent it" (Isa. 55 : 11). "In many and various ways God spoke of old to our fathers by the prophets; but in these last days He has spoken to us by a Son, whom He appointed the heir of all things, through whom also He created the world. He reflects the glory of God and bears the very stamp of his nature, upholding the universe by his word of power. When He had made purification for sins, He sat down at the right hand of the Majesty on high" (Heb. 1 : 1-3).

God's will for the Church was that it should be the place *par excellence* where his word abounded: "Let the word of Christ dwell in you richly" (Col. 3 : 16); the dwelling place of "the word made flesh" where we are to "see his glory, glory as of the only Son from the Father", "full of grace and truth" (John 1 : 14); the place where the Word of God "lays bare" and is "living and active, sharper than any two-edged sword ... discerning the thoughts and intents of the heart" (Heb. 4 : 12). In short, conversion to what St John wrote in the Apocalypse: into servants like John "who bore witness to the word of God and to the testimony of Jesus Christ" (Rev. 1 : 2), and to what is declared by the servant of Yahweh: "The Lord God has given me the tongue of those who are taught, that I may know to sustain with a word him that is weary. Morning by morning he wakens, he wakens my ear to hear as those who are taught. The Lord God has opened my ear ..." (Isa. 50 : 4f.).

2. "Immersion" in the history of the oppressed: Next to conversion to the Word as God's praxis in the history in which He reveals his glory comes baptism, that is, "immersion" in this same history as the location of "the birthpangs of this expectant creation which waits for the revealing of the sons of God" (Rom. 8 : 19-21). "The whole creation has been groaning in travail until now" (Rom. 8 : 22). The poor and the oppressed long for their liberation, for a more just and a more fraternal, participatory world.[6] History, whether ancient or modern, is one great building site where the work is always unfinished. What is taking place here is a creation still in progress, constantly unfolding, whether by advance or by retreat, with its heights and its depths. The poor and the oppressed are hammering out here their own liberating praxis, whether within the Church or outside it, whether with the Church or against it. In the last two centuries, this liberating praxis has been developed overtly despite the Church or by ignoring it in practice.[7] Yet this praxis is authentically human in its profoundest levels. It is "loaded" with hope right at the heart of the struggle and the suffering for a more fraternal world, even if this thirst for justice

operates ambiguously as always in our human condition, always historically and contingently, always exposed to the dangers of being dragged
back, domesticated and established in a new form of oppression once it
has achieved power as history continues to illustrate to us. It is nevertheless a groping for a certain absolute anchored in the very centre of the
human heart, for the human being has been created in the image and likeness of God.

The life of the Church in the context of liberation

In this struggle for more justice, moving towards a world that is more
fraternal despite its contingencies and limits, the oppressed have not
recognized in the Church this witness on behalf of the peoples, a sign
established by God among the nations. Christian institutions, for their
part, have not been able to read in it the signs of the times.[8] How often
fear has been the standard reaction in ecclesiastical institutions to this
march of the oppressed. Is this due to the moralizing attitude of the ecclesiastical bodies, or to their inability to read these signs of the times, when
in fact they should grasp the deep inspiration and breath of life in what is
being built? Has this fear also been prompted by apprehension about the
loss of certain acquisitions and privileges, a certain mode of existence, a
way of life, the risk of being upset by what is being lived elsewhere? Does
this pose the temptation to exclusion and withdrawal?

God's practice and the praxis of the oppressed

Yet, all through the Bible we observe that nothing that men do, create,
invent, undertake or construct frightens God, even an act of defiance as in
I Sam. 8, when the people demanded a king.

The God of the Bible, the God revealed in Jesus Christ, is a God who
is not afraid of human beings, and because He is not afraid, He does not
set up barriers. On the contrary, He pulls down those that exist, those that
men are constantly putting up between one another. Jesus is not the
bringer of a new morality, but the friend of people, passionately concerned for human beings, seeking out those that they wanted to exclude
and isolate by barriers. He compromised himself with them, only to end
up himself "hanged" on a "barrier", a tree (Deut. 21 : 22; Gal. 3 : 13) on
account of his practice of destroying barriers: "For He is our peace, who
has made us both one, and has broken down the dividing wall of hostility
. . . that He might reconcile us both to God in one body through the cross,
thereby bringing the hostility to an end" (Eph. 2 : 14-16).

The eschatological tension of Jesus' practice and human history

From end to end of the gospels, especially that of John, it is impressed upon us that the Word was made flesh, dwelt among us, and we have seen his glory (John 1 : 14). Jesus was a real man, fully human, that is the experience that the Gospel conveys. But in that human life of Jesus of Nazareth, John translated for us another reality which it reveals: the glory which He had from the Father.

That life of Jesus of Nazareth did not begin or end within the limits of merely human reality; that reality bore the glory of God — that glory that was manifested in a very precise moment, unexpected for the people. In St John, the whole life of Jesus of Nazareth bears the mark of his hour (John 16 : 16-24, especially v. 21). There is an hour which must come: the hour has come for the woman to give birth (John 16 : 21). Jesus' hour is the time to reveal his life, where it came from and where it is going, to show forth the full dimensions of his human life. In other words, in Jesus of Nazareth we have a fully human being who opens out a much vaster dimension and goes very much farther into human reality and much farther than human reality. By opening out completely his own human history in this way, He opened it out for the whole of humanity. Jesus returns to the Father, but with all humanity, so as to bring it into the place from which He came (John 17 : 24; 14 : 2).

The incarnation of the Word is not static; it is a whole itinerary, a path. Jesus is thus continually travelling with us on new roads to Emmaus, adapting himself to the weakness of our intelligence and short-sighted views, desiring as the sole sign of his presence the sharing in the Word and the Bread. Is not the first community of believers described in the Acts as the "way" (Acts 9 : 2; 18 : 25-26)?

Human history as the locus of the eschatological Pasch (Passover)

The God of the Bible is the God who passes, who gets human beings on their feet and on the move. He is the God of the nomads; with him there is no stopping. God moves through the life of Abraham, comes to Moses, goes into Egypt to make his people pass from oppression to freedom, sends Elijah to face Jezebel and the false prophets, and so on. He passes indeed so straight that He is only seen from behind. By the time we realize who He is, He has already passed. It is always a case of going after him, following in his steps.

The incarnation of the Word in Jesus of Nazareth is part of the same dynamic movement. It is essential for Jesus to be in this world, to be that human reality He was, but it is also essential for him to pass from this world: "It is good for you that I should go." The hour to which Jesus was looking forward eagerly was the hour of his passing from this world to the Father, not out of contempt for this world, but so that we might go with him.

And now, after his resurrection, He continues to "go before us" and awaits us "in Galilee", that "Galilee of the Gentiles", the "Galilee of the poor", we could say, the land of hope where "the people who sat in darkness have seen a great light, and for those who sat in the region and shadow of death, light has dawned" (Matt. 4 : 16).

The Kingdom as radical novelty

Christ became man to inaugurate the Kingdom of God as a radically new reality at the very heart of the human condition. "Behold! I make all things new" (Rev. 21 : 5). "If any man is in Christ there is a new creation; the old has passed away; behold the new has come. All this is from God ... (II Cor. 5 : 17). St John tells us in fact that "God so loved the world that He gave his only Son that whoever believes in him should not perish but have eternal life. For God sent the Son into the world, not to condemn the world but that the world might be saved through him" (John 3 : 16f.), who, "although He was a Son, [He] learned obedience through what He suffered; and being made perfect, [He] became the source of eternal salvation to all who obey him" (Heb. 5 : 8f.).

The Kingdom of God is that element of reality in history which opens the road to fulfilment of God's purposes for the world. That is to say, the Kingdom of God opens the way to the fulfilment of the human future. Those who shape the future, rejecting change and this radical novelty of the Kingdom, are closing themselves to its reality. This is why Rubem Alves points out: "Perhaps this is why the Gospel is so sceptical about the wealthy and the powerful, to the point of exclaiming: How difficult it is for a rich man to enter the Kingdom of God! The rich and the powerful want to preserve their 'now'. The Kingdom, on the contrary, is the presence of the future that forces men out of every 'now' towards a new tomorrow. The suffering of the slave, however, is no virtue. If it were, the slave would have to find his happiness in the act of his suffering. He could not have the right to hope to overcome it. Suffering is rather the starting point for the dialectics of liberation that negates the old and stretches itself, in hope, towards the new."[9]

This reality of the Kingdom is manifested through all those who strive for justice, fellowship, joy, peace, love, participation. People's movements, communities of believers of other faiths, men and women with ideologies foreign to Christianity, when they seek the values just mentioned, are looking for this reality called the Kingdom of God.

The Kingdom as liberating power

This gift which comes to us from God in Jesus Christ through the Spirit is a *power* of resurrection, "the power of an indestructible life" (Heb. 7:16), a liberating power. "For freedom Christ set us free" (Gal. 5:1). The Gospel is the proclamation of this deliverance in Jesus Christ by the power of the Spirit.[10] It is a total liberation which goes right to the roots of our human condition, to the very root of our sin, of every form of injustice and exploitation, the spring of the breach of all the bonds of friendship and love. "He who does not love remains in death. Anyone who hates his brother is a murderer" (I John 3:14b-15a).

Consequently, the Kingdom must not be sought out in our human world, but at the heart of historical realities. As St John stresses most emphatically in chapter 3 of his first epistle, it is impossible to interpret this liberation in any purely spiritualizing way, such as we find so deeply rooted in certain Christian circles. Starvation and injustice do not point merely to economic and social problems; in a more inclusive sense they are human problems which represent a challenge to our very way of practising our Christian faith. Love and sin are historical realities which are experienced and practised in concrete situations. This is why the Bible speaks of liberation and justice in opposition to the enslavement and humiliation of the poor in history and the Book of Proverbs tells us that "God guards the paths of justice" (Prov. 2:18) and "he who oppresses a poor man insults his Maker" (Prov. 14:31a). We see God "rising up" whenever injustice becomes flagrant and intolerable. "Because the poor are despoiled, because the needy groan, I will now arise", says the Lord; "I will place him in the safety for which he longs" (Ps. 12:5). Injustice is a challenge to his sovereignty over history (for example, Amos chapter 4).

Liberation and the incarnation of the Word

This liberating action is continued in an even more radical way in the incarnation of the Word: "But when the time had fully come, God sent forth his Son, born of woman, born under the law, to redeem those who were under the law, so that we might receive adoption as sons" (Gal. 4:4f.).

This gift of being his children is thus an experience in history and is continued throughout history thanks to the Spirit who makes us cry out:

"Abba, Father!" (Gal. 4 : 6). And it is by actually treating others as brothers and sisters in practice that we receive this free gift, *not in word only but in deed.* This is what it means to receive and to live the Father's love and to bear witness to his name.

Once again, this liberating love is in essence a gift which we receive gratuitously: "But God shows his love for us in that while we are yet sinners, Christ died for us" (Rom. 5 : 8). But we are all called to be witnesses and ministers of this love: "For this I toil, striving with all the energy which He mightily inspires within me" (Col. 1 : 29). It is the vocation of the Church to be the sacrament of this: "He who says he abides in him ought to walk in the same way in which He walked" (I John 2 : 6).

Liberating love as source of conflict

The proclamation of a God of love, saviour and deliverer of all human beings, and especially of the most disadvantaged, is meant to find its embodiment in history. The proclamation of this liberating love in a society characterized by injustice and the exploitation of one social class by another, or of one country by others, helps to provoke a different history and inspire challenge and conflict.[11]

The liberating praxis of the love of Jesus was an occasion of conflict, dissension and "schism" in the etymological sense of the term, the final outcome of which was the putting of Jesus to death. On several occasions John refers to this desire of the Jews to put Jesus to death because of his praxis: "This was why the Jews sought all the more to kill him . . ." (John 5 : 18; 7 : 1, 19; 11 : 53).

It was to this same praxis that Jesus was referring when He said: "Do you think that I have come to give peace on earth? No, I tell you, but rather division" (Luke 12 : 51).[12]

Liberating love as a gift and as a task to be fulfilled

In short, this liberating love of the Lord is a gift which questions and challenges us, which presses us to commit ourselves, to love "not in word or speech but in deed and in truth" (I John 3 : 18) so that God's glory might be manifested. To take up the cause of the poor and the oppressed is to acknowledge God to be true in the midst of a society rent by the conflict of classes, the existence of those relegated to the edge of society and the systematic looting of the poor countries. To choose this liberating praxis of the Lord means not just "waiting for" but also "hastening the coming of" the day of God, as St Peter reminds us. For "according to his promise we wait for a new heaven and a new earth in which righteousness dwells" (II Pet. 3 : 12-13).

Israel and God's liberating praxis: a call to the churches

God insisted on associating with himself in this praxis from the earlier times a people whose calling it would be to represent a sign in the midst of the nations, a witness for the nations (Isa. 55 : 4), a light for the nations: "I am the Lord, I have called you in righteousness, I have taken you by the hand and kept you; I have given you as a covenant to the people, a light to the nations, to open the eyes that are blind, to bring out the prisoners from the dungeon, from the prison those who sit in darkness. I am the Lord, that is my name; my glory I give to no other, nor my praise to graven images" (Isa. 42 : 6-8).

Israel's faithlessness: a word of alert to the churches

But God's experience with his people was bitter in the extreme: "From the day that your fathers came out of the land of Egypt to this day, I have persistently sent all my servants the prophets to them, day after day; yet they did not listen to me or incline their ear but stiffened their neck. They did worse than their fathers ... they went backward and not forward" (Jer. 7 : 25, 26, 24). The consequence? "God no longer knows at what point to attack his people, so rebellious have they become. The whole head is sick and the whole heart is faint. From the sole of the foot even to the head there is no soundness in it ..." (Isa. 1 : 5f).

Exile and captivity: a warning to the churches

The consequence of Israel's double crime of idolatry and injustice will be the road into exile and captivity. "You have become guilty by the blood you have shed, and defiled by the idols you have made; and you have brought nearer your day, the appointed time of your years. Therefore I have made you a reproach to the nations, and a mocking to all the countries ... Father and mother are treated with contempt in you; the sojourner suffers extortion in your midst; the fatherless and the widow are wronged in you. You have despised my holy things and profaned my sabbaths ... You take interest and increase and make gain of your neighbours by extortion; and you have forgotten me, says the Lord God ... I will scatter you among the nations and disperse you throughout the countries, and I will consume your filthiness out of you ..." (Ezek. 22 : 4, 7-8, 15).

Exile and captivity are the logical result of Israel's faithlessness, of her "prostitution", of her praxis which is an insult to the "glory" of the Lord: "For Jerusalem has stumbled and Judah has fallen, because their speech and their deeds are against the Lord, defying his glorious presence ... The

Lord has taken his place to contend, He stands to judge his people. The Lord enters into judgment with the elders and princes of his people: 'It is you who have devoured the vineyard, the spoil of the poor is in your houses. What do you mean by crushing my people, by grinding the face of the poor?', says the Lord God of hosts" (Isa. 3 : 8, 13-15).

The "remnant" and the poor of Yahweh

The churches must not forget that Yahweh in his faithfulness and mercy will raise up a "remnant" among the deportees (Ezek. 6 : 8-10; 12 : 10) and God will gather them together in exile for the messianic restoration (Jer. 22 : 3; 31 : 7). This "remnant" will be recognizable in the "poor of Yahweh" spoken of by the prophet Zephaniah: "On that day you shall not be put to shame because of the deeds by which you have rebelled against me; for then I will remove from your midst your proudly exulting ones, and you shall no longer be haughty in my holy mountain. For I will leave in the midst of you a people humble and lowly. They shall seek refuge in the name of the Lord, those who are left in Israel" (Zeph. 3 : 11-13).

Christ the "seed" of the new Israel

In fact, it is the Messiah who will be the true "seed" (Jer. 23 : 25) of the new Israel; born of the Virgin Mary, daughter of the people of Israel, of the humble remnant of Israel, whose unshakable confidence in this liberating God and Saviour who "has regarded the low estate of his handmaiden" and who has "put down the mighty" and "exalted those of lowly degree" finds incomparable expression for all ages in the Magnificat (Luke 1 : 46ff).

Jesus' practice and political practice

After He multiplied the loaves, the crowd said: "This is indeed the prophet . . . they were about to come and take him by force to make him king . . . Jesus withdrew again to the hills . . ." (John 6 : 14, 15). If at that moment Jesus had accepted kingship, He would no longer have manifested the whole dimension that He came to reveal: He multiplied the loaves and fed the people, but that is not the end of everything. Everything does not finish there in the history of those crowds: "This is the work of God, that you believe in him whom He has sent" (John 6 : 29), and Jesus announces the bread which is God's gift and which does not dispense with the other bread. Jesus announces, shows, and reveals this bread of life which pierces hearts, penetrates people to open their hearts to a hunger and thirst which will never end, and which John translates as eternal life: "Do not labour for the food which perishes, but for the food which endures to eternal life, which the Son of Man will give to you: for on him God the Father set his seal" (John 6 : 27; also Matt. 6 : 25-33). The true bread, from heaven, the bread of God, is a gift from the Father, "it is that which comes down from heaven and gives life to the world" (John 6 : 32-33).

This "bread of life" comes from farther away and has no limit. It is the "bread" which opens out innumerable possibilities for human abilities and for the future of humanity. There is no contradiction between the two actions of feeding the crowd and giving the bread of life. The contradiction is to remain on a single level. For Jesus, sin is not to be found on the moral or spiritual level only; it consists in making an absolute of some situation: "Little children, keep yourselves from idols" (I John 5 : 21); the sin consists in refusing to let this situation break up in order to begin again farther on, for the heart of the human being remains hungry and thirsty even when satisfied with bread: "Blessed are those who hunger and thirst for righteousness, for they shall be satisfied" (Matt. 5 : 6).

Jesus Christ and the exercise of power

Power is understood as the exercise of influence, through coercive or non-coercive means, in order to achieve the aims defined by those who are exercising influence. There are different kinds of power: economic, social, intellectual, military, and so on. Jesus had to face various manifestations of power: religious (the Scribes and the Pharisees, Matt. 21 : 23-27; Mark 11 : 27-33; Luke 20 : 1-8); social and cultural (the Saducees, Luke 21 : 27-33); political (Pontius Pilate, Luke 23 : 1-25 and parallels). These powers, according to the witness of the Gospel, can be understood as dehumanizing powers. Jesus' power, however — the power of his Kingdom — is not a power like that of others, because his "Kingdom is not of this world" (John 18 : 36).

This has been understood by representatives of established theologies to mean that a sharp division has to be established between Christianity and the powers that be. The result has been an implicit support of the powers by ecclesiastical institutions (though this has not always happened). Unfortunately this position does not see the problem of the relationship between Jesus and the worldly powers in a larger perspective.[13]

For Jesus of Nazareth, the important thing is that He comes from the Father and goes again to the Father. Being the Son and only the Son, this is the very heart of his being and his existence. He joyfully acknowledges this gift. It is this which makes him the poor man *par excellence.*

To be a disciple of Jesus Christ is to be always referred further on, for Jesus is the Son and refers us constantly to the Father who is the inexhaustible source, like the burning bush. In the case of Jesus any cult of personality is ruled out because of this constant reference back (and forward) to the Father.

The whole action and the whole being of Jesus of Nazareth run counter, therefore, to absolutism of any sort, to everything which closes things down. On the contrary, He constantly releases fresh energies, new perspectives, new creations: "Behold, I make all things new" (Rev. 21 : 5).

If the Church claims to be prophetic, if it is the continuation of the prophets in Jesus Christ through the Spirit, it owes it to itself to become aware of, and to proclaim, God's absolute and that of the human created in God's image, by denouncing the power of every idol, the power of all that hinders human potentialities, and the power of all closed systems, the power of every absolute trust in anything which is no more than a human creation, beginning, of course, with itself in its own institutions and in its own life-style.

At the very end of the Gospel of Matthew, Jesus says: "All power has been given unto me in heaven and on earth" (Matt. 28 : 18). The Risen Christ disposes of all power and it is this power which He confers on his Church.

In the Gospel of St John, we find Jesus telling Pilate, his judge: "Yes, I am king. My kingship is not of this world. . . . For this I was born, and for this have I come into the world, to bear witness to the truth" (John 18 : 36f). The same set of problems is also met with in the synoptic gospels, in respect of Jesus and power. In the temptations in the wilderness, the tempter says to Jesus: "If you are the Son of God, you have all power; command these stones, therefore, to become loaves of bread; rule over the nations of the earth" (cf. Matt. 4 : 1ff and parallels). As we saw previously, we find the same temptation again in chapter 6 of the fourth gospel, in the story of the multiplying of the loaves. Jesus rejects all this. This is not the road He has mapped out for himself.

What matters for Jesus is this: "All power has been given me." For Jesus, his power, his kingship, is a gift which He receives, a gift of the Father. And Jesus does not jealously take tight hold of what has been given him, as if it were something He had stolen (cf. Phil. 2 : 6ff).

Consequently, "as Christians and churches we cannot speak about or work for a new world order in the midst of situations of domination and structures of oppression without referring to the liberating power of Jesus Christ. He liberates us from sin, both personal and social. We recognize that the Gospel expresses this liberating strength. The prophetic word of Yahweh's drawing near to the humble, to the powerless, finds an echo in fundamental passages of the Gospel (Luke 4 : 17-21; Matt. 25 : 31-46, and others). The Gospel has been brought to the poor, to the powerless, to the oppressed, to the captives, to the sick. In the person of Jesus, Yahweh has put himself decidedly in the place of the poor; He has searched for those who are 'nothing' (I Cor. 1 : 26-31). The word 'nothing' refers not to intrinsic moral quality but to the very fact that the poor are marginal, leaving their very destiny to the powerful." [14]

It is in this line of thought that the relationship between Jesus and the powers helps us understand the role of the Church in the process of liberation.

The Church: new Israel

The "seed" of the new Israel is presented to us by St Paul as he who "is before all things, and in him all things hold together". He is also "the head of the body, the Church" (Col. 1 : 17-18) which is "the fullness of him who fills all in all" (Eph. 1 : 23). This Church, the combination of the strength of God and the weakness of man, of the grace of the Spirit and the sin of man, of the power of resurrection and the weight of death — this Church is a supreme sign of tension and paradox.

For the multitude of the poor, despite the assistance received from the ecclesiastical institutions, with their undeniable signs of renewal and of hope, ecclesiastical bodies seem often to have been in their practice in history an obstacle, a barrier between Christ and human beings, or else simply ignored. It is not easy for the people of the poor, or the poor of the peoples, to recognize in it this sign set up in the midst of the nations, this witness for the peoples and this lamp "on a stand" which is meant to "so shine before men ... that they may give glory to your Father, who is in heaven" (Matt. 5 : 14).

The Church as "sacrament"

Following its Master, the Church is called in the strength and power of the Spirit to be the sacrament of this eschatological tension, this Pasch, this "passing", brought into the history of humanity by the death of Christ on the cross and by his resurrection from the dead. It is not required to possess economic and political proficiency.

Christ through his Pasch broke open our human condition of mortality, engrafting eternity on it, thus opening out the history of mankind to the fullness of the Kingdom. The last word will never be said as long as Christ has not yet "filled the universe" (Eph. 4 : 10), recapitulating in himself all humanity by leading it to the Father: "All is yours; and you are Christ's, and Christ is God's" (I Cor. 3 : 22-23).

Christ willed his Church to be the sacrament of his plenitude (Eph. 3 : 19), comprising the universe renewed and ruled by the Lord, the sacrament of "all is yours, and you are Christ's, and Christ is God's". He willed it to be the "salt of the earth", the "light of the world" (Matt. 5 : 13-16), and the "leaven in the midst of the masses" (Matt. 13 : 33).

When the Church "loses its savour" and ceases to be the leaven at the heart of the struggles for liberation and the fight of the oppressed for greater justice and fraternity, when its "light" weakens on the path of those who bend under the burden only in order to straighten up and get on the move, the Church is failing in its mission as a particularly favourable meeting-place for the liberation effected by the oppressed and the salvation offered in Christ, thus opening out to that liberation its true dimension in Christ which is to share in the building of the Kingdom.[15]

The Church's mission is not to be a member or guarantor of political and economic powers and authorities, established or to be established. Its mission is not limited to the political order. The political order is not a priority for the Church. Rather, its mission is to be always on the move, to get people going,[16] to live this "passing" with suffering humanity, to be the witness in the midst of unjust human realities, social, economic and political, of that hope which "does not disappoint us, because God's love has been poured into our hearts through the Holy Spirit which has been given to us" (Rom. 5 : 5). Its mission is to be always in the breach in defence of the right of the oppressed: "The people of the land have practised extortion and committed robbery; they have oppressed the poor and needy, and have extorted from the sojourner without redress. And I sought for a man among them who should build up the wall and stand in the breach before me for the land, that I should not destroy it; but I found none" (Ezek. 22 : 29-30). Its mission is, in imitation of its founder, to be willing to become poor instead of rich in order to enrich by its poverty the combat of humanity (cf. II Cor. 8 : 9).

For if the Church were stripped of all political power and were freed from all economic wealth, having nothing more to fear or to lose, it would be freer to devote itself to the struggle to raise what is bowed down and to give back strength to what is weak, like Peter to the man who was lame from birth: "Now Peter and John were going up to the temple at the hour of prayer, the ninth hour. And a man lame from birth was being carried, whom they laid daily at that gate of the temple which is called Beautiful to ask alms of those who entered the temple. Seeing Peter and John about to go into the temple, he asked for alms. And Peter directed his gaze at him, with John, and said, 'Look at us.' And he fixed his attention upon them, expecting to receive something from them. But Peter said, 'I have no silver and gold, but I give you what I have; in the name of Jesus Christ of Nazareth, walk.' And he took him by the right hand and raised him up; and immediately his feet and ankles were made strong. And leaping up he stood and walked and entered the temple with them, walking and leaping and praising God." (Acts 3 : 1-8).

The Church's mission is to be the witness in the march of humanity to what St Gregory of Nyssa says in his commentary on the Song of Solomon: "He who truly gets up on his feet will always have to be doing it; for the man who is hastening towards the Lord will never lack space. So the man who is climbing upwards never stops going from one starting-point to another, in beginnings that never end." By taking its place by the side of the oppressed, by the tension it maintains at the heart of history, of which it is the sign and witness, the mission of the Church is to "hasten" with the Holy Spirit, in the very heart of the ambiguities of human realities, "the coming of the day of God", of those "new heavens and a new earth in which, according to his promise, righteousness dwells" (II Pet. 3 : 12-13).

The Church's mission is by that same commitment to be an anticipation already experienced of that *koinonia* in which the poor will feel at home because all men will be brothers, of one heart and soul, where none will say that any of the things he possesses are his own, but all have everything in common (cf. Acts 4 : 32). To be credible, this *koinonia* can only be lived through a diakonia, the only form of "power" that the Church must exercise.

Conclusion

In conclusion, we return to the passage already cited from St Paul: "All are yours, and you are Christ's and Christ is God's" (I Cor. 3 : 22-23). That sums it all up. What the Church has to proclaim to the poor as good news to them, is that "all things are yours": the work of creation and of human history, this is your domain. "But you are Christ's and Christ is

God's." Christ comes from further away and goes further. Being the Son, He is the poor *par excellence* and He possesses this total freedom.

Ultimately what gives the Gospel its radical character, its root, is the sign of the cross. The Jews demanded signs of power and authority, the Greeks demanded a scientific rationality, an argument (cf. I Cor. 1 : 22). But liberation, the fullness of light, authentic liberty, springs forth from the complete weakness and folly of the cross of Jesus Christ. There is no place in it for triumphalism, but only for obedience to Jesus. It is this sign of the cross that we need to be able to contemplate and constantly seek to understand in the realities of our human world and history, into which we are baptized, in order there to rediscover the strength, the power, and the radicalism of the Gospel.[17] This is an experience which must constantly be begun afresh and gone through step by step.

"But far be it from me to glory except in the cross of our Lord Jesus Christ, by which the world has been crucified to me and I to the world" (Gal. 6 : 14). It is a sign which first of all crucifies us to ourselves, to everything which we do and think or find it possible to do and think. We must place this sign of the cross over every reality, all realities. Everything has not yet been, or been said, in this world, and yet it is there that we must struggle and be passionately involved.

Everything is not perfect, everything is relative, but this sign of the cross means that everything becomes possible for us and for others, it means that something new can be done, and should be done and created. The Church must be involved in this process of change, in this struggle, in order that it may become:

1. This place where the Word of God is read and confronts the signs of the times and, at the same time, the place where the signs of the times are read in confrontation with the Word of God — in other words *a place of permanent conversion.*

2. This place of fellowship, *koinonia,* of an already experienced sharing, of the solidarity in which the oppressed can recognize themselves — in other words, according to the Book of Acts, the Christian kind of fellowship is a manifestation of his witness of the mission that the Church fulfils on behalf of Jesus and in the power of the Spirit (Acts 4 : 32-35).

3. This place of diakonia, of launching by the power of him who dwells in us, and who commits and "immerses" us in the world, in order there to reveal his justice and the power of his love — in other words, a place of eschatological tension, of Exodus and of "passover".

Therefore, the role of the Church in the process of liberation is to become the sign of this reign of justice and love, by keeping constantly before itself the picture of Jesus on the cross. The message to be proclaimed is undoubtedly one of love, but of crucified love, which remains victorious, thanks to the trust which we have in the righteousness of God. We are therefore summoned to recognize the face of Christ in that of every human brother and sister oppressed and persecuted by the injustice of human beings and by the existing structures, and to struggle together so that he or she may be less disfigured and may discover in the meaning of his or her suffering the power of the redemption which sets us upright and directs us along the road towards the light of the resurrection: "The sun of righteousness shall shine with healing in its rays" (Matt. 4 : 2).

NOTES

[1] In more than one sense, this is a result of the current process of secularization, so closely linked to the evolution of the "free-market" system. Religion has been pushed to the private sector of life: its influence on public issues is not considered relevant by those who control and handle the laws of the market, except where religion supports the dominant ideology. Curiously, something similar happens in centrally planned economies, where the rejection of the role of religion in sociopolitico-economic aspects of life is expressed in very hard terms (though at present this rejection is not as strong as in the past).

[2] This has been the case of groups who supported *coups d'état* of a reactionary kind in Latin America: the so-called group "Patria, Familia y Propriedad" ("Homeland, Family and Property") has supported them in several countries. Cf. JAIME ROJAS and FRANZ VANDESCHUEREN: *Chiesa e Golpe Cileno.* Torino: 1976. Claudiana.

[3] Cf. *To Break the Chains of Oppression*, p. 76: "For those who take this point of view (or rather points of view, since there are more than one among those who are working in solidarity with the poor), '*orthopraxy*' is nearer the truth than 'orthodoxy': the latter has to link on to and give account of the former, otherwise it can be no more effective than ideological talk; very often, all it can do is reflect the ideology of the dominators. Only active involvement in the fate and struggles of the poor will achieve credibility for a message which seeks to be a sign of a new way of life." Geneva: CCPD/WCC, 1975.

[4] Cf. JULIO DE SANTA ANA (ed.): *Separation Without Hope?*, especially André Biéler's chapter, pp. 23-24. Geneva: WCC, 1978.

[5] Cf. GUSTAVO GUTIÉRREZ: "Evangelio y praxis de liberación social." *Fe cristiana y cambio social en América Latina*, p. 244: "In this context, theology will be a critical reflection in and on historical praxis in confrontation with the word of the Lord lived and accepted in faith ... To reflect on faith as liberating praxis is to reflect on a truth which is being done and not merely stated. In the last resort, our exegesis of the word, to which theology seeks to contribute, is given in deeds." Salamanca: Sigueme, 1973. Cf. also of LEONARDO BOFF: *Qué es hacer teología desde América Latina*, pp. 7-8. Lima: Miec-Jeci, 1977.

[6] Cf. Ian Fraser: *The Fire Runs*, pp. 3-41. London: SCM Press, 1975.

[7] Julio de Santa Ana (ed.), *op. cit.*, especially the chapters by Nikolai Zabolotski: "The Russian Orthodox Church and the Poor in the 19th and 20th Centuries", and Metropolitan George Khodr: "Social Action and Thought among Arab Orthodox Christians (1800-1920)."

[8] Nikolai Berdyaev: *Christianity and Class War*. London: Sheed & Ward, 1933.

[9] Rubem Alves: *Theology of Human Hope*, p. 115. Washington: Corpus Books, 1969.

[10] Cf. Jürgen Moltmann: *The Church in the Power of the Spirit*, p. 209: "The truth of Jesus' proclamation, his preaching of the Gospel to the poor, his forgiveness of sins and his healing of the sick is ratified through his giving himself up to death and his resurrection from the dead. The apostolic preaching of the calling, justification and liberation of men comes from this event of truth. But it is directed for its part towards the parousia and the resurrection of the dead, that is, the new creation. Its verification takes place between the remembrance of Christ and hope for the Kingdom through the presence of the Spirit and the power of the resurrection." London: SCM Press, 1977.

[11] Cf. Robert A. McAfee Brown: *Theology in a New Key*, p. 180: "Conversion means looking at things from a different perspective because one has been 'turned around'" (and this happens often when we are receptive to challenges). "If we look at the world from the perspective that it is *working well for us*, we simply try to preserve it as it is. If we see that the world needs *reform*, we try to make the present system work better by education and other persuasive means. But if we see that the systems *won't work anymore*, we move toward more radical change." Philadelphia: Westminster Press, 1978. Cf. also Rubem Alves, *op. cit.*, pp. 16-17.

[12] In this respect, it is appropriate to recall what is said in *To Break the Chains of Oppression, op. cit.*, pp. 64-65: "We believe that within the Christian community, where theological reflection takes place, we must clearly recognize that *our God is Father of all*, of rich and poor, and that He seeks to make the Church the sacrament of universal reconciliation in Jesus Christ. But at the same time, we must also recognize that the reconciliation God seeks and to which we are called cannot be achieved by covering up the injustice and inequality which separate his children, but by seeking to reach a situation of true brotherhood, which means that we must participate in efforts to bring true liberation and equality to the oppressed, anticipating among them the provisional signs of reconciliation in Christ."

[13] This perspective appears in *To Break the Chains of Oppression*, chapter IV, pp. 36-45. Also in the report of Section VI of the WCC's Fifth Assembly on "Human Development: the Ambiguities of Power, Technology, and the Quality of Life", paras 35-40. David M. Paton (ed.): *Breaking Barriers: Nairobi, 1975*, pp. 129-130. Grand Rapids, Mich.: Wm B. Eerdmans, and London: SPCK, 1976.

[14] *Ibid.*, p. 130.

[15] Cf. James Cone: *Black Theology and Black Power*, pp. 62-115. New York: Seabury Press, 1969.

[16] See Robert McAfee Brown, *op. cit.*, pp. 162ff, especially 179-182.

[17] The Greek word which indicates this attitude of mind, this spirituality in the struggle, is *parresia.* It appears few times in the Gospels, but is transparent in each gesture and speech of Jesus. His life expresses better than anything else the meaning of evangelical boldness — *parresia.* This is the word used by Luke in Acts 4 : 13 describing the attitude of Peter and John when they were arrested in order to be tried. *Parresia* is needed to give witness to the Word of God (Acts 4 : 29). *Parresia* is the fruit of conversion, as St Paul's experience proves. Since his conversion (cf. Acts 9 : 20-30) he preaches the Gospel with *parresia* till the end of his life (Acts 28 : 31). For this, the Spirit sustained him as all other believers — that is the work of the Parakletos (John 16). The normal context of *parresia* is conflict. It is what helps to overcome fear, shyness, weakness ... It is normal for those who preach the Gospel, because the "Good News" brings conflict into the world. "Because of this, *parresia* is a constitutive element in ecclesial life in any period in which God's action in history is intensively experienced". Cf. DAVID MOLINEAUX: *La Audacia Cristiana — Parresia en el Nuevo Testamento,* in *Páginas,* No. 07, p. 16ff. Lima: CEP, December 1976.

3.
The Way Ahead:
Proposals for Action

XI · Evangelization, the Bible and Liturgy in the Church of the Poor

The purpose of this chapter is to reflect upon evangelism, Bible reading and the liturgies of the churches of the poor. A theology of the underdogs is expressed through preaching of the Good News of God to human beings, through new ways of considering the written witness of the Word of God, and new manifestations of Christian worship. It is at these levels that Christian communities find the Church of the poor manifests itself similarly.

The poor: evangelized and evangelists

The teachings of Jesus were heard by the poor as "good news" (Luke 7:22). But that proclamation was substantiated by concrete facts that made the poor hopeful and happy: the sick were healed, the blind could see again, the lepers were cleansed, the dead were raised up, and the oppressed tried to break the structures of captivity in which they were caught. Simple-minded people — fishermen, persons without education — received the power to do the same. This is the meaning of the call to the twelve, who received authority from Jesus "over all demons and to cure diseases, and He sent them out to preach the Kingdom of God and to heal" (Luke 9:1-2; Matt. 10:1, 5, 7-11, 14; Mark 6:7-12). The poor received the Good News, and also the power to communicate the Good News to others.

The history of the Christian Church is proof that privilege of the poor has not been exclusive to the disciples of Jesus. Over centuries, the Gospel has been communicated through the words and deeds of persons who generally were neither rich, nor powerful, nor highly placed in their own societies. Of course, there have been exceptions, but it is possible to say that the message of the love of God with promises of justice and liberation to all human beings has been channelled mainly through the poor themselves. Unfortunately, the separation that took place between the ecclesiastical bodies and the poor has not favoured the continuation of this process.[1] What is more, the close relationship between ecclesiastic institutions and powers that dominated in society, made people doubtful about the liberating and saving strength of the Gospel.

Fortunately, the concern of the Church to be with the poor, to be the church of the poor, is increasingly manifested in our time.[2] As previously indicated, there are sectors of the churches which have taken a conscious option to work *with* the poor, and by doing so they affirm that they are "rediscovering the Gospel" through the sharing of the life, the expectations and the struggles of the poor. Through this experience they can not only say that the poor receive the Gospel, but also that they are the true evangelists of our time.

What does this mean? Is there not a danger, in such an affirmation, of idealizing the poor? Can it be true that they preach "good news" when their lives, due to the oppression they suffer, are expressions rather of evil than of "abundant life"? First, the poor bear in themselves a clear judgment of prevailing social, economic and political structures which generate oppression and inequality. The lack of satisfaction of their basic human needs is a verdict condemning a life-style of affluence and waste, of which a minority is guilty in today's world. This is the experience all those live through who try to share the life of the poor from a situation of wealth: they experience a feeling of uneasiness, almost of guilt, which moves them to change, to repent, to be converted. In this sense, the poor are a challenge to the rich to a new life.

Secondly, through all the evils they suffer, the poor are bearers of hope. They know that they have almost nothing to lose, but expect much. Their hopes are not easy ones. Their expectations cannot be fulfilled from one day to the next. They long for what they want. But they do not give up! For centuries, indigenous communities in Latin America have been standing up for their rights. For centuries, African people have been struggling for freedom. For centuries, Asian communities have been claiming justice and respect for their cultures. For centuries workers everywhere have been looking for a more just and participatory society. For centuries, women have been longing for acknowledgment of their rights as human persons *de facto*, and not only *de jure*. And, what is more important, they have paid the price for it, and they are ready to continue to do so. Their costly hope has the support of their historical involvements.

Thirdly, when we look back in history, it is clear that change has been produced by people who were not in power, but were rather looking for reform of economic, social and political structures. Of course, the results achieved were not entirely what they expected; nevertheless there was progress on the structural level. In this sense too, the poor are bearers of good news.

Fourth, the poor are those who provide the signs of the Kingdom of God. Their life is more naturally a life of sharing than the life of the rich, who are very much conditioned by the demons of possession and individualism (cf. Luke 12 : 16-21). The poor more easily experience joy than those who are trying to accumulate wealth. In this too they bear the marks of the Kingdom, which is not "food and drink, but righteousness and peace and joy in the Holy Spirit" (Rom. 14 : 17). Perhaps the clearest signs of the Kingdom that they manifest are, on the one hand, their claim for justice and equity and, on the other, their claim for participation, an idea that cannot be separated from the meaning of Christian fellowship, of *koinonia*, a real expression of the Kingdom of God in history.

Because the poor judge the wrong ways of the powerful and the rich, calling them to repentance, because they are bearers of hope, because they bring change into historical reality, and because they provide signs of the Kingdom of God, it is possible to affirm that they are *heralds of the Gospel.* This implies that the Church is not the real Church if it is not the church of the poor, if it does not share their struggles for justice. However, the evangelistic task of the poor is not a clear one, for their plight is ambivalent. For example, they are also called to repent; sometimes they compromise their hopes in order to survive; at other times the change that they could have brought to history has helped the rich even more. So their manifestations of the Kingdom of justice are not always clear: they are not unequivocal.

This is true. No one can deny it, unless the poor are to be idealized. Nevertheless, none of these affirmations can definitively cancel the role of the poor as evangelists, firstly, because the preaching of the message of the Gospel by ecclesiastical institutions has been and still is ambivalent: peace is a component of the Gospel, but Christian bodies have encouraged wars. Freedom is a sign of the children of God, but Christians have participated in colonial oppression and slave trading. That is to say, Christian institutions have compromised in many ways, and very often, in the preaching of good news to non-Christian peoples. Ambivalence has to be overcome through faithfulness to Jesus, and this implies paying the cost of discipleship for which one of the requirements is not to compromise with Mammon.[3]

In the second place, no Christian community has the right to disqualify the poor as evangelizers unless the members of the community are ready to share their life, hopes and struggles with the poor. Christian groups whose ministry is *with* the poor find an evangelistic power among the needy and the oppressed. They also find that, among the poor, their voices are not dissonant from the Word of God. There is a new kind of evangelization being developed among the poor which is characterized by effective appropriation of the message of Jesus by oppressed people who eagerly try to make the liberating Good News of the Gospel come true.[4]

Having said all this, we must remember certain elements of the narratives of the Gospel which declare the poor to be carriers of the message of the Kingdom of God. For example, the blind who received sight from Jesus (John 9 : 1-12), and the paralytic who, for more than thirty years, had been hoping to be healed and who was liberated from his pain by Jesus (John 5 : 1-18). About the first case Jesus said that the problem was less important than the manifestation of the power of God: "It is not that this man sinned, or his parents, but that the works of God might be manifested in him" (John 9 : 3). In the second case, the paralytic himself began to witness the liberating event that happened to him through Jesus: the law (imposing the day of rest — the sabbath) was less important than God's action and the act of communicating it through the paralytic. Both persons, the blind and the paralytic, were poor. Both became bearers of the message of good news, because they lived the meaning of the Gospel.

That is to say, Jesus has a different perspective of the poor than the rich. For the rich, the poor are their chance to show how charitable they are. But for Jesus, the poor are in themselves a potential manifestation of the Kingdom. Jesus and the rich looked at the poor in different ways: Jesus saw them as mediators of the Kingdom of God. Something similar can be said about the story of Jesus healing the leper (Mark 1 : 40-45, especially vs. 44-45).

What is even more important is the fact indicated several times already in this book: that Jesus Christ himself is present incognito among the poor (Matt. 25 : 31-46). If to evangelize means to make it possible to meet Jesus Christ, then the poor are the people among whom Christ is present in unknown ways. They are also the evangelists who bear Christ, *Christophoros!*

Bible reading in the church of the poor

The Bible has often provided the dynamics for social and cultural changes throughout the history of the Christian faith. But the domestication of theology and Church has produced a view of the Bible which has robbed it of its liberating force. If our churches wish to be churches of the poor, they must rediscover this liberating power so as to use the Bible as an instrument in the struggle for deliverance from oppression and injustice.[5] The capacity of the Bible to serve as such an instrument is proved by the practical use made of it in widely differing circumstances by various groups who find it an aid to reflection on daily experiences. They use the Bible to help them in their daily life, read it for its secular message and wrestle with the biblical texts so as to obtain guidance for their political activities.[6] This approach to the Bible matches its actual character. We must grasp the fact that the Bible is a collection of documents reflecting on how peoples have lived liberation, and learn to read it as such.

At the beginning of the history of Israel we find the Exodus from the "house of bondage", the laborious journey of an oppressed people to freedom. The statements later developed in Israel relative to a theology of creation were not intended to establish a theology of the orders and to buttress the *status quo*, but speak of the creation of a human habitat — the prerequisite of real human development (cf. Ps. 8). The prophetic protest against social injustice reflects an awareness of God's direct identification with the cause of the poor and the exploited (cf. Hos. 6 : 4-10; Micah 3 : 9-12; Amos 6 : 1-8, etc.). The New Testament tells the story of Jesus Christ as an act of solidarity on God's part with the despised and the suffering. The message of Jesus Christ is a summons to human beings to be changed and to acknowledge the sovereignty of God. The trial of Jesus was a political act and proves that his enemies correctly understood his message. If we wish to claim legitimately to be his followers, we too must learn to understand him correctly. The gospels with their miracle stories document the liberation and humanization which took place at that time when, by the power of the Spirit of Jesus Christ, human life was radically changed. Paul focuses his message on the idea of justice in the sight of God (cf. Rom. 3 : 21-26), while at the end of the Bible we find the vision of a transfigured and renewed world (Rev. 21-22). The central concepts of the Bible speak above all a political language. The keywords of the Bible (justice, shalom in the OT; gospel in the NT) are not only borrowed from the political realm but clearly used and directed towards that realm.

Does this explanation iron out the dialectic between "horizontal" and "vertical" proclamation? The Bible is certainly not meant to be understood as a political pamphlet. It is and it remains the fruit of human experiences of the God who does not disappear without trace into our human history but whose purpose is to enter wholeheartedly into it.[7] Consequently it alerts human beings even today to God's work in history. And the biblical message still inspires human beings today and even creates political movements in consequence.[8]

Since Bible study leads directly to the political struggle and involves human beings in movements of opposition to poverty, exploitation and oppression, we have here a clear expression of the liberating spirit of God.[9] In fact, it is a specific mark of the Holy Spirit to create an emancipatory movement and to draw human beings into it. In the church of the poor, therefore, it is not possible to separate a "spiritual" Bible reading from a political Bible reading. Spirituality and political struggle are inseparable and the study of the Bible is an essential element in the development of a new spirituality, a spirituality in the struggle of the poor.[10]

But to describe the Bible as a collection of documents of a theology of liberation is still not sufficiently precise. Liberation is no isolated, disconnected act but something accomplished always in processes rich in contradictions and conflicts. The biblical books also provide evidence of these conflicts. For example, behind I Sam. 8-10 there are two very different political positions.[11] Amos 7 : 10ff narrate the direct clash between two theological positions and their political background.[12] And when Paul and James express different theological opinions (compare Rom. 3 : 28 with James 2 : 14 and context), the explanation is to be sought in contrasting social contexts. At all events, behind the biblical tradition many concrete choices are visible which did not avoid conflicts and when necessary even invited and produced them.[13]

In this connection a lot can be learned from the way in which the canon of the New Testament came to be established. It reflected a discussion of theological principles the outcome of which was the present collection of New Testament writings with all their mutual tensions. The last inference that could be drawn from this combination of documents into a single book is that it represented an attempt to iron out the tensions between them. On the contrary, the purpose was to *affirm* them. The best proof of this is the fact that the *Diatesseron*, Tatian's Harmony of the Gospels, failed to establish itself in the Church.[14]

Once it is recognized that in establishing the canon the early Church was not seeking to cover up theological differences, which in fact always represent a divergent interpretation of social reality, the way is open to a *conflict-oriented Bible reading* which can help us better understand and describe contemporary social conflicts.[15] Since the struggle of the poor against exploitation and oppression includes conflict as an essential factor, a Church which wishes to be a church of the poor should not discourage but rather promote conflict-oriented Bible reading of this kind. It is both politically necessary and, as we have seen, biblically justified.

Obviously this approach to the Bible calls for new forms of Bible reading. It needs discussion in groups and between groups. When people from different backgrounds (of race, class or status) arrive at a deeper understanding of their world as a result of common Bible study and are thereby inspired to social action, Bible reading becomes itself an element of social advance.

We should realize that every kind of Bible reading is culturally and socially conditioned and has political consequences. If the churches wish to be churches of the poor, they will have to promote forms of Bible reading which play an emancipatory role in the process of liberation. Every Bible reading achieves its *precise* significance only through social involvement. Conflict-oriented, emancipatory Bible reading only achieves its precise significance when the poor are the subjects of such social actions and not merely their objects. Conflict-oriented Bible reading is an element in dynamic catholicity which can see itself as *one* movement in the process of liberation, even if it finds expression in widely differing choices and actions.

Liturgy in the church of the poor

There is a distinct tension in Christian worship. It is an area of freedom, an offer of "sabbath" rest, an anticipatory celebration of a new world order, but at the same time it is worship with the life of everyday affairs in view, challenged by and in the conflicts of daily life. It can be genuinely Christian worship only as it lives with these conflicts. But in practice there is a constant danger of ironing out this dialectic. The liturgy is a good place to study this evasion. Although the diversity of church liturgies makes any blanket assessment impossible in practice, attention is drawn to three points which are important for any assessment of the liturgical praxis of a church of the poor.

1. The liturgies of our churches are the fruits of a long tradition. They therefore tend to conserve the past. To *avant-garde* church groups and outsiders they often seem to be fossilized. Since the traditionalist approach to the liturgy is often backward looking and involves the danger of consolidating and sanctifying the *status quo* in Church and society, it becomes

essential to make the celebration of the liturgy sensitive to contemporary experiences and especially to those of oppressed groups.

2. Even traditional liturgies have one major positive value, namely, that of providing congregations with the opportunity of discovering and developing their identity. The different liturgical traditions of the churches are an obvious form of this quest for identity in a variety of cultural and social contexts.[16]

Since liberation is not just an economic process but also includes the development of the outlook of the oppressed, the Church of the poor should make its liturgy an expression of the work and culture of the poor as a setting in which they can both discover and experience their own identity.[17]

To this end it will be vital for the liturgy to make room for the congregations to develop their own activities; their *own* natural and free activity and not some prescribed activity laid down by lectionaries and service books — which have certainly been very appropriate in other circumstances — in advance.

One main question which must be faced by a church of the poor in respect of its liturgy is this: "How can the liturgy become the means whereby the church of the poor can discover and celebrate its identity? How can the liturgy help the mass of the poor become a human community?"

3. In the Orthodox tradition we find reference to a "liturgy after the liturgy".[18] This is the point where the transfer is made from the edification and worship of the assembled congregation to the everyday life of the world.

This idea of a "liturgy after the liturgy" invites further reflection. The preparatory stage of worship has acquired such importance for many of the groups which are concerned with the renewal of worship that it can be described as a "liturgy *before* the liturgy" in which experiences can be considered, material for worship collected and the various elements in the service thoroughly weighed.

If our churches wish to become churches of the poor, this will depend largely on their incorporating people's experiences in the act of worship and making these experiences the formative principle of worship. The thoughts and feelings of the poor must find a place in the liturgical celebrations of the Church of the poor.[19]

This means that "transfer points" must be created so that everyday experiences can be introduced into worship. There are many different ways in which this can be done: for example, by project groups or action groups which deliberately prepare the services, but also and especially by using elements from daily life in worship. Suitable material should be systematically collected for this purpose and distributed. These collections of material should include:

- *People's music from daily life:* hymns and songs used in the struggle of the poor. The music and songs of the poor are a vital expression of their suffering as a result of iniquitous conditions and of their hope of liberation, of their quest for identity and their discovery of identity. Musical forms of expression are an indispensable level of communication and participation for the church of the poor.

- *Prayers and meditations* which can justifiably claim to be a relevant form of liberating spirituality.[20] In prayer, the sufferings, anxieties and hopes of people are set in their overall context by being brought before God. Prayer is a vital form of the congregation's participation in the problems of its world as well as an expression of its hope in the transforming power of God. A socially committed church must therefore be a praying church. A church which has decided to identify itself with the cause of the poor must learn to pray in the spirit of poverty.[21]

- *Secular and biblical texts*, symbolizing and describing action patterns suitable for the expression of basic human responses to life (such as fear or hope).
It is vital that the basic responses of the poor should irrigate the worship of the churches. There should be a specially thorough search for symbols which can serve as a bridge between everyday experience and the Christian message. New symbols will only be possible as key themes and key words of daily life are discovered.

- *Suggestions* for a fresh understanding of the sacraments and for giving them a new form. *Baptism and the Lord's Supper* are an expression of God's involvement in the everyday world.[22] The church of the poor should regard and use them as material signs of transformation.[23] In its use of the sacraments especially, the Church's readiness and capacity to deal with the tension between the present realities of poverty and oppression and the hope of a new world order become clear. It does so when the sacraments are seen both as an anticipatory celebration of a new world and as a protest against the present structures of injustice. The Lord's Supper, in particular, is both the congregation's participation in the material problems of human beings and also its anticipatory joy in the prospect of a new world order.[24]

● *Popular symbols and elements* which play key roles in the struggle of the poor. All popular elements have their proper place here. In their acts of worship, the churches should take into account the fact that other religious and non-religious movements also play their part in the battle against poverty. Taking their forms of expression into account is an act of solidarity and a demonstration of the catholicity of the Church.[25]

NOTES

[1] Cf. JULIO DE SANTA ANA (ed.): *Separation without Hope?*, especially "Conclusion". Geneva: WCC, 1978.

[2] Cf. "Ministry with the Poor", *International Review of Mission*, Vol. LXVI, No. 261, January 1977. Also JETHER PEREIRA RAMALHO: "Basic Ecclesial Communities in Brazil". *The Ecumenical Review*, Vol. 29, No. 4, October 1977, pp. 395-397. Cf. CCPD Dossier No. 13: *Good News to the Poor*. Geneva, 1978.

[3] See JULIO DE SANTA ANA: *Good News to the Poor*, chapter 3, pp. 27-28. Geneva: WCC, 1977.

[4] DIEGO IRRARÁZABAL: "Las clases populares evangelizan: ¿cómo?" *Páginas*, Vol. III, No. 14, February 1978, p. 6.

[5] As stated by JOSÉ PORFIRIO MIRANDA: "(. . .) for the Bible law is nothing like the 'neutral arbitration' which the Greco-Roman tradition imposed on us, a so-called neutral arbitration whose unimpeded task is to preserve the *status quo* by overcoming with force whoever challenges it. For the Bible, (. . .) law consists in finally achieving justice for the poor and the oppressed of this world. Completely opposite to the defence of the *status quo*, the realization of justice not only subverts it, (. . .) the West has tried to cover this over, even by theological means." *Marx and the Bible: a Critique of the Philosophy of Oppression*, p. 30. London: SCM Press, 1977.

[6] Cf. JETHER PEREIRA RAMALHO, *op. cit.*, p. 397: "In reading the Bible, they (the poor) want to discover in it the reality of life, and in their life they want to find the reality of the Bible. They use the Bible spontaneously as an image, a symbol or mirror of that which they experience every day. They almost arrive at the point where they mix the two and say: 'Our Bible is our life'. But they do not always manage to make the connection between the Bible and life. They sometimes establish arbitrary relationships without basis in the Bible or in the reality of the life today. But this should not deter nor impede the profound intuition present in all the uses made of the Bible by the people: 'The Bible is related to life'."

[7] In a similar line, though focused on the person of Jesus, JON SOBRINO indicates: "It would be anachronistic to look to Jesus for an analysis of classes such as we find in the work of present-day sociology. Yet his general attitude makes it clear that in trying to understand justice, Jesus adopts a stance that is rooted in the poor and is meant to benefit them. Justice as a universal ideal cannot be understood or rendered operational unless one somehow does that through concrete experience of injustice. In that sense the first principle for concretizing moral

values is nothing else but the first principle of Christology itself, i.e. incarnation. One must deliberately adopt some partial stance in order to comprehend the totality." *Christology at the Crossroads: a Latin American Approach.* London: SCM Press, 1978.

8 Cf. José Porfirio Miranda, *op. cit.*, chapter 5, especially pp. 250ff.

9 Cf. José Míguez Bonino: *Revolutionary Theology Comes of Age*, pp. 89-90. London: SPCK, 1975.

10 Cf. M. M. Thomas' report, as moderator of the WCC's Central Committee, to the Fifth Assembly. David M. Paton (ed.): *Breaking Barriers: Nairobi 1975*, pp. 237-240, especially para. 31: "All these issues bring us to the need for a 'spirituality for combat' — an expression that comes from David Jenkins. (...) The rediscovery of the Bible and the liturgy is basic here. In this context the Orthodox concept and practice of *theosis*, and the centrality of the eucharist as the celebration of a humanity in community with transfigured nature, society, and cosmos, need to be redefined and reaffirmed in relation to the spirituality of contemporary struggles for the defence of the *humanum* and the unity of mankind. Let us not forget that our struggle is not merely against others but also ourselves, not against flesh and blood, but against the false spiritualities of the idolatry of race, nation, and class, and of the self-righteousness of ideals which reinforce collective structures of inhumanity and oppression. Any spirituality of righteousness must start with a turning in repentance from idols to the living God and justification by faith". Grand Rapids, Mich.: Wm B. Eerdmans, and London: SPCK, 1976.

11 Although Samuel stood for a more "democratic" position, the majority of the people (and this is the ruling principle in the practice of democracies) claimed monarchy. It is important to see that between the theoretical principle and the practice, God made an option in favour of the practice (v. 22). Justice is not a theoretical goal, but the result of people's action.

12 The controversy between Amos, a prophet of God, and Amazi'ah, the priest of Bethel, about the government of Jorobo'am is not theological in the first place, but political. But theology is not separated from politics.

13 Cf. St Paul going to Jerusalem: conflict with the Jews was unavoidable in that case (cf. Acts 21 : 15-40, especially vv. 27-32).

14 Cf. Hope W. Hogg: "The Diatessaron of Tatian". Allan Menzies (ed.): *The Ante-Nicene Fathers*. Grand Rapids, Mich.: Wm B. Eerdmans, 1951, Vol. X, pp. 35-41. Cf. Feine, Behm and Kuemmel: *Einleitung in das neue Testament*, pp. 359, 387. Berlin: Evangelische Verlagsanstalt, 1965. Also Hans Freiherr von Campenhausen: *Die Entstehung der Christlichen Bibel*, pp. 205 and 206. Berlin: Evangelische Verlagsanstalt, 1975.

15 Sergio Rostagno helps to clarify this position when he states: "(...) the practice of the ancients will not help us to 'situate' their theology. It is precisely our own practice, for which we have complete responsibility, that will help us understand the virulence of the unfortunate ancients." *Essays on the New Testament*, p. 50. Geneva: WSCF, 1975.

16 It is in this perspective that the quest for indigenization of the Church must be understood; one of its major expressions is at the level of the liturgical life of the Christian community. It must be noted that "indigenization" does not only imply that cultural elements be taken into account in the celebration of Christian worship,

but also that *social aspects* and emphases be integrated in the liturgy. Cf. KNOLLY CLARKE: "Liturgy and Culture in the Caribbean". In IDRISH HAMID (ed.): *Troubling the Waters*, pp. 141-157: see especially p. 154: "The Jamaicans have been introduced to new words through the Rastafarian movement. For example in order to describe the struggles of the poor and the difficulties they face, the word 'downpress' is used. Free love or a promiscuous person is said 'pussycratic'. To describe one's sexual urges the word 'ital' is used. It is also used to relate human nature with animals, flowers and the earth. Apart from these innovations the Rastafarians deliberately use the nominative for the accusative and objective. The example is their well known hymn 'O let the power fall on I, O Lord, let the power fall on I'. Of course Jamaicans are noted for using 'him' as the subject of their sentences. 'Him thief a bread'." San Fernando, Trinidad: Ramahan Printery, 1973.

[17] "Within this perspective there is a very vital question: creation and *liturgical freedom.* As a matter of fact, liturgy touches the daily life of community. It is very sensible and very close to life's reality." To be creative in social life means at the same time to be creative at the liturgical level of the life of the Church. Cf. J. B. LIBANIO: "Uma comunidade que se redefine". SEDOC, Vol. 9 on *Comunidades ecclesiais de base,* col. 325, October 1976.

[18] Cf. the report of the WCC Consultation of Orthodox Theologians, New Valamo, Finland, September 1977: *The Ecumenical Nature of the Orthodox Witness.* Geneva: WCC, 1978.

[19] In this sense, the best biblical example is the Psalms. Ernesto Cardenal has provided beautiful examples in putting them into present-day language and context.

[20] Cf. FREI BETTO: *Christo: Oração na Ação.* Rio de Janeiro: supplement to CEI, No. 18, July 1977.

[21] When the poor pray, their prayers are open, not formal or ritualized.

[22] I Cor. 11 : 26: "For as often as you eat this bread and drink the cup, you proclaim the Lord's *death until he comes.*"

[23] Concerning baptism, see the Faith and Order document on: *One Baptism, One Eucharist and a Mutually Recognized Ministry,* para. 7, p. 11. Geneva: WCC, 1975.

[24] Cf. TERTULLIAN: *On Patience*, MPL, T.I., Col. 1371.

[25] The WCC and CCPD have published liturgical calendars and prayer books. These efforts should be welcomed and intensified. However, suitable materials should also be published in other forms, for example, as a lectionary (as in *Risk,* Nos. 2 and 3, 1975) for direct use in public worship; as a report which includes stories of people's struggles for liberation; and as hymns, prayers and other liturgical elements, so that it will be more than just a dry document.

XII · On Church Structures

The search for a Christian Church which is really representative of the poor and shares in their struggles and expectations, their sorrows and hopes, must inevitably include the issue of Church order and Church structures. This is, of course, a delicate and sensitive matter, because the different denominations are more ready to consider innovation at the level of ideas, values and programmes than to discuss the organization of the church. However, it is becoming increasingly clear from the experiences of the different churches and Christian communities which have opted for the poor that the challenge the latter present to the Church also involves the problem of Church order.[1] At the same time, the churches which look squarely at the problem of their relationship with the poor know that most of the needy and the underprivileged are in other parts of society rather than in the Church. The poor feel that Church structures are foreign to them, whereas the early Christian communities did not (Acts 2 : 42-47; 4 : 32-37; I Cor. 1 : 26-29, James 2 : 5-7).

As we have already said several times in this work, there are in our time many Christian communities which have taken a clear option for justice and liberation in the social conflicts in our world. They are becoming increasingly involved in movements of solidarity with the oppressed and they are urging their constituencies to involve themselves in efforts to combat racism, in struggles aimed at changing social, economic and even political structures. Most of these Christian communities which opt for social transformation feel the need to show a consistent attitude in the Church. Such an option in society demands clear involvement in the renewal of the Church.[2] They recognize that the problem of Church structures cannot be tackled in the same way as the issue of the general organization of society, but they feel that sometimes Church order has to become more flexible to respond to the aspirations and needs of common people.[3] The Church is called to be the body of Jesus Christ among human beings;

that is, it is called to be the body of a servant.[4] Yet sometimes it seems as though people are called to serve the structures rather than the structures being designed to serve the people, above all the most underprivileged.

Any reform of the Church must be guided first and foremost by the action of the Holy Spirit. In the eyes of those churches which are seeking to become the church of the poor, the Spirit of God is calling the churches to repentance and transformation in the challenge of the poor to the Church today. They know that they themselves are being profoundly renewed by new gifts of the Holy Spirit when the poor begin to feel that the Church is becoming their own. The poor bring new insights and give fresh impetus to the work of the Church and call the institutional churches to change their organization and reform their structures. This is therefore not simply a question of adjustment to the signs of the times; it is a pilgrimage towards becoming an instrument of God's service in the process of human liberation, being faithful to Jesus Christ.[5]

For example, peoples all over the world — including in particular the poor — are demanding greater participation in the discussion and decision-making processes which affect their lives. More and more we hear it said that development cannot take place without the participation of the people. No matter how widely informed the people who carry responsibility for making decisions, and no matter how deep their knowledge, it is clear that the people in the pew are not prepared to resign their right to let their views be known and to take their part in the decisions that have to be made. But most of the Christian churches are still very hierarchical institutions which do not have the openness necessary to allow participation of lay people at all levels of their life.[6] A sociological analysis of how church decision-making bodies are composed shows that they tend to reproduce the structures of domination prevailing in society; these are not conducive to participation by the lowest sectors of society; women, the poor, etc. and, while most of the clergy is dependent, the inherent patterns enable clergy to dominate in a variety of ways.[7]

In this respect, *koinonia* and the eucharist are dramatic reminders of the essential oneness of the Church. The root meaning of *koinonia* points to "that which is held in common". The fellowship or the communion of the Church is premised on a common faith, a common commitment, a common task in the world. Christians share and participate in the same reality, and they are one. The recognition of the common commitment to one Lord highlights the meaning of the eucharist. It is not only a celebration of the presence of Christ in his Church, it is also a joyful thanksgiving for the transforming power of his Spirit in Christian community and in the world. The eucharist and *koinonia* belong together as aspects of a single Christian reality.

Churches which are trying to respond positively to the challenge of the poor feel that their structures must correspond to those of the community life of the people they are trying to serve. This is the experience, for example, of the Evangelical Methodist Church in Bolivia, most of whose members belong to the Aymara nation. This church has embarked on a process of transforming its structures in an attempt to serve Jesus Christ more faithfully among the people.[8] It is also the experience of some sectors of the churches in the Philippines, in South Korea and in several African countries.[9] This is to say that church structures must be adapted to people, they must be flexible enough to accept their challenges, their ideas. The basic ecclesial communities in Brazil are one example of this renewal in the Church. Instead of following an organizational pattern which maintains the vertical relationship between the superior hierarchical authority and the clergy (and keeps the laity in the passive position of a mere recipient of services who does not participate actively in the dynamics of the church), grassroots communities, in their experience, affirm the real life situation of the people of God as the main aspect of the Church, while the organization is a consequence of the reality expressed. "The power of Christ *(exousia)* is not in the hands of a few only, but in the whole people of God who bear the threefold service of Christ: witness, unity and worship. This power of Christ is diversified according to specific functions, but it does not exclude anybody."[10] In other contexts, for example in some socialist countries such as the USSR, where most of the believers do not belong to the ruling sectors of society, the existence of the Church provides the opportunity for the people to participate in religious life.[11]

This new awareness in the life of the Church poses a clear challenge to the different branches of the ecumenical movement and in particular to the WCC. For a long time, ecumenism has been the concern of exclusive circles in the churches and this seems an appropriate time for us to set about finding new ways of expressing in institutionalized ecumenical circles the kind of Christian unity that is being expressed and developed at grassroots level in many places, where unity in service and worship seem to be more easily achieved. It is an ecumenism of the people, an ecumenism of the poor which does not care about the formal aspects of Christian unity or inter-religious/inter-ideological dialogues, an ecumenism of people who believe that institutional ecumenism should follow what is being practised instead of claiming to set the norms for something that people are keen to live out.[12] This challenge is addressed not only to the WCC but also, and perhaps in even stronger terms, to ecumenical bodies operating at national and regional levels. It is essential to be alert to what lay people, women and young people are trying to practise and communicate about Christian unity. For the cause of Christian unity, orthopraxis is more relevant than orthodoxy in the minds of the poor.

The new forms of ecclesial life emerging from a church of the poor clearly emphasize that the Church, in its concrete expression at local or diocesan level, is to be understood as a community of ministries which seeks to be obedient to Jesus Christ in serving all human beings and, in particular, the poorest. The problem posed here is the following: Who takes care of the whole, who ensures order and harmony between the different charismas so that everything works together for the edification of the same body? In this connection, in Brazil, for example, those involved in the experience of the basic ecclesial communities talk about the "ministry of unity" to be exercised by the minister (the presbyter, the bishop or the lay person designated for this responsibility). This is different from the "ministry of authority" in which authority is exercised from above, sometimes even from outside the community. In contrast to this, the ministry of unity is at the centre of the ecclesial community which is trying to express the reality of the church of the poor in our time.[13] Similar experiments are being lived out in India, Africa, Italy and many other places. They are formulating new proposals for structures of churches which merit serious consideration from the authorities. We should not forget that, like the wind, "the Spirit of God bloweth where it listeth".

The ministry of unity stresses the aspect of participation, of responsibility assumed within the Christian community. The language frequently used of being "set apart" for ecclesiastical responsibility is thus unfortunate since it connotes geographical separation rather than identification with the needs of the community. Originally this language referred only to the task to be performed, as evidenced in Paul's letters. In many instances he underscores "being with" the Christian community as a crucial factor. This emphasis was maintained in the ancient Church. Church leaders have often provoked awareness of the plight of the poor in instances when the dignity of their office made their voices heard and their actions visible. The record is nevertheless a mixed one.

The churches, having shown in the last centuries of their history that they have not been, and still are not, very close to the people (cf. *Separation Without Hope?*), should give the attention they deserve to the many and varied developments going on in the life of the church of the poor. These indicate that inadequate church structures must be reformed. This does not mean that all experiences at the grassroots level need to be institutionalized. The essential thing is for them to be seen as expressions of the pilgrimage of the people of God through history, always marching forward, looking to the future, to the promised kingdom and not remaining captive to the past and its traditions (Heb. 12:1-2). We feel that, in view of this situation, the WCC should take the initiative in looking for channels and ways by which these expressions and cultures can be shared. Further search is needed in this area, not only in justice and service programmes, but also in those of faith and witness.

NOTES

[1] Cf. LEONARDO BOFF: *Eclesiogênese: as Comunidades eclesiais de base re-inventam a Igreja*, especially No. 4-5. *SEDOC,* Vol. 9, No. 95 on *Comunidades eclesiais de base,* October 1976, col. 410-418. Also, by the same author: "As Eclesiologias presentes nas Comunidades Eclesiais de Base". *Uma Igreja que nasce de povo,* pp. 201-209. Petropolis: Vozes, 1975.

[2] JOSÉ MÍGUEZ BONINO, following Diez Alegría, states in this respect: "A Christian committed to liberation becomes therefore involved in the struggle for the reformation of the Church, or to put it more drastically, for the reconstitution of a Christianity in which all forms of organization and expression will be humanized and liberating." *Revolutionary Theology Comes of Age,* p. 159. London: SPCK, 1975.

[3] Cf. among others MARCELO PINTO CARVALHEIRA, Bishop of Paraíba: "A caminhada do povo de Deus na America Latina". *Revista eclesiastica brasileira,* Vol. 38, fasc. 150, 1978, pp. 316-319. CHRISTIAN LALIVE D'EPINAY: *Haven of the Masses,* pp. 50ff. London: Lutterworth, 1969.

[4] Cf. DIETRICH BONHOEFFER: *Ethics,* pp. 17ff. London: SCM Press, 1955.

[5] MARCELO PINTO CARVALHEIRA, *op. cit.,* p. 326: "In face of the powers of this world and their capacity for manipulation to achieve their projects of technological and political greatness, the community of faith, the bearer of God's project, may feel itself filled with a feeling of impotence which saps hope. It is in this context that the christological faith becomes most decisive. In Jesus crucified God showed the destiny of the power of this world; it is not a means towards the Kingdom of God. For this God chose 'what is foolish in the world to shame the wise, what is weak in the world to shame the strong, what is low and despised in the world, even things that are not, God chose, to bring to nothing things that are' (1 Cor. 1:27-28). The mission of faith is constantly to represent and actualize that power of God, given concrete form in the way followed by Jesus Christ. That power passes through weakness, poverty and death, loving, hoping and serving all. The resurrection shows the strength of the weak: it is they who will inherit life and inaugurate the new world. The Christian community lives by this hope and is organized in the power of the resurrection. It does not fear the strong of this world, because it knows the Lord has overcome this world (John 16:33). Ultimately it is not the powerful but God who is the Lord of history and guides it to its happy ending, despite human zigzagging and the dead weight of sin."

[6] Cf. the report of the WCC general secretary, Dr Philip A. Potter, to the Fifth Assembly. DAVID M. PATON (ed.): *Breaking Barriers: Nairobi 1975,* p. 252: "Everyone has the privilege and responsibility to develop and share his or her gift in the fellowship of the Spirit. It is, therefore, the task of the ecumenical movement and of the World Council to encourage the churches to further this participation of all who are made in God's image and are empowered by his Spirit to play their part in the life of the congregation and of the community." Grand Rapids, Mich.: Wm B. Eerdmans, and London: SPCK, 1976.

[7] As it is stated in the *Report of an Asian Ecumenical Consultation on Development: Priorities and Guidelines,* pp. 59-60: on "Church and Societal Structures": "1. We recommend the decentralization of services with the attendant breakdown and relocation of service structures ... 2. We believe that elitist and hierarchical church structures no longer provide the dynamism to reflect the new ethos and promote true development with people's participation. 3. We want structures initially to be more open and receptive to genuine innovative attempts and programmes aimed at promoting this new development ethos, however unorthodox they may be." Singapore: Christian Conference of Asia, 1974.

[8] Cf. CENPLA: *Evaluación de la obra de la Iglesia Metodista en Bolivia.* Rio de Janeiro, 1978 (mimeo).

[9] See chapter X of this book.

[10] Cf. LEONARDO BOFF, *op. cit.,* col. 413.

[11] Cf. ERICH WEINGÄRTNER (ed.): *Church Within Socialism: Church and State in East European Socialist Republics,* p. 55: "(...) church life shows no signs of being moribund or obsolescent. On the contrary, indications are that religion is enjoying a revival, especially among the young, and despite Orthodox theology's essential traditionalism, the Church has not been blind to the challenge of the times." Rome: IDOC, Dossiers 2 and 3, 1976.

[12] Cf. for example STANLEY J. SAMARTHA (ed.): *Towards World Community: the Colombo Papers,* pp. 126-129, on "A Common Commitment to Reconstruct Community" and "Ways of Working Together". Geneva: WCC, 1975. Also C. S. SONG: *Christian Mission in Reconstruction: an Asian Attempt,* p. 190: "We cannot, therefore, dismiss religions, be it world religions or primitive religions, as nothing but the product of man's own imagination or his sinful nature. ... A realization such as this should make Christians at once humble and joyful — humble because Christianity is not the sole custodian of the truth of God, and joyful because the love of God in Jesus Christ also embraces those outside the Christian Church in a way that has to do with salvation." Madras: Christian Literature Society, 1975. GUSTAVO GUTIÉRREZ, from a different context says, in *Theology of Liberation,* pp. 278-279: "Unity will thus be forged not among those who say, 'Lord, Lord', but among those who 'do the will of the Father'. For the ecclesial community to recognize the fact of class struggle and to participate actively in it will not be a negation of the message of unity which it bears; rather it will be to discover the path by which it can free itself from that which now prevents it from being a clear and true sign of brotherhood." Maryknoll, NY: Orbis Books, 1973.

[13] Cf. LEONARDO BOFF, *op. cit.,* col. 414-415.

XIII · Social Involvement

One important common characteristic of the churches wherever they are opting clearly for the poor is their refusal to regard social action as an appendix to the Church's mission but rather to consider it as the form of praxis which substantiates the Christian community's proclamation of the Gospel to the poor.[1] Social involvement in this sense is an indispensable part of the Church's life. In the experience of the church of the poor, it is impossible to separate action in society from the proclamation of the liberating message of Jesus Christ. It is Christian mission.

Implicit in this view is a corrective of the idea that the proclamation of the Word is more important than social action. For those who support this latter view, the preaching of the message has a normative function in relation to social involvement. The meaning of the proclamation of the Word provides the framework within which Christian social action should operate. Usually the message is proclaimed in such a way that it transmits the outlook of the dominant group in society. There are exceptions to this general rule, of course, but they tend to attract the attention of those who control the system whereby ideas are produced and very often anyone who dares to oppose or criticize those who manipulate the levers of domination is called to order and silenced. However, if the presentation of the message is made in ways which are correlative to the praxis of the believing community, it becomes more difficult for the social implications and the meaning of the message to be controlled in such a way. This message has a substance which derives not from theory or abstract concepts but from concrete life.

A Church which is inclined favourably towards the poor knows that social involvement goes hand in hand with the presentation of the message.[2] But it must be realized that to be involved in action also means to proclaim the message. The Church is in both word and deed a "confessing community". The deeds support the preaching and the preaching accompanies the social action of the Christian community.[3] In the life of a church whose social involvement is not determined *a priori* but develops out of its alignment with the poor, it could not be otherwise. As has been stated earlier in these pages, the church of the poor not only believes that God in Jesus Christ has taken the side of the poor, but also that Jesus is himself sacramentally present among the poor today.[4] The action of the poor, their struggles for justice and liberation, must therefore be taken into account when the Church becomes involved socially and also when it proclaims the Gospel of liberation which God in Christ is offering to every man and woman, to all human beings.

Does this mean that the Church has to be like a political party? We think not. The Church is open to all; it is the gathering of the *called*, and God excludes no one from this calling.[5] If the Church becomes like a "political party", it is no longer the fellowship of the *called*, it has become an exclusive group. The church of the poor does not exclude other social groups and social classes if they express in action and in words the concern for justice and liberation for the underprivileged as manifested by Jesus at the outset of his ministry (Luke 4 : 17-21). This is the direction in which the Church looks as it seeks to be faithful to Jesus Christ: serving him among the poor, aligning itself with them. This alignment will guide political action. Jesus Christ, present in the "least" (Matt. 25 : 31-46), and the poor themselves, require the meaning of the message to be expressed in a social praxis of solidarity with the poor, made clear and specific by such social involvement.

As has already been pointed out, a constant element in the social praxis of the poor is the search for liberation. What the Hebrews wanted while they were oppressed in Egypt under the pharaonic domination was liberation for the whole of their people. What the black slave communities in the Americas wanted was liberation.[6] What the people who strove for independence from colonial power wanted was liberation. What people whose rights are being violated want is liberation. What those who feel crushed by the oppressive mechanisms which reflect the "law of the market" are looking for is liberation. Liberation, therefore, is the permanent quest of the poor and the oppressed.[7] They are sometimes so oppressed that they are unable to give effect to this search. The experience of history shows, however, that they do not give up but continue to strive: the struggle continues! And those Christian communities which are involved with them know that the struggle continues.

The social involvement of the churches implies their being aligned with the poor in their struggle. It is not social action *for* the poor. If it were so, it would have to be called social assistance rather than "social action", and social assistance implies a paternalistic approach to the poor.[8] Again, if social action were to be identified with social assistance, it could be described as not essential for the Church's mission. When the Church is aligned with the poor, therefore, and shares their concerns and struggles, the proclamation of the Gospel is substantiated by its being rooted in the praxis of liberation which opens up the way in history for a new, more just and more participatory society.

Those Christian communities which have already decided to go this way are trying to keep hope alive for the oppressed. This is a costly commitment, since it is not easy to be hopeful when poverty is as scandalously prevalent as it is now. But the churches which retain this hope and believe in Jesus Christ also believe that He is at work among the poor. They are therefore ready to persist in their hope because they have confidence in who they are and what they are about.[9] They therefore share in their resistance to oppressive power, as the churches in the Philippines did, or those in Chile, by their efforts against forces which repeatedly violated human rights. Their advocacy of the cause of the poor was a clear consequence of their alignment with those same poor.[10]

In western Europe, there are Christian communities who stand for rights of migrant workers, and who combat racism within their own societies as well as in other parts of the world. In some countries, such as South Africa, South Korea or Brazil, they have also been involved in struggles with a view to opening up new free spaces for popular action. Through commitment of this kind some of the churches in these countries have demonstrated their solidarity with the poor and the oppressed in their desire to create a better society. The intention of these churches has not been to lead the way but simply to accompany the peoples in their pilgrimage to freedom and justice.[11]

For those involved in it, this option has meant enduring a painful transformation process. It has been necessary to end old traditional alliances with those who control the mechanisms of domination from the centres of power. It has then been necessary to show solidarity with the poor without wishing to lead them or to tell them what to do. It is on the contrary the social practice of the poor themselves which gives substance to the social involvement of the churches. This is educating the Christian communities to be humble. They are not the leaders in the liberation process. They can only be the servants of the poor through involvement of this kind. And they have to be prepared to pay the price for it, as the poor have paid the price throughout history.

Witness and service inseparable

Being allied with the poor, the churches must strive for the achievement of the goals and objectives of the underprivileged: social justice, a society not subject to economic exploitation or sexist or institutionalized oppression but in which basic human needs are satisfied and life shared. In India, for example, it will mean that the churches must try to offer a radical challenge to the social system.[12] In Latin America it will mean opposing militaristic regimes which use new forms of organized national security to violate human rights and to institutionalize authoritarianism and torture.[13] In Africa, it will mean challenging the neo-colonialist structures which hold down the peoples of that continent in a state of dependence, and struggling against racist powers. In North America it will mean being in solidarity with oppressed minority groups. In Europe it will mean supporting the cause of foreign workers. Throughout the world it will mean opposition to oligarchic political operations by transnational capital, particularly when it is deeply implicated in military production and armaments trade.[14] It should be noted that it is not primarily the churches which propose involvement of this kind but above all the poor in their struggle against the evils that oppress them.

Certain sections of the ecclesiastical establishment often disregard involvement of this kind because it is viewed as merely "rhetorical". It is then asserted that the only valid action at the social level is assistance or charity. Maybe those adopting this position should listen more attentively. They would then realize that the struggle of the poor is far from being merely rhetorical. It has in practice cost the lives of hundreds of young people in Southern Africa, Nicaragua, Lebanon and elsewhere. It is a movement which demands of the churches far more than charitable aid. It calls for a practical demonstration of love in action, tackling the root causes of injustice and not merely its effects.[15] When this actually happens, the poor know that they are not alone in their struggle. Then, they can recognize the church of the poor. What is even more important, they can see the presence of Jesus Christ in the Church.

For the churches themselves, it means that there is no longer any separation between *martyria* and *diakonia*, between witness and service. Witness is substantiated by the service expressed in this concrete alignment. At the same time, the service can only be explained in terms of the proclamation, when someone enquires the reason for this service. It is impossible, therefore, for the churches to impose on the poor their own ideas as to how the struggle against the causes of oppression should be conducted or as to how hunger is to be eliminated. On the contrary, it is the churches which must be aligned with the people, in accord with the meaning of the Gospel. For example, in recent years many requests have been received from various sections of the poor asking the churches to give financial support to training courses for agents in social mobilization. In Indonesia they are known as "motivators", in certain parts of Africa as "animators", in Asia as "catalysers", and in Latin America as "agents of pastoral action". The label is not important. What really matters is that it is the poor themselves who make such a request. They feel the need to train people to work competently in the various situations they are faced with. At this level they do not want to be dependent. We believe that requests of this kind call for adequate responses from those churches which have the resources to support programmes of this kind, and also from the WCC.

To summarize our views on social involvement — on the basis of the experiences of those Christian groups and parishes which are working along the lines indicated above — it can be said that the social involvement of the churches must be seen and formulated in organic relation to the aspirations of the poor themselves. To work "in organic relation to" means to play an "instrumental role". Sad to say, however, the churches have all too often acted in society as instruments of the rich.[16] In thus acting "in organic relation to" the rich, they have been completely unjustified from the standpoint of the Gospel (Luke 18 : 24ff; Matt. 19 : 23ff; Mark 10 : 23-25). But the signs referred to in these pages indicate that the churches now wish to work in organic relation to, in an instrumental role in relation to the poor, and in this way to become the church of the poor. As already emphasized, this decision, this choice, *excludes no one who wishes to be faithful to the call of Jesus Christ.* This way, we avoid the trap of a paternalistic approach with "assistantialist" and "charitable" modes of operation. It is not a "triumphalist" option. In our view it is an option for those who wish to be disciples of Jesus Christ and who are ready to follow him where He is and wherever He is going. We therefore welcome the declaration by the Nairobi Assembly of the WCC that the churches' participation in development means "joining hands with all who are engaged in organizing the poor in their fight against poverty and injustice".[17] This is part of the prophetic ministry to which God is calling the churches, both in denouncing the unjust structures which oppress the poor and reminding men of the various signs of the Kingdom of God in history.

A call for solidarity

The Church in New Testament times expressed this concern through sharing. The community in Jerusalem shared with others the wisdom it had and the gifts of the Spirit. The community of Antioch shared with other Christian communities of that time its concern for the missionary work of the Church. St Paul asked the Corinthians and others to share their wealth with the poor of Jerusalem (cf. II Cor. 8 : 9ff). This mutual sharing must be understood as an expression of solidarity which exists among different members of the same body (I Cor. 12). The Early Church practised and affirmed solidarity. This solidarity, through other ways and means, is also manifested among the poor. They generally share the few things that they have. It is not surprising that the New Testament idea of *koinonia*, the community of those who share the gifts of the Holy Spirit and the table of the Lord, can be more really and fully expressed among the churches of the poor than in churches of rich people. It cannot be a surprise because the poor live more naturally in a sharing attitude than the rich.

However, it must be noted that the problems created by the existence of mass poverty have challenged the consciousness of the rich during the last two or three decades. In order to respond to these challenges, aid has been organized and institutionalized. Massive sums of money, tons of food, thousands upon thousands of foreign experts have been channelled from the rich to the poor. In a few cases the results achieved were good; where this happened, the main reason for it was the decisive will of the people directly concerned with the problem to change the situation. That is to say, in these cases material aid played a supportive role, being an expression of solidarity with the unprivileged. However, in most cases, the results were not in proportion to the amount of assistance given to the poor by the rich.[18] This kind of aid was not without vested interest, as recent research has shown very well.[19]

Internationally, the organization of the aid system has been mainly through the presentation of projects by those affected by given problems. They then receive (or sometimes do not) financial support through "funding agencies" (international, non-governmental, mixed, benevolent, etc.). In some cases, aid provided in this way has helped people to overcome poverty and become self-reliant. However, in most others this kind of aid has consolidated situations of domination and dependence. When this happens, there is no real solidarity, no real partnership, but rather asymmetric relationships, in the context of which the possibilities of interference by the "donors" are great.[20] Hence there is a relation of unevenness, of inequality. It is the logical result of the application of the "laws of the market" to the project system, which then becomes a "market of projects". It is clear that poverty is not being tackled at its roots when aid is channelled in this way. Aid must be in terms of solidarity, and the ways through which aid is implemented should be in accordance with solidarity.

In a perspective such as this, sharing may help to make the liberation of the poor possible, which means for all of us:

a) liberation of the exploited poor of the Third World where the vast majority of people are languishing in hunger, physical poverty, obscurity, cultural alienation and political oppression which generate all kinds of problems;

b) liberation also of the "prosperous poor" section of the world, capitalist and socialist, which calls itself "civilized" — what is more "Christian civilization" — where a tiny minority of lobbies ignore the human dimensions of their real human poverty, seeking blindly and avidly ways and means to assure their own socio-economic domination based on selfish expansion and enjoyment of possessions and, all too often, sinful and shabby interests.

So it should be noted that the exercise of solidarity liberates the rich,[21] in that, when a materially well-off Christian becomes responsibly and prophetically aware of the need for human solidarity, he also clearly sees that all of us are both rich and poor at the same time. Therefore, because we can, we must share together all the material, cultural and human potential and factors which guide our common aspirations for development, for the fulfilment of the whole human being and of all human beings (II Cor. 8:8-15).

Thus, while we are not of this world, but "placed in the world" (John 17:15-18) to regenerate it, we are all of us privileged, we are all called to reflect the immeasurable love of Christ, the Word made flesh. The Son of God who became a son of man offers to share with us all the brimming abundance of his Kingdom of justice. He asks nothing more than to have us share in the treasures of his rich and sovereign Kingdom.

Social involvement in socialist countries

One might think that the demands of social involvement of the churches with the poor are only addressed to Christian communities of the capitalist world, both in rich and poor nations, and that the churches in socialist countries are not concerned. But it must be noted that they are very much aware of the challenge that the poor put to their social involvement. For example, in a recent publication of the Evangelical Lutheran Church in Hungary, it is said of the orientation of participation of Christians in development: "Speaking of wealth and poverty we move in a vacuum unless we consider the historical development which has led in the life of mankind today to the untenable contrast between wealth and poverty. Even if we admit that it would be impossible and even wrong to realize an equal standard of living for every citizen of the world, it is also beyond doubt that the appalling contrast between wealth and poverty has been caused by the system of imperialistic capitalism, and that the radical help which, in the present situation, would go beyond occasional acts of alleviating misery, can only be given by socialism. Since the solving of the problem involved in the contrast has become a vital issue for mankind, we should make our orientation towards socialism, even if we know that the socialist camp itself, while liquidating the past, is grappling with problems ... The believer too must reckon with these realities when he carries on his service in the world. If the Christian looks today for a radical solution of the problem posed by the conflict between wealth and poverty, then he cannot escape the question as to his cooperation with the forces of socialism." [22]

The same kind of conviction is expressed by the "Confession of Faith" of the Presbyterian-Reformed Church in Cuba: "The Church lives in the real, concrete practice of human freedom which its members achieve throughout committed participation in quantitative growth and qualitative development of 'love-justice', in the socio-political and economic structures of human society, including the structures of the Church itself as a socio-juridical institution ... The Church neither supports nor serves the interests of the oppressing classes which take away men's vocation as responsibly free trustees, exploiting the labour of the many in order to increase the wealth of the few at the cost of a general growth in human misery, which is a 'sign' of the frustration of the love of God." [23]

NOTES

[1] Cf. report of Section I of the World Conference on Salvation Today, on "Culture and Identity", para. 7f: "The moment the 'agents of salvation' are even equivocally on the side of the oppressor, the Christian message is distorted and Christian mission is in jeopardy." *Bangkok Assembly 1973.* Geneva: CWME/WCC, 1973, p. 74. Also, in the report of Section I on "Confessing Christ Today" of the WCC's Fifth Assembly, on "The Whole Gospel" it is stated: "The Gospel always includes: the announcement of God's Kingdom and love through Jesus Christ, the offer of grace and forgiveness of sins, the invitation to repentance and faith in him, the summons to fellowship in God's Church, the command to witness to God's saving words and deeds, *the responsibility to participate in the struggle for justice and human dignity,* the obligation to denounce all that hinders human wholeness, and a commitment to risk life itself." DAVID M. PATON (ed.): *Breaking Barriers: Nairobi 1975,*

p. 52 (italics mine). Grand Rapids, Mich.: Wm B. Eerdmans, and London: SPCK, 1976.

2 Cf. Evangelical Methodist Church in Bolivia: *Manifesto to the Nation*, CCPD Dossier No. 1, *Churches in Development*. Geneva: WCC, 1973.

3 James 2 : 14-17: "What does it profit, my brethren, if a man says he has faith but has no works? Can his faith save him? If a brother or a sister is ill-clad and in lack of daily food and one of you says to them, 'Go in peace, be warmed and filled', without giving them the things needed for the body, what does it profit? So faith by itself, if it has no works, is dead."

4 Cf. JULIO DE SANTA ANA: *Good News to the Poor*, chapters II-III, pp. 12-35. Geneva: WCC, 1977. Also see chapters XIII and XIV of this book.

5 It is God who gathers his *ekklesia* through his Word, with the power of the Spirit through the apostolic witness. This explains why the groups of believers are characterized by names which point   out the fact that it is a godly action which leads them to meet each other in the church. They are "called" (Rom. 1 : 6): to be saints (Rom. 1 : 7; Rom. 8 : 27). The Greek word *ekklesia* is related to the verb *kaleo*, to call. There is no Church without God's calling.

6 Cf. the expression of this effort through JAMES CONE's *Black Theology and Black Power*. New York: Seabury Press, 1969.

7 Cf. GUSTAVO GUTIÉRREZ: *Theology of Liberation*, pp. 300-301. Maryknoll, NY: Orbis Books, 1973. See also M. M. THOMAS: *Towards a Theology of Contemporary Ecumenism*, pp. 148-149. Madras: Christian Literature Society, 1978.

8 Cf. Bishop PAULOSE MAR PAULOSE: *Church's Mission: 1. Struggle for Justice. 2. Involvement in Political Struggles*, pp. 21-22: "Today the Korean church lives under political dictatorship, and . . . believes that oppressive political power is in contradiction with the Christian faith and the mission of the Church. A responsible Church cannot be indifferent to this kind of situation, for 'if we disregard our responsibility as Christians for the preservation and promotion of the dignity of man it would be forsaking one's faith in Christ Jesus'. Therefore, the Korean church, in the midst of repression and persecution, is engaged in a struggle to establish democratic principles in the country, and 'for the ordering of society in the fullest recognition of the basic dignity of man'. They have taken the Gospel seriously. They know that the Gospel is the word of reconciliation. They also know that the ministry of reconciliation involves not only bringing together the alienated opponents, but also struggling for the liberation of the oppressed and exploited." Bombay: Build, 1978. In a different situation, the statement of the bishops of central-western Brazil: *Marginalization of a People*, expresses a similar commitment on the social level. Goiania, 1973, especially pp. 41-44.

9 GUSTAVO GUTIÉRREZ: *Signos de lucha y esperanza: testimonios de la iglesia en América Latina 1973-1978*, introduction, p. xlii: "The poor know that history belongs to them and that though they weep now, tomorrow they will laugh (Luke 6 : 21). That laughter springs from deep confidence in the Lord — the kind found in the canticles of Hannah and Mary — which the poor live in the midst of a history which they seek to transform. A joy which is subversive of a world of oppression, and which on that account disturbs the powerful, denounces the fear of the hesitant and reveals the love of the God of hope." Lima: CEP, 1978.

[10] Cf. JOHN PERKINS: "What It Means To Be the Church". *International Review of Mission*, Vol. LXVI, No. 263 on "Human Rights", July 1977, pp. 244-247.

[11] See chapter X of this book.

[12] Cf. ROBERT F. CURRIE, SJ: *The Church: Credible Sign of People's Liberation? Socio-political and Theological Analysis of a Church Movement in Bihar, India.* Mermajal PO, Mangalore: Centre for Human Concern. 1978.

[13] Cf. GUSTAVO GUTIÉRREZ, *op. cit.*

[14] Cf. the report of a WCC *Consultation on Militarism*, Glion, Switzerland, 13-18 November 1977, pp. 8-11. Geneva: CCIA/WCC, 1978.

[15] Cf. THOMAS CULLINAN, OSB: *The Roots of Social Injustice*, pp. 8ff. Privatization of ownership is for him one of the main roots of social injustice. London: Catholic Housing Aid Society, 1973.

[16] Cf. JOHN KENT: "The Church and the Trade Union Movement in Britain in the 19th Century". JULIO DE SANTA ANA (ed.): *Separation Without Hope?*, pp. 30-37. Geneva: WCC, 1978.

[17] Cf. the report of Section VI on "Human Development: the Ambiguities of Power, Technology, and Quality of Life", of the WCC Fifth Assembly. DAVID M. PATON (ed.), *op. cit.*, para. 12.1, p. 123.

[18] JOHN WHITE: *The Politics of Foreign Aid.* London: Bodley Head, 1974.

[19] THERESA HAYTER: *Aid as Imperialism.* Harmondsworth, UK: Penguin Books, 1971.

[20] Cf. CCPD Dossier No. 8 on *Quality of Aid.* Geneva: CCPD/WCC, 1976. See especially "Combined Analysis of the Replies to the Questionnaire on 'The Quality of Aid'", p. 21.

[21] This is what the rich young ruler did not understand: cf. Matt. 19: 16-22; Mark 10: 17-22; Luke 18: 18-30. See JULIO DE SANTA ANA, *op. cit.*, pp. 24-28. This liberating experience was lived through by Pierre Vaudès, the founder of the Waldensian Movement, in the twelfth century. Cf. JEAN GOUNET and AMEDEO MOLNAR: *Storia dei Valdesi*, col. I, pp. 10-13. Torino: Claudiana, 1974.

[22] Study contribution of the Evangelical Lutheran Church in Hungary to the Sixth Assembly of the Lutheran World Federation in Dar-Es-Salaam, 1977: *In Jesus Christ a New Community.* Budapest: Magyarországi Evangélikus Egyház, Sajtoosztálya, 1977, pp. 114-115.

[23] Quoted by SERGIO ARCE-MARTÍNEZ in "Development, People's Participation and Theology". *The Ecumenical Review*, Vol. 30, No. 3, 1978, p. 271.

XIV · Striving with Others for a New Society

It has already been pointed out that human society today is divided between rich and poor — the haves and the have-nots, oppressors and oppressed. We are all concerned about the fact of poverty and understand that the main cause of poverty is oppression and exploitation.[1] The forces of oppression, though numerically a minority, are powerful and united and their action is systematic and thorough. Such forces maintain their oppression and carry on exploitation, keeping people on the periphery, playing the subtle game of dropping "crumbs" in the forms of charity or aid, while keeping the major share of the world's resources and wealth to themselves.[2]

The poor of the world are slowly waking up to the situation. In all societies and nations there are signs of this. The fight against colonialism in this century is an example. There are growing unrest and conflict all over the world, and "principalities and powers" are being challenged by the people. The oppressive forces retaliate with more oppression and we see the rise and fall of dictators, especially in Asia, Africa and Latin America, where the majority of the world's poor live and struggle.[3]

Search for a new society

The struggles and conflicts which we see around us are signs of an ongoing search for a new society. The people in Asia and Africa under western colonialism thought that if they were able to throw out western imperialism they would be free. It is being realized that the present rulers, though not outsiders, are agents of neo-colonialism and continue oppression of their own people.[4] Out of this experience and frustration, the search for a new society is emerging. There are two major influences in this search. First, that of ideologies: without entering into a discussion on the merits or limitations of the experiences of Russia and China in this century, one can say that their experiences have made an impact in the world which cannot be ignored.[5] The ideologies which promoted these developments are taken seriously in many countries in the search for a new society. The tools provided by these ideologies are being used by many to understand their situation without idealizing these experiences. Gandhism is another ideology which is a part of this search in the Indian context.[6] *Sarvodaya* (welfare of all) is still an Indian dream which has deep roots in the Indian socio-cultural milieu. Nationalism is another ideology which may not be well defined and may be reactionary, but which is yet a reality in some situations.[7]

The second influence of this search for a new society is that of religions and faiths. The Asian scene is predominantly of people other than Christian. Islam is gaining ground in many parts of the world. The bulk of the people involved in the search for a new society are rooted in their religio-cultural base which predominantly is not what may be described as "Christian". The search for a new society in the context of their religious and cultural background has resulted in the renaissance of these religions during the closing decades of the nineteenth century and still goes on, especially in Asia. There is a growing recognition that certain elements of the religions and cultures are bondages, and breaking away from such forces is part of the search for a new society.[8]

The Church in the search for a new society

Jesus Christ announced the Kingdom of God and his apostles spoke of a "new heaven and a new earth". Jesus preached, taught and healed the sick in the context of the announcement of the new society. He was not prepared to institutionalize his "services" of healing the sick and feeding the hungry. He used such interventions in the everyday life of the people to show new possibilities and encourage them to be part of a movement towards a real human community devoid of exploitation of one by the other.[9] It was not his help to the poor that threatened the oppressors of that time, but his preaching and teaching of the Kingdom of God and the signs of the awakening of the people. The Good News He preached is still echoing in the world and his spirit is working in movements both inside and outside the Church. Great men like Mahatma Gandhi were not members of the organized Church, but yet they were front-line fighters for freedom and human dignity which are an essential part of the Good News Jesus preached. The expression of the search for a new society going on in the world today, especially in Asia, is seen mostly outside the Church, a fact which we should be prepared to deal with in humility but with gratefulness to God.

The Church in the developing countries, except in a few cases, is the result of the missionary enterprise of western churches with the support of colonial expansionists from the sixteenth century onwards. The attitude of this missionary enterprise was one of aggressiveness as bearers of "light" to the "children of darkness" living in the heathen lands. So it called for a conversion of people which meant cutting off their roots at their socio-cultural and religious base and adopting the values and practices of a different culture and background.[10] This implied being "separate" from their fellow men and community and becoming an exclusive group. The message preached by the missionary enterprise mainly belonged to the metaphysical realm and drew the attention of the converts to the other world. This later created an unfavourable reaction in the countries and communities which were the objects of the missionary work, and the community at large viewed the new converts with suspicion and prejudice. This in turn made the converts rather insecure, with the result that they withdrew into their assemblies and meetings, further alienating themselves from the mainstream of the life of the people. The Indian situation is a typical example of this, where the Christians as a community played no significant part in the freedom struggle, and the minority complex of the churches even today prevents them from entering into the struggle of the people.

The churches in Asian, African, Latin American, Middle Eastern and Pacific countries have to prove their credibility before they can join the search for a new society. They have to understand the mission in the given context, taking into consideration other faiths, and should not just follow the ways of the western church in preaching the Gospel today.[11] The Church in each situation has to further prove that it belongs to that situation and is not an agent of any outside body.[12] It also has to prove that it is deeply committed to social change and the search for a new society by siding with the oppressed, and not with the oppressor. The credibility of the Church in South Korea and the Philippines among their own countrymen and outside is very high because of its willingness to take risks in spearheading the fight against oppressive regimes. The churches in the Indian sub-continent have a poor image among the people except for their "service", though the emergence of church-related micro-level action groups is opening up channels of communication and they are becoming a part of the search for a new society. In the situations where the Church is a minority and where it does not have the image of a participant in the ongoing search for a new society, it is presumptuous to think that it can undertake a search by itself or provide leadership. The Church, after proving its credibility, can become a "handmaid" in the process.

Value and implications of a common search

In dealing with the value and implications of a common search, three main areas can be pointed out.

1. *The quality of the search:* The quality of the search will be enriched by joining hands with people of other faiths and ideologies.[13] The experience of the churches, especially in minority situations, in understanding the dynamics of the society and the realities, is rather limited. The common search is very important if the problem is to be seen in all its dimensions and manifestations and the root causes are to be identified. Some local experiences in Asian countries, where men and women of different faiths and ideologies are acting and reflecting together, have proved extremely useful.[14] This process should not be confined to local or national levels. The churches and bodies like the WCC should try to include, in their study and reflection process, people of other faiths and ideologies to make such process rich in quality.

2. *Common search leads to genuine dialogue:* The conversation which is going on between Christians and men and women of other faiths is very much on the theoretical or academic level. However, where men and women of different faiths and ideologies work together with the people in local situations, genuine dialogue takes place. They discover each other's faith and hopes about the future society. Such dialogue is meaningful and ordinary people can fully participate. It is done in the context of a common commitment to the search for a new society.[15] The churches and the WCC should take note of such experiences and encourage the process at all levels.

3. *Common search develops unity and solidarity:* Discovering persons and movements and a common search with them for a new society, bring about unity and solidarity. The only means of breaking free of oppressive forces is united action by the oppressed.[16] The people who support such movements should be united in the cause of strengthening the solidarity of the people. If this does not happen, unwittingly the oppressor is strengthened. So the Church has to take seriously all persons and movements which are active in the struggle of the people and support them in all possible ways, including financial.

In closing, one may say that in all situations and struggles of the poor the Church should not try to strive alone, especially where other faiths and ideologies are major influences, and a large proportion of the people actually follow other religions.[17] The Church must discern the work of the

Holy Spirit in all movements, secular or religious, which are working for a just and creative human society. This process is important not only for the cause of the poor, but also for enriching the insights and experiences of the Church itself.

NOTES

[1] Cf. chapters I and II of this book.

[2] As DIEGO DE GASPAR has stated: "In a first approach I want to address myself to the more entrenched charitable practices of everyday life, related to systems of long-term assistance. Most, if not all, of these practices would fall under the heading of 'symmetrical' solutions. They address themselves to 'symptoms' or 'victims' of a determined system, and are rarely even aware that the 'symptoms' or the 'victims' exist because of basic defects in the social and economic system prevailing in the particular geographic region. Let us review some of the features of charitable behaviour. The first is that charitable behaviour does not call for 'measurement' at both the giving and receiving ends. What is given does not relate to the wealth of those who give. It is for them (individuals, institutions, countries) to decide how much they will release from their fortunes. Neither is there any adequate measurement of the needs. The receiver may receive less than is necessary or more than is required. It is usually only by coincidence that needs and charity given match each other. Therefore, from a strictly economic point of view, such charity giving is an act of 'irresponsibility'. As a corollary, the receiver is supposed to be 'eternally grateful' to the donor, and expected to be fully loyal. No wonder, then, that from the psychological and political points of view so many surprises are constantly disclosed." In "Some Comments on Changing Life Styles". *Study Encounter*, Vol. XII, No. 3, 1976, p. 14.

[3] See the report of the general secretary to the WCC's Fifth Assembly. DAVID M. PATON (ed.): *Breaking Barriers: Nairobi 1975*, pp. 252-253. Grand Rapids, Mich.: Wm B. Eerdmans, and London: SPCK, 1976.

[4] See the classic book of KWAME NKRUMAH: *Neo-Colonialism as the Last Stage of Imperialism*. Accra: Ghana Press, 1965. Cf. also JAMES O'CONNOR in "The Meaning of Economic Imperialism": "Neo-colonialist policy is first and foremost designed to prevent the newly independent countries from consolidating their political independence and thus to keep them economically dependent and securely in the world capitalist system. In the pure case of neo-colonialism, the allocation of economic resources, investment effort, legal and ideological structures, and other features of the old society remain unchanged — with the single exception of the substitution of 'internal colonialism' for formal colonialism, that is, the transfer of power to the domestic ruling classes by their formal colonial masters. Independence has thus been achieved on conditions which are irrelevant to the basic needs of the society, and represents a part denial of real sovereignty, and a part continuation of disunity within the society." In K. T. FAUN and DONALD C. HODGES: *Readings in US Imperialism*, p. 40. Boston: Porter Sargent, 1971.

[5] Cf. CHOAN-SENG SONG: "New China and Salvation History: a Methodological Enquiry", and JULIO DE SANTA ANA: "Liberation for Social Justice: the Common

Struggle of Christians and Marxists in Latin America." In STANLEY J. SAMARTHA (ed.): *Living Faiths and Ultimate Goals: a Continuing Dialogue*, pp. 68-89 and 90-107 respectively. Geneva: WCC, 1974.

[6] The influence of Gandhi appears clearly in the thought of SAMUEL PARMAR, the well-known Indian economist. Cf. his contributions to *Beyond Dependency: the Developing World Speaks Out* (GUY ERB and VALERIANA KALLAB eds. Washington, DC: Overseas Development Council, 1975) and RICHARD D. N. DICKINSON: *To Set at Liberty the Oppressed.* Geneva: WCC, 1975.

[7] As stated in the World Conference on Church and Society, Geneva 1966, in the report of Section II on "The Nature and Function of the State in a Revolutionary Age", paras 47-49ff, especially paras 47-48ff: "A sense of nationalism is essential for the building of a new nation. But this nationalism must not be confused with some kinds of aggressive nationalism which have led to wars, nationalisms which deify the nation and provoke feelings of national superiority. . . . People who today have understandable objections to nationalism have to consider without prejudice what nationalism and the nation-state really mean for nation-building in young nations: nationalism embodies the concept of national purpose; it is the means of striving for real independence; its goal is a new freedom from the former colonial structures within which the new nations were built; it is a means of achieving unity within the nation-states bequeathed by the colonial powers at independence, nation-states within which are peoples of diverse ethnic groups and languages, it is a means to find national personality." *Christians in the Technical and Social Revolutions of Our Time*, pp. 106-107. Geneva: WCC, 1967.

[8] Cf. STANLEY J. SAMARTHA (ed.), *op. cit.*

[9] See chapter XIV of this book.

[10] Cf. in JULIO DE SANTA ANA (ed.): *Separation Without Hope?*, especially the chapters by JULIO BARREIRO: "Rejection of Christianity by the Indigenous Peoples of Latin America"; C. I. ITTY: "The Church and the Poor in Asian History"; and SAM M. KOBIA: "The Christian Mission and the African Peoples in the 19th Century." Geneva: CCPD/WCC, 1978.

[11] Cf. CWME/WCC: *Bangkok Assembly 1973*, pp. 78-80. Geneva: WCC, 1973.

[12] *Ibid.*, pp. 60-61.

[13] Cf. STANLEY J. SAMARTHA, ed., *op. cit.*, pp. vi-xvii.

[14] Cf. Friends of the Philippines: *Makibaka: Join Us In Struggle!* A documentation of five years of resistance to martial law in the Philippines. London: Blackrose Press, 1978.

[15] Cf. the report of Section III on "Seeking Community: the Common Search of People of Various Faiths, Cultures, and Ideologies" of the WCC's Fifth Assembly: "Many stressed the importance of dialogue in view of the necessity of cooperation of all people in order to establish a righteous and peaceful society. Dialogue helps people in their search for community." DAVID M. PATON (ed.), *op. cit.*, p. 77.

[16] Cf. *To Break the Chains of Oppression*, chapter V, especially pp. 48-55. Geneva: CCPD/WCC, 1975.

[17] Cf. chapters XIV and XVI of this book.

XV · Proposals to the Churches

The commitment to being a church of the poor, and to working with and for the poor, immediately faces the fundamental problem that inherited and prevailing patterns of work in all phases of the life of ecclesiastical institutions reflect commitments to other options and tend to perpetuate those options. For a shift of commitment, the Church must understand clearly not only the new directions and reasons for the shift, but also and especially the new methods necessary to equip the churches and their members for the new work of ministry.

1. Prevailing methods need to be identified and understood in the process of changing or replacing them. They appear in various aspects of the Church's work and organization:

1.1: *Structures* which are not open to people's participation.

1.2: *Objectives* of the Church's ministry based on the rich and the powerful rather than on the poor.

1.3: *Evangelism* which emphasizes the growth of the constituency in numbers rather than sharing the Gospel with the poor and oppressed.

1.4: *Education* in the ecclesiastical bodies from catechetics for the young to training of the laity and professional education for the clergy which produces an institution concerned about itself and its internal life rather than one whose members go forth to work with God for justice in the world.

1.5: *Social action* which reflects practices and strategies that mirror the class interests of those who are not poor rather than those who are materially needy. Charity as a response implies that the poor are not equal partners.

1.6: *Aid* from one church to another which moves from one controlling minority to another rather than to the broad participation of people that would ground its use in their deeper needs while serving needs that are immediate.

2. Those negative judgments, to whatever degree they might be true in any part of the Church Catholic, face an increasing surge of new counter-movements that signal renewal of the Church towards being a church of the poor. The stories of some of these movements in chapter I point to such developments. In less dramatic ways the churches in many places are moving towards grounding their work in the poor through such efforts, through redirected activities with the poor, and through courageous and startling advocacy for the poor. The signs are there in the churches.

3. In the light of the irrelevance of inherited methods and these new counter-movements, what specific proposals can help the churches to become a church of the poor, working with and for the poor and oppressed?

3.1: *Alignment:* If the Church is born from the poor and for them (Acts 2 : 42-47; 4 : 32-35; 6 : 1-7), then it must judge every part of its life from the perspective of the poor. That solidarity can be real only when the Church is where they are. Only when direct contact with the poor and their oppression is maintained can that solidarity be continuous. The Church can then become a tool of the poor as their Lord works through it. Churches whose members are from the poor classes therefore become the front line of the Church's efforts, bringing from their Bible study and action/reflection reliable guidance in the struggles for justice. Churches whose members are not primarily from the poor can have solidarity with them through participation in their struggles directly or through advocacy, by giving "voice to the voiceless".[1] In those situations, however, churches must carefully align themselves with the poor and their viewpoint, using as a plumbline in all decisions the simple question: "Will this act express solidarity with the poor?"[2] In this way ecclesiastical bodies become faithful witnesses to the Gospel.

We propose that the churches align with the poor by sharing at appropriate levels, but mainly in direct ways, their struggles for justice, and by judging every decision by whether it helps the poor to fulfil their hopes and expectations.

3.2: *The Bible:* Churches of the poor witness to the importance of the rediscovery of the Bible and its relevance for daily life.[3] In their struggles for justice poor people read the Bible and find that it comes alive in new ways as the liberation to which it witnesses is seen as their liberation in action. Overcoming the dichotomy between spiritual and historical interpretations that plagues Christian communities of privileged people, the poor see immediately the Bible's relevance for their lives. As they discuss the concrete problems of their communities, as they fight against different kinds of oppression, they practise Bible study in action. In the conflicting options for liberation in Scripture they find indications which help them to formulate their own response. They find help in the Bible for understanding and preparing their conflict. In their fresh mixing of struggle and Bible they are developing a didactic of conflict which opens up a new understanding of the scriptures. As Alves generalized, the western churches have emphasized a rational approach to Scripture; the eastern ones, a mystical; and the Third World and poor, a militant and active approach.[4] Mind, heart and will — it takes all three to be human. The new vitality of Bible study among the poor restores a wholeness and offers to churches of the poor and those with and for the poor exciting possibilities of Bible study in action.

We propose that the churches develop and support action-study of the Bible among those who share the struggles of the poor for justice.

3.3: *Theology:* For a Church committed to the option of being of the poor, inherited theological concepts born or shaped in historical experience under other commitments stand as obstacles to the new directions. Popular values and popular religiosity, even if sometimes indicative of the alienation of the poor, also express their resistance to oppressors. Therefore fundamental theological concepts and ways of understanding the faith must be reformulated from the perspective of the liberating praxis of the poor.[5] A new plumbline measures the distortions of the old structures of thought and provides clear guidance for construction of the new. But the task is not easy, for familiar structures of theology assume an aura of certainty that must be radically rejected. The new commitment to become a church of the poor can provide the motive and the strength for ploughing up the old and planting the new, for it contains the judgment that without this commitment the ecclesiastical bodies lose their character as the Church of Jesus Christ. The Church must undertake serious efforts to ground its theological work in the new life and perspective of the poor, and those already existing at this level must be encouraged. Theologians should leave the positions they have in dominant centres and share the life of the poor and their struggles.

We propose that the churches search out groups of the poor from whose struggles new theological formulations may be arising, and commit resources of biblical and theological analysis to participation in those actions. We also propose to the churches that they support programmes which can help the development of theological thought rooted in the practice of the poor for justice and liberation.

3.4: *Solidarity, empowering the powerless:* Faithfulness to the Word of God in the context of the world today means siding with the poor in their struggle for justice.[6] The aims and purposes of such participation in people's struggles have to be defined according to each situation. Generally speaking, it means the search for liberation and what it means to be fully human. The Bible points to Jesus as the perfect expression of humanness. Unfortunately, there are structures and systems which prevent human growth to the stature of Jesus Christ (Eph. 6 : 10ff). In these situations the challenge is not just for participation or acceptance but for a radical change of the society. In various situations the gulf between the rich and poor is wide and the poor's consciousness of their own needs and their own rights is very low. Historically the poor have been subjected to exploitation and manipulation by the elite and the rich, through the creation of structures of exploitation.

The purpose of work for liberation in this context is not to give a ready-made ideology to the poor but to create awareness and power in the people so they can become the subjects of change for the kind of society they want to live in. This process of empowering the powerless to become the subjects of change occurs mainly through helping them organize themselves to face immediate local power structures.[7] Such conflicts and confrontations at the micro-level within the perspective of the macro-level help people to become conscientized and organized to deal with major issues on a larger scale. Appropriate sharing of resources must be organized in order to improve the efforts of the poor.

We propose that the churches support this kind of work by all means (including financial), provide communication linkages for it around the world, redirect traditional mission energies towards this kind of liberation praxis with the poor, and use this engagement for learning from the poor themselves.

3.5: *Involvement as basis of reflection:* The learning of the poor comes not from cool thinking remote from action, but from the struggle itself. Nevertheless, careful analysis must be part of it if in the long run that learning is to overcome oppression and liberate people. An essential part of active learning is reflection on the context within which the action occurs.[8] The structural situation and the linkages with other forces which go along with the struggle must be identified and understood as the liberation process moves forward. Analysis of strategy and tactics must be made carefully, in anticipation of resistance and the need for alternative approaches. The essence of the learning process is what some call popular pastoral action, that is, direct shared engagement with the poor in their struggles against oppression, and the help that action can give in analysing the realities which the poor face in their liberating praxis. Both living in misery and existence under the powerful conditioning forces of modern society hide the contextual realities from people. Traditional methods in schooling[9] do not tie together active engagement and relevant analysis in ways which overcome the blindness. To avoid either mere activism or escapist analysis, new ways must be developed to forge practical analysis out of the struggle, and to use that analysis in an ongoing praxis for justice, participation and liberation.

We propose that the churches commit resources of community organizers and action educators to the task of developing ways of analysing the structures and contexts within which the struggles for liberation occur, through direct engagement with the poor, and that the methods thus learned be used in the formation of agents for the search of a just, participatory, sustainable and liberated society.

3.6: *Struggle in situations of conflict:* "The fight is the best teacher," said a community organizer in a Buenos Aires slum.[10] Deep in the movement for liberation lies an inevitable contradiction with the oppressive forces that dominate the lives of poor people. Whether overt or hidden, those forces represent the demonic, the baalism that offends the God of righteousness (Hos. 4:7-14). That demon cannot be expelled without tearing up some of the body it has inhabited. Conflict in the liberation process must be accepted and understood as a necessary element. It also serves as a means of liberation, and can be prepared and used in the strategy of liberation praxis.[11]

When poor and oppressed people stand up for their liberation against the powerful who oppress them, that very act humanizes and empowers them. The established ecclesiastical bodies have been historically conditioned to avoid conflict and to expect the Church not to disturb the calm of ongoing life. That conditioning must be overcome with more open ways of engaging in conflict when fundamental causes are at stake. Since conflict is unavoidable, the potential of violence in the reactions of the powerful must be anticipated and even used. But whether dealing with the strong forces of oppression in structures of society or the embedded patterns of attitudes and behaviours, some violent reaction to change must be faced. It must be made clear that it is not a question of the churches opting for or against violence. In situations of oppression, the poor are objects of aggression committed against them daily, and the churches must decide what must be their position in relation to this type of violence. Again the plumbline of identification with the poor is essential to keep a clear direction through conflicts. The Church needs to work with integrity to support the stand of the poor, and to open up its praxis of engagement against evil forces without abandoning the pastoral sensitivity and community support that frees persons to change.[12]

We propose that the churches seek active partnership with those movements for liberation which revindicate the rights of the poor, and from that participation work for new models of growth in the faith towards liberation.

3.7: *Education:* The education of the people of God likewise must be convergent with the new commitment to be the church of the poor. Pedagogical practices that reinforce value systems of privilege, the behaviour patterns of the dominant classes, and the privacy and charity of personal piety must be radically challenged and transformed into fellowship and solidarity. Building awareness of and action against the contextual forces that form the milieu for Christian liberation must become central in Christian popular education. This is people's education, not that of professors or leaders. It starts in the experience of the people where they are, and builds successive levels of awareness as they struggle against oppressive forces.[13]

This radical approach to education in the Church calls for abandonment of or radical change in the traditional school-type learning which imposes and reinforces passive behaviour and negative self-images upon those who are being educated. Getting rid of those concepts that oppress requires getting rid of or radically reorienting the structures of education that condition those concepts in persons of all ages: patterns of authority throughout society that "teach" submission, mass media "value education" through advertising, and schools that educate for dependency. Liberation of the Church to become the church of the poor means nothing less than a radical revolution of how its members are formed. Only through participation in the struggle for liberation, in a praxis of action and reflection through successive stages, can true disciples of the Liberator be nurtured.[14]

We propose that the churches develop radical new experiments in action/ reflection models of learning and that they pursue a strategy of replacing the old educational ways with new types of popular education.

3.8: *Formation of agents of change:* The preparation of agents for the work of the church of the poor also involves radical changes in the inherited patterns of training for church leadership, clergy and lay. Only those committed absolutely to sharing the struggle of the poor, and having demonstrated an appropriate understanding of people's struggles, should be indicated for the work of agents, and their selection should involve the direct participation of the people.[15]

Their readiness can then be directed further into specific identity with the people without losing their own identity. They must learn first in the praxis of liberation with the people, sharing their insecurities and dangers, learning not to draw attention to themselves and being ready to withdraw when the people's strength warrants it. Their development must include preparation in understanding the ideological framework of societies, and must go beyond traditional theological training into analysis of the contexts and correlation with other fields that contribute towards that end. Present methods of theological education and lay training need to be radically challenged to provide active engagement in the struggles for liberation and a new and deeper education on the contextual, ideological and theological dimensions of the praxis of the poor towards liberation. Just as the inherited structures of education reflect and support the oppressive structures of dominant societies, so the new forms of education must reflect the new commitment to the poor. Agents immersed in their struggles can thus be developed further only by new methods that reflect the fight for liberation and the praxis of the poor.

We propose that the churches challenge their programmes of lay and clergy education to explore radically new methods of engagement in the search for a just, participatory and liberated society and the educational patterns possible in that search.

3.9: *Assistance in the quest for justice:* Liberation movements of the poor need support structures and linkages among themselves. Faced with global forces of oppression, the struggle for liberation which begins with local poor people fighting against specific oppressive forces needs the collegial support and protection of networks of the poor. The churches

have an important role to play here, for they have direct access to the poor
through congregations and connectional structures that can help provide
support. In some countries and given historical moments, churches are
almost the only institutions which can provide such support. Sometimes
these support structures need to provide livelihood to protect against
economic pressure upon the agents of liberation. Sometimes they need to
facilitate communication for mobilization of force against certain
enemies. Sometimes they need to challenge local groups struggling for justice and liberation to look at the broader situation and to ally themselves
with other movements. A problem comes when the poor try to organize
beyond the local situation of struggle without becoming bureaucratic and
remote from the communities at the base. But the attempts must be made,
and the Church with its extensive network of persons and groups and
resources can be of great help at this level of the liberation struggle.

*We propose that the churches activate their various networks of support
for the struggle of the poor, analyse their potential for the fight, and develop
means of strengthening the connectional structures that can support the
struggle against poverty and oppression.*

3.10: The church of the poor needs to get rid of the encumbrances and
burdens of heavy structures. Vertical patterns of relationships, wealthy
endowments and luxurious furnishings inevitably alienate the poor. When
the churches look at their structures from the viewpoint of the poor, much
of their institutional inheritance is seen as useless and dangerous in the
struggle against oppression which this legacy itself perpetuates. At their
best the churches provide a lean and muscular body for the struggle. They
offer free space for the people to resist and organize their conflicts, and
consolatory sanctuary for the hurt. Their pastoral and prophetic functions
help to unite in liberating praxis, exposing their administrative apparatus
as unnecessary or overbuilt. Flexibility becomes a major objective for the
mobilization of churches' resources for the fight, and an undue accumulation of structures limits that flexibility. The ecclesiastical institutions need
to look upon their own organization in order to reappraise radically the
structures needed for the new commitment to become the church of the
poor.

*We propose that the churches reconsider their organized structures to
permit maximum deployment of their resources to the struggles for a just,
participatory, liberated and sustainable society.*

NOTES

[1] Cf. DOM HÉLDER CAMARA: *Les conversions d'un evêque: entretiens avec José de Broucker*, pp. 183-192. Paris: Editions du Seuil, 1977.

[2] This was precisely the line followed by the Brazilian bishops of central-western Brazil who wrote the document *Marginalization of a People*, Goiania, Brazil, May 1973.

[3] Cf. chapter XIV of this book.

[4] Cf. RUBEM A. ALVES: "Libertad y ortodoxia: ¿opuestos irreconciliables?" *Cristianismo y Sociedad*, XVI year, No. 56-57, 1978, pp. 37-42.

[5] Cf. GUSTAVO GUTIÉRREZ: *Teología desde el reverso de la historia.* CEP: Lima, 1977. Also his appendix to chapter IX of this book. See also FRED RODRIGUES KAMATH: "Community Resurrection in Mermajal Village". In BOBBI WELLS HARGLEROAD (ed.): *Struggle to Be Human: Stories of Urban Industrial Mission*, pp. 62-68. Geneva: CWME/WCC, 1973.

[6] Cf. the statement "Structures of Captivity and Lines of Liberation" adopted by the CCPD/CICARWS Joint Consultation at Montreux, December 1974. *The Ecumenical Review*, Vol. XXVII, No. 1, January 1975, pp. 44-47, especially p. 45.

[7] Cf. "Letter of Mgr Pedro Casaldáliga to his Spanish friends". GUSTAVO GUTIÉRREZ: *Signos de lucha y esperanza*, pp. 254-255. Lima: CEP, 1978.

[8] Cf. the minutes of the *Sociological Symposium on Active Research, Cartagena, Colombia, 1977.* Bogota: Fundarco, 1977. Orlando Fals Borda, organizer of that symposium, is one of the main social scientists working in this line, together with G. Huizer, Miguel and Roziska Darcy d'Oliveira, and others.

[9] See the book by PAULO FREIRE, IVAN ILLICH and PIERRE FURTER: *Educación para el cambio social,* especially the chapter by Illich: "Critica a la liturgia de la enseñanza", pp. 99-115. Buenos Aires: Tierra Nueva, no date.

[10] For more information about this line of experience, see BOBBI WELLS HARGLEROAD (ed.): *Struggle To Be Human, op. cit.,* pp. 31-34.

[11] See chapter V of this book.

[12] The rich can change. Their salvation is an act of grace of God who challenges the rich to repent and be converted. Cf. Luke 18:18-30, and JULIO DE SANTA ANA: *Good News to the Poor,* chapter III. Geneva: CCPD/WCC, 1977.

[13] Cf. PAULO FREIRE: *Pedagogy of the Oppressed.* New York: Herder & Herder, 1973. Also, by the same author: "Education, Liberation and the Church". *Study Encounter*, Vol. IX, No. 1, 1973.

[14] In his address to the WCC's Central Committee meeting, August 1977, PHILIP A. POTTER, commenting on Hebrews 13:13-16, stated: "It also means that the struggle for liberation from all structures of injustice, the violations of human rights, and the human carnage of war is a struggle of suffering. ... We are here reflecting concretely on what it means to bear the cross for the sake of the Gospel and God's Kingdom of justice and peace. As in Christ the cross was the event which authenticated the integrity of his witness of the truth, the revelation and faithfulness of the Father, so the churches and the World Council are challenged to take on the suffering of the healing and victorious cross as they confront themselves and others who refuse to accept the call to repentance, *metanoia*, the radical change of

thinking and living towards obedience to the Gospel. When the 'principalities and powers', the structures of destructive concealment and mistrust, which refuse to receive Christ as Lord, attack the people of God, suffering for the truth of the Gospel is the way through which doctrine, confession and social involvement become the vehicles of the truth we have to live and proclaim.

"For us, there is no escape from this calling to suffer. Christ promised us no less. He warned that when we live the way of truth through the Spirit, when we expose the world's sin and evil, when we manifest loyal trust in our fellow human beings by committing ourselves to their well-being, we attract the hatred of the world. It is in the midst of the world and its hatred that he promises us the Spirit, the *Paracletos*, he who is called beside us, who hears and expresses our speechless groans, who empowers and guides us to continue in the fellowship of Christ's sufferings. This spirituality in suffering becomes light and hope in the struggle for a new world in which dwell God's justice and peace. It is a spirituality — that life in the spirit, which is life-giving and life sustaining . . ." *The Ecumenical Review*, Vol. 29, No. 4, October 1977, pp. 363-365.

[15] This is the line of involvement in development work defined by the Development Commission of the Council of Churches in Indonesia, and several Latin American churches and Christian groups, all of them with the support of the WCC's Commission on the Churches' Participation in Development.

LETTER TO THE CHURCHES
from the contributors to this book

Grace to you and peace in our Lord Jesus Christ.

The foregoing pages reflect the experience of a growing number of Christian congregations and groups all over the world. They express grief, but also hope; their words denounce injustice but at the same time echo the actions of those who sigh in longing for the coming of the Kingdom of God. Their aim, even beyond the views they express, is to try to give an account of the continual and transforming work of the Spirit of God in the Church and in society. In other words, they are not primarily the outcome of a theory, but principally of an actual practice of faith which is taking root among the poor of the earth. This faith is what is impelling groups of the poor to be the Church of Jesus Christ, who was poor himself, in the midst of mankind. We wish in fact through these pages, in the name of the poor themselves, to invite churches and the World Council of Churches to enter deeply into the transforming experience of becoming the church of the poor, being in solidarity with them, sharing in their struggles, their sorrows, hopes and joys.

Those of us who, on the basis of our commitment to the poor, met in Ayia Napa, Cyprus, to reflect on the implications of this practical process of transformation of the Christian community, wish to invite you to live this revivifying experience by the power of the Spirit of God. For us, it is a wonderful thing to witness a process (we have been caught up in it and are taking part) in which the people of God are taking shape and form out of the mass of the disinherited of our time. It means sharing in that movement which strengthens the weak, makes it possible for those who have no voice to have their say, aids the development of faith among those who in the logic of the powerful of this world would have no right to hope. We experience the wealth of what we are living through, the hope that is growing in us, the urgent need that injustice should be curbed and the liberation of the oppressed extended, with something like the joy of the first Christians when they received the Holy Spirit: it has to be shared with all who, like us, believe in Jesus Christ.

To invite them to share in the struggles and hopes of the church of the poor is not to point out a triumphal course for them to follow. Just as Jesus Christ in his poverty had the Cross prepared for him, so the Church of the poor cannot hope for any other fate than its Lord, especially if it remains faithful to him: "For I have given you an example, that you should do as I have done to you. Truly, truly, I say to you, a servant is not greater than his master; nor is he who is sent greater than he who sent him. If you know these things, blessed are you if you do them" (John 13: 15-17). This invitation is made so that the Christian community may be enriched by the life of the poor of our time, among whom, Jesus has said, it is possible to serve him incognito. It is not an invitation to an exercise of this world's power, but to humble service of the humblest of the earth.

The experience of our brothers and sisters who have actually made this choice serves as a basis for the expression in a new way in our time of a *church of disciples,* that is, of persons disposed to follow to the very end the path which following Jesus implies. Among the needy and silent of the world, a *koinonia of the poor* is coming into being, who not only share between them the little they have, but in particular join together in hopes and struggles to which the Spirit of God moves them, as He opens up ways in the midst of history — with terrible distress and unimaginable pangs — towards the full manifestation of a new humanity.

In this sense, the church of the poor is the one that affirms, perhaps with greater force than any other type of Christian community, our faith's dimension of hope. There are things which there is no "realistic" reason to hope for, but which are longed for and striven for eagerly; justice for the millions of dispossessed is one of them. Now, this hope is firmly held in the church of the poor. Those who constitute that church are paying a high price for that hope. There are things scarcely glimpsed but which are gradually taking shape, being demonstrated by the very action of the poor in history: the example of a really sharing society. The poor are not renouncing their rights, however much they may be trodden under foot. And the churches in South Korea, Chile, South Africa, Brazil, the Philippines and so many other places in both east and west, north and south, are making this hope and demonstrative action of the poor their own. In all these places there is a real manifestation of faith which, according to the author of the Epistle to the Hebrews, "is the assurance of things hoped for, the conviction of things not seen" (Heb. 11 : 1).

This makes the church of the poor *a community that is open towards the future;* it is the people of God who live attentive to the manifestations of the Kingdom and seek its justice perseveringly. It is not a community looking only towards the past; of course, it is nourished by the memory of the mighty deeds of God in history, but its gaze is turned towards the fulfilment of the judgment of God when there will be a new heaven and a new earth, the new Jerusalem in which there will be no tears of the exploited and greed of exploiters, in which justice will flow like the waters of mountain torrents. Some may say this is Utopian. The same term would doubtless have been applied to the idea of Jesus' resurrection by those who condemned him to death or when He was put to death. Would not the growth of the Church have been considered Utopian on the eve of Pentecost? No, those affirmations are not Utopian. They are affirmations of the poor who are entering the Church and who in their daily practice of faith show that they have genuine historical substance. They are not vacuous ideas or idle words; they are expressions of the faith of a community that has nothing materially to lose and, at the same time, has everything to hope for. And it is hoping, and struggling for what it hopes for. And through its sufferings it is gathering strength as the church of the poor.

It is a community which in its poverty demonstrates *vigorous missionary activity.* It cannot be otherwise when we remember that it is sharing something very valuable, which gives meaning to personal and social life. That existence would be empty were it not for this gift of God — the hope which prevents human beings, in particular the poor, from being defeated by death and the destruction to which they appear to be destined by the agents of the Leviathan who obstruct the manifestation of the justice of the Kingdom promised by Jesus to all the peoples of the earth; it would be empty, however gorged it were with material goods on which it claimed to live, for it is well known that when the will to possess dominates us, we end up by things possessing us. The church of the poor, like Peter and John in front of the lame man at the gate of the temple, has neither silver nor gold to give. Instead, in the name of Jesus of Nazareth it declares to the outcasts of the earth: "Get up and walk! On the move! Go forward, do not allow yourselves to be overcome by the forces that rule the market, nor by the multinational agencies that reassert injustice, nor by that trade in death that helps to violate the rights of peoples." This mission of sharing Jesus' power, of sharing the love that God has given fully to mankind in Jesus Christ, is in fact a message of good news; it is the Gospel. And it is the poor who are evangelizing! A wonderful experience, which is revivifying the Church and transforming into a community of historical significance the shapeless mass of the disinherited of our world.

It is also a *diaconal community*, which humbly and with deep love serves its equals. The poor have been suffering for centuries the injustices which the powerful have imposed on them. Their service is a vicarious one, which gives them strength not only to suffer but also to want to change the situation. The church of the poor is laboriously opening up places that make it possible for the dispossessed actually to be human beings, at least when they meet as a community. Then the embarrassed overcome their inhibitions, the oppressed feel freer, those who are exploited meet a community of equals, those who experience the fierce hatred of the world dominated by the law of the market have the living experience of love and communion in the grace of God. This is not a service that can be counted like money; it is, instead, a service of those who are "less than human", so that they can be really men and women growing "to the measure of the stature of the fullness of Christ". This service is beyond the lists of projects of agencies. It is not an expression of "charity", but of deep solidarity. That which was manifested in Jesus Christ "who, though He was in the form of God, did not count equality with God a thing to be grasped, but emptied himself, taking the form of a servant, being born in the likeness of men. And being found in human form, He humbled himself and became obedient unto death, even death on a cross" (Phil. 2 : 6-8).

We are aware of the price that must be paid to give concrete shape to this church of the poor. That awareness comes from the actual experience of brothers and sisters who are fully committed to this undertaking. They form confessing communities, perpetually on the move: today consoling the victims of oppression and torture; tomorrow perhaps confronting economic powers that do not pay the workers proper wages; the day after, very possibly struggling for the rights of the peasants, who are often forced to emigrate because the mechanisms that permit the application of the laws of the market appear to condemn them to poverty. This church, the church of the poor, is no longer a prop for the interests of the powerful. With Hannah and Mary it sings that the Lord is to put down the mighty from their thrones and exalt those of low degree, filling the hungry with good things and sending the rich empty away (cf. I Sam. 2 : 1-10; Luke 1 : 47-55). It is not a case of a church that hates the powerful and the rich; the Church of Jesus Christ cannot hate any human being. Nevertheless, it is a matter of a community that denounces the evils brought about by irresponsible accumulation, egoism, greed for property and power.

In this sense the church of the poor is a *prophetic community:* it gives expression to the voice of the Lord in our time, summoning the rich to change their lives, to live fraternally and not in self-idolatry. When the rich and powerful are faced with the poor, they become more clearly aware of social inequalities, of the injustices produced by the structures that support their wealth, of the oppression which is so often unleashed to defend an established order of things in which the majority of people cannot be really human, and minorities are not respected. That kind of awareness involves a challenge to change, because the condemnation of the situation which it implies cannot be ignored by anyone who really has a spirit of responsibility and care for the dispossessed of the world. The church of the poor appeals to the heart and mind of the powerful for their transformation: "One thing you still lack. Sell what you have and distribute to the poor" (Luke 18 : 22). This is impossible for the mere will of human beings, but it is possible to God. This is once again an announcement of good news, the voice of the Gospel, coming to us from the poor themselves.

The poor of our time call for change and herald a new world, that of the Kingdom and its justice. A testimony to this is their opposition — not always clear, it is true, and unfortunately not always unanimous, but opposition all the same, something that is not generally found among the rich and powerful — to an unjust social order, to human relations that tend to deny that the human being was made in the image and likeness of God. That opposition is sometimes expressed in a struggle against "principalities and powers, against the world rulers of this present darkness" (Eph. 6 : 12), and in many cases this provides the necessary correctives to make possible an advance in justice and human liberation. It is a *prophetic community in action*, often silent, but in many places paying for the growth of the life of the Church with the blood of new martyrs.

It is to this Church, then, that we invite you. We invite you to the living experience of giving priority to the poor, not only in programmes of service but in actual evangelization, to learn from them, to travel with them, to draw up church programmes and projects from their side of history, which means doing so *with* them, so that they are really *their* projects and programmes, not simply *for* them. This church is the Church of Christ, to whom we all desire to be faithful. The experience of our brothers and sisters is that the poor find in that Church the presence of him who was called Emmanuel: God with us. The poor, just as they are, without being obliged to lose their identity as regards social class and personal integrity, meet there a community which in deeds, in the practice of faith, manifests Jesus Christ. Thank God, these are manifestations of a transformed church which has assumed the spirit of the poor, whose members have the hearts of the poor and so share in the aspirations, the struggles, the expectations of the disinherited of the earth.

We invite you to this vicarious community which shoulders the suffering of the world in order to transform it into a motive of hope. In fact, to encounter Jesus Christ. When? How? When we give food to the hungry and drink to the thirsty, when we clothe the naked, make the stranger welcome, care for the sick, free the imprisoned. When we do this for him for no other motive than love. Then, as happens in Matto Grosso or in Alabama, in Seoul or Beirut, Santiago, Berlin or Lusaka, out of the unhoped-for, but with increasing clarity, the face of Jesus Christ will begin to emerge in the midst of the institutions of the People of God.

Brothers, sisters, beloved churches, we invite you to this profound experience of faith. We do so in the name of Christ who was himself poor, and of his love, and in the power of the Spirit who is the power of those who are without power and the strength of the weak and humble. The poor are waiting for you, and among them, Jesus himself.

Appendix

LIST OF PARTICIPANTS

CCPD Workshop on "The Church and the Poor" Ayia Napa, Cyprus

BAYIGA, Rev. Alfred (Cameroon)
BINDEMANN, Rev. Walther (German Democratic Republic)
BOERMA, Dr. Coen M. (The Netherlands)
BROWN, Mr. John, Jr. (United States of America)
BRUMMEL, Dr. Lee (Argentina)
DEVASUNDARAM, Mr. Alex (India)
EKOH, Mr. Jean-Marc (Gabon)
HINKELAMMERT, Dr. Franz J. (Costa Rica)
KAZAH, Rev. Makram (Algeria)
KENNEDY, Dr. William (United States of America)
NINAN, Mr. George (India)
RAMALHO, Dr. Jether P. (Brazil)
SOMERVILLE, Rev. James (United States of America)
TARYOR, Dr. Nya Kwiawon (Liberia)
WIETZKE, Dr. Joachim (Federal Republic of Germany)

ZABOLOTSKI, Prof. Nikolai (WCC/Unit II Staff)
DE SANTA ANA, Dr. Julio (WCC/CCPD Staff)
HALLER, Ms. Erna (WCC/CCPD Staff)

COMBA, Mrs. Fernanda (Interpreter)
GOERTZ, Rev. Marc (Interpreter)
RICHTER, Ms. Madeleine (Interpreter)
RUBINE, Ms. Elisabeth (Interpreter)
SALEM, Ms. Nimet (Interpreter)
VALERO-BOVET, Mrs. Maria (Interpreter)

LEWIS, Mr. David (Translator)
O'HARA, Mr. William (Translator)
REILLY, Ms. Joan (Translator)

Other Orbis books . . .

THE MEANING OF MISSION
José Comblin

"This very readable book has made me think, and I feel it will be useful for anyone dealing with their Christian role of mission and evangelism." *New Review of Books and Religion*
ISBN 0-88344-304-X CIP   *Cloth $6.95*

THE GOSPEL OF PEACE AND JUSTICE
Catholic Social Teaching Since Pope John

Presented by Joseph Gremillion

"Especially valuable as a resource. The book brings together 22 documents containing the developing social teaching of the church from *Mater et Magistra* to Pope Paul's 1975 *Peace Day Message on Reconciliation.* I watched the intellectual excitement of students who used Gremillion's book in a justice and peace course I taught last summer, as they discovered a body of teaching on the issues they had defined as relevant. To read Gremillion's overview and prospectus, a meaty introductory essay of some 140 pages, is to be guided through the sea of social teaching by a remarkably adept navigator."

National Catholic Reporter
    "An authoritative guide and study aid for concerned Catholics and others." *Library Journal*
ISBN 0-88344-165-9   *Cloth $15.95*
ISBN 0-88344-166-7   *Paper $8.95*

THEOLOGY IN THE AMERICAS
Papers of the 1975 Detroit Conference

Edited by Sergio Torres and John Eagleson

"A pathbreaking book from and about a pathbreaking theological conference, *Theology in the Americas* makes a major contribution to ecumenical theology, Christian social ethics and liberation movements in dialogue." *Fellowship*
ISBN 0-88344-479-8 CIP   *Cloth $12.95*
ISBN 0-88344-476-3   *Paper $5.95*

MARX AND THE BIBLE

José Miranda

"An inescapable book which raises more questions than it answers, which will satisfy few of us, but will not let us rest easily again. It is an attempt to utilize the best tradition of Scripture scholarship to understand the text when it is set in a context of human need and misery."

Walter Brueggemann, in Interpretation

ISBN 0-88344-306-6 *Cloth $8.95*
ISBN 0-88344-307-4 *Paper $4.95*

BEING AND THE MESSIAH

The Message of Saint John

José Miranda

"This book could become the catalyst of a new debate on the Fourth Gospel. Johannine scholarship will hotly debate the 'terrifyingly revolutionary thesis that this world of contempt and oppression can be changed into a world of complete selflessness and unrestricted mutual assistance.' Cast in the framework of an analysis of contemporary philosophy, the volume will prove a classic of Latin American theology." *Frederick Herzog, Duke University Divinity School*

ISBN 0-88344-027-X CIP *Cloth $8.95*
ISBN 0-88344-028-8 *Paper $4.95*

THE GOSPEL IN SOLENTINAME

Ernesto Cardenal

"Upon reading this book, I want to do so many things—burn all my other books which at best seem like hay, soggy with mildew. I now know who (not what) is the church and how to celebrate church in the eucharist. The dialogues are intense, profound, radical. *The Gospel in Solentiname* calls us home."

Carroll Stuhlmueller, National Catholic Reporter

ISBN 0-88344-168-3 *Vol. 1 Cloth $6.95*
ISBN 0-88344-170-5 *Vol. 1 Paper $4.95*
ISBN 0-88344-167-5 *Vol. 2 Cloth $6.95*

LOVE AND STRUGGLE
IN MAO'S THOUGHT

Raymond L. Whitehead

"Mao's thoughts have forced Whitehead to reassess his own philosophy and to find himself more fully as a Christian. His well documented and meticulously expounded philosophy of Mao's love and struggle-thought might do as much for many a searching reader." *Prairie Messenger*

ISBN 0-88344-289-2 CIP   *Cloth $8.95*
ISBN 0-88344-290-6   *Paper $3.95*

WATERBUFFALO THEOLOGY

Kosuke Koyama

"This book with its vivid metaphors, fresh imagination and creative symbolism is a 'must' for anyone desiring to gain a glimpse into the Asian mind." *Evangelical Missions Quarterly*

ISBN 0-88344-702-9   *Paper $4.95*

ASIAN VOICES
IN CHRISTIAN THEOLOGY

Edited by Gerald H. Anderson

"A basic sourcebook for anyone interested in the state of Protestant theology in Asia today. I am aware of no other book in English that treats this matter more completely." *National Catholic Reporter*

ISBN 0-88344-017-2   *Cloth $15.00*
ISBN 0-88344-016-4   *Paper $7.95*

FAREWELL TO INNOCENCE

Allan Boesak

"This is an extremely helpful book. The treatment of the themes of power, liberation, and reconciliation is precise, original, and Biblically-rooted. Dr. Boesak has done much to advance the discussion, and no one who is interested in these matters can afford to ignore his important contribution." *Richard J. Mouw, Calvin College*

ISBN 0-88344-130-6 CIP   *Cloth $4.95*

THE PRAYERS
OF AFRICAN RELIGION

John S. Mbiti

"We owe a debt of gratitude to Mbiti for this excellent anthology which so well illuminates African traditional religious life and illustrates so beautifully man as the one who prays." *Sisters Today*
ISBN 0-88344-394-5 CIP   *Cloth $7.95*

POLYGAMY RECONSIDERED

Eugene Hillman

"This is by all odds the most careful consideration of polygamy and the attitude of Christian Churches toward it which it has been my privilege to see." *Missiology*
ISBN 0-88344-391-0   *Cloth $15.00*
ISBN 0-88344-392-9   *Paper $7.95*

AFRICAN TRADITIONAL RELIGION

E. Bolaji Idowu

"A great work in the field and closely comparable to Mbiti's *African Religions and Philosophy*. It is worthwhile reading." *The Jurist*
ISBN 0-88344-005-9   *Cloth $6.95*

AFRICAN CULTURE
AND THE CHRISTIAN CHURCH

Aylward Shorter

"An introduction to social and pastoral anthropology, written in Africa for the African Christian Churches." *Western Catholic Reporter*
ISBN 0-88344-004-0   *Paper $6.50*

TANZANIA AND NYERERE

William R. Duggan & John R. Civille

"Sympathetic survey of Tanzania's attempt to develop economically on an independent path." *Journal of World Affairs*
ISBN 0-88344-475-5 CIP   *Cloth $10.95*